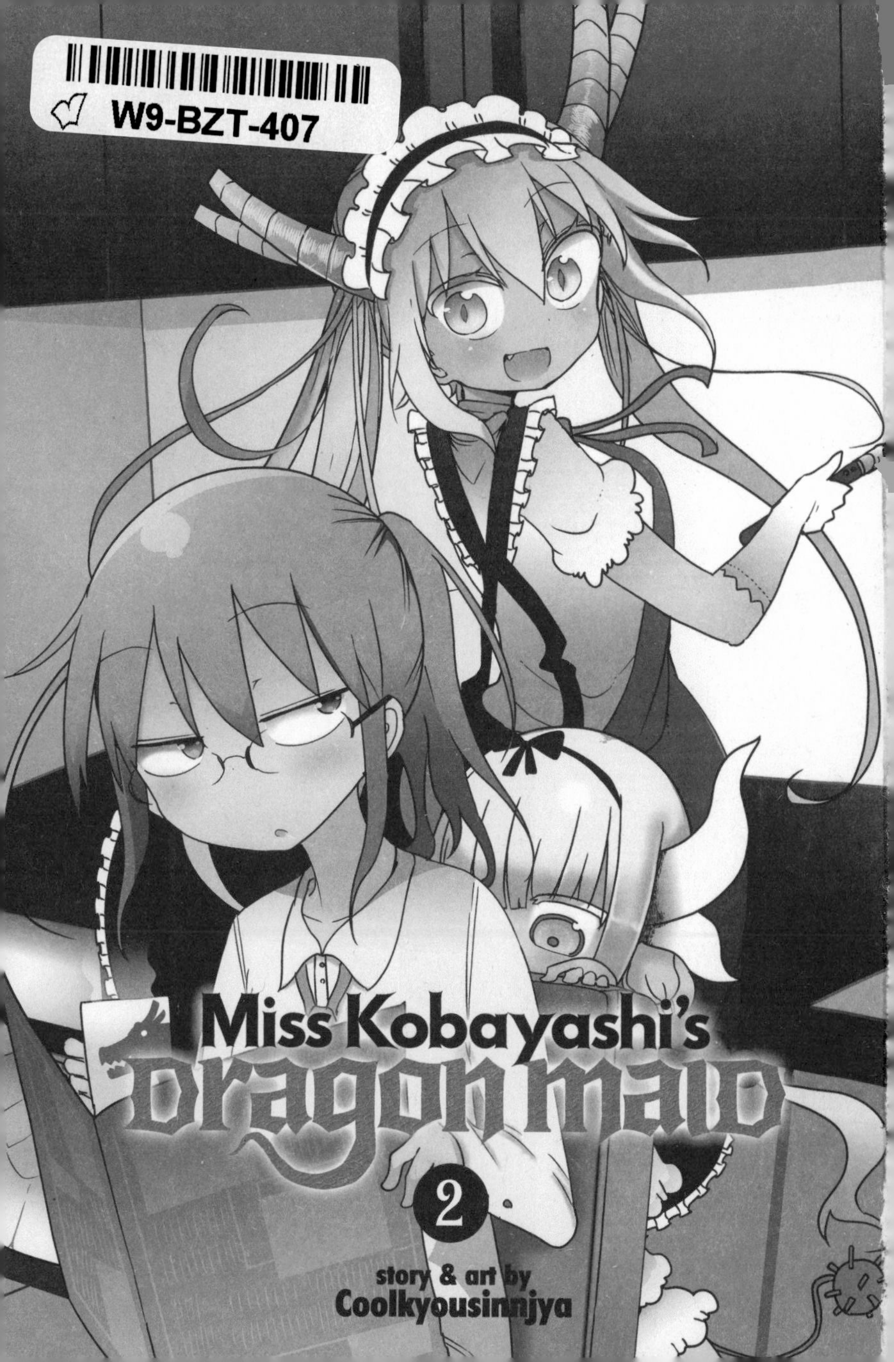
Miss Kobayashi's
Dragon Maid
2
story & art by
Coolkyousinnjya

Miss Kobayashi's
Dragon Maid

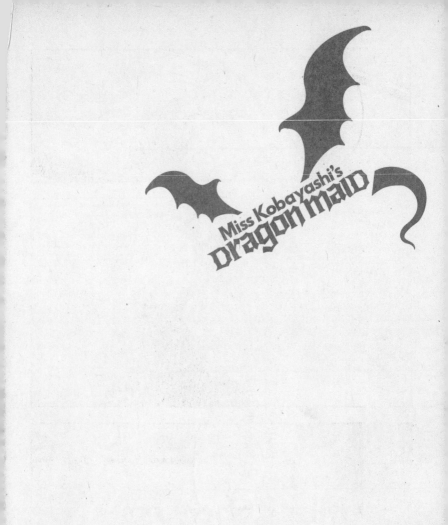

CHAPTER 11 : TOHRU & CLEANING

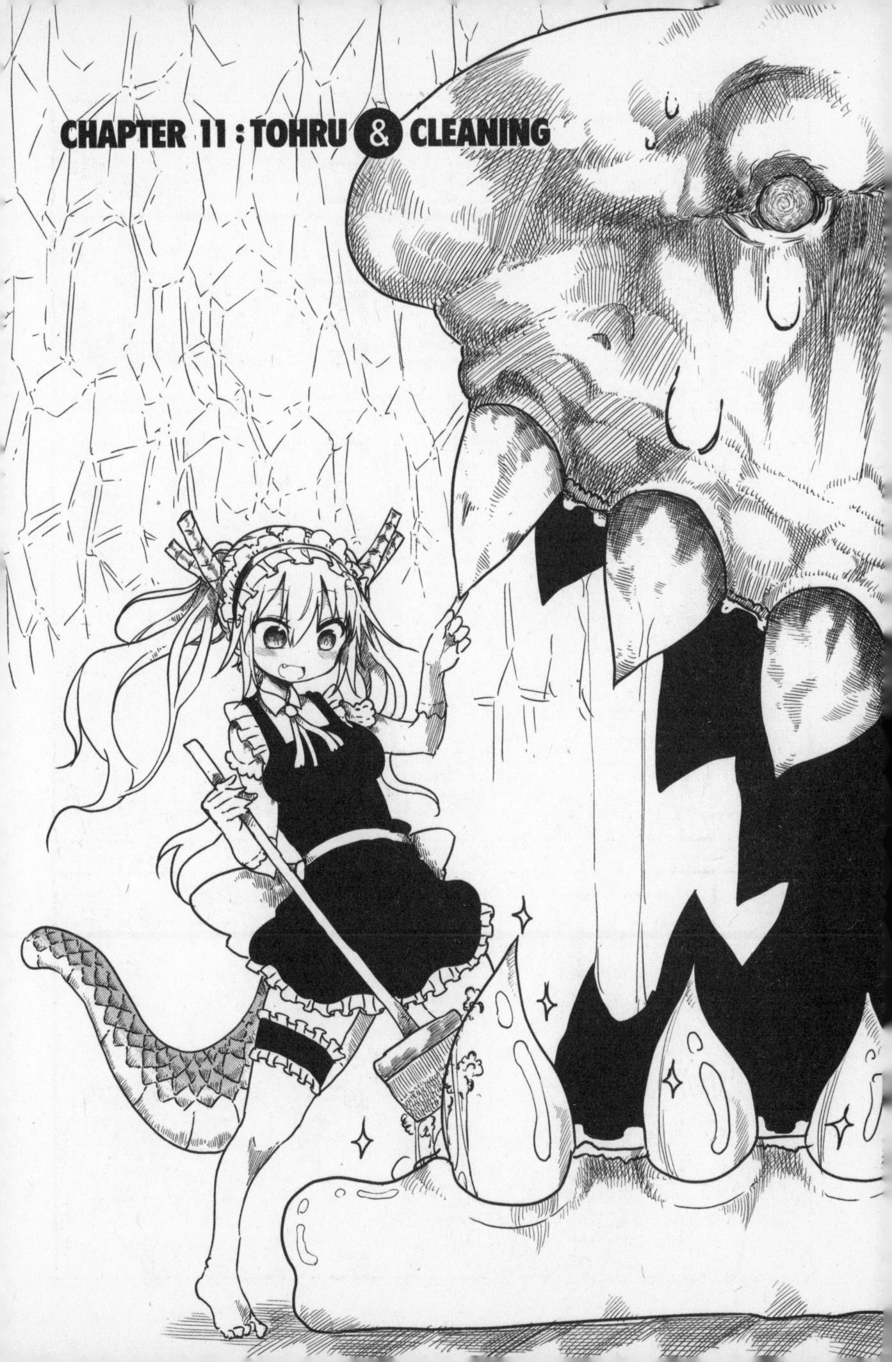

CHAPTER 11

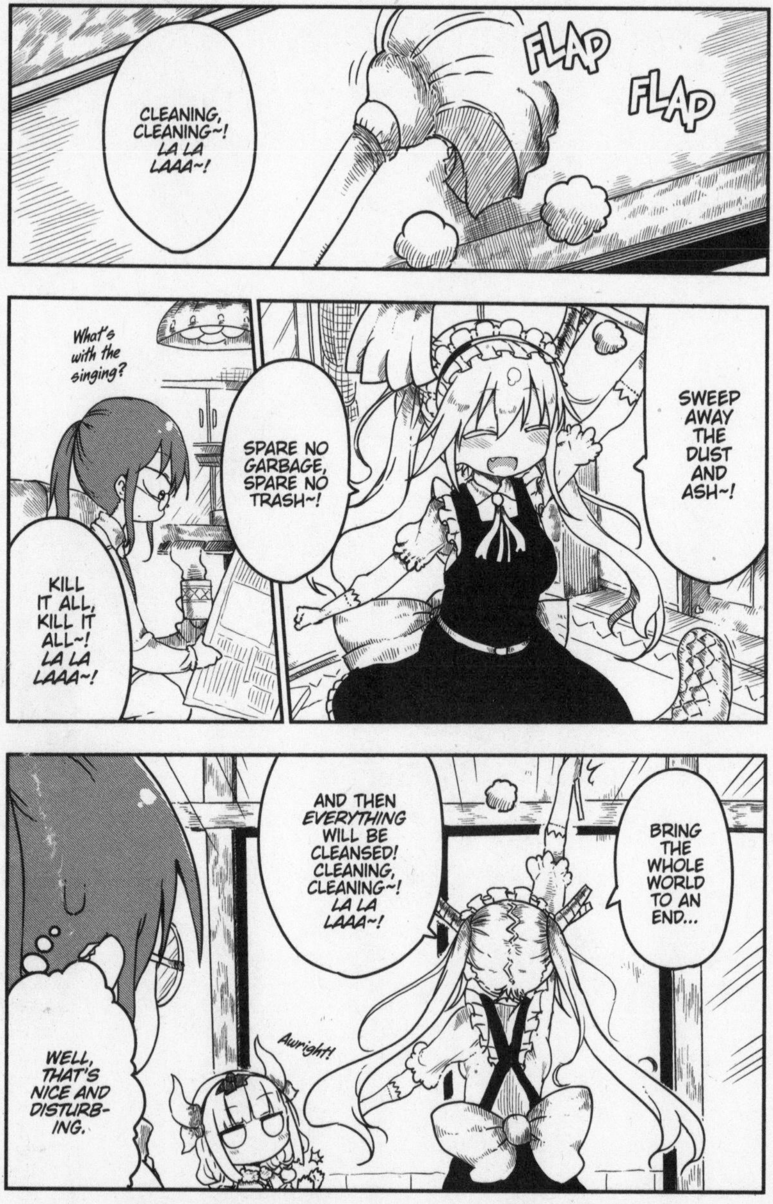
FLAP
FLAP
CLEANING, CLEANING~! LA LA LAAA~!
SWEEP AWAY THE DUST AND ASH~!
SPARE NO GARBAGE, SPARE NO TRASH~!
What's with the singing?
KILL IT ALL, KILL IT ALL~! LA LA LAAA~!
BRING THE WHOLE WORLD TO AN END...
AND THEN EVERYTHING WILL BE CLEANSED! CLEANING, CLEANING~! LA LA LAAA~!
Awright!
WELL, THAT'S NICE AND DISTURB-ING.

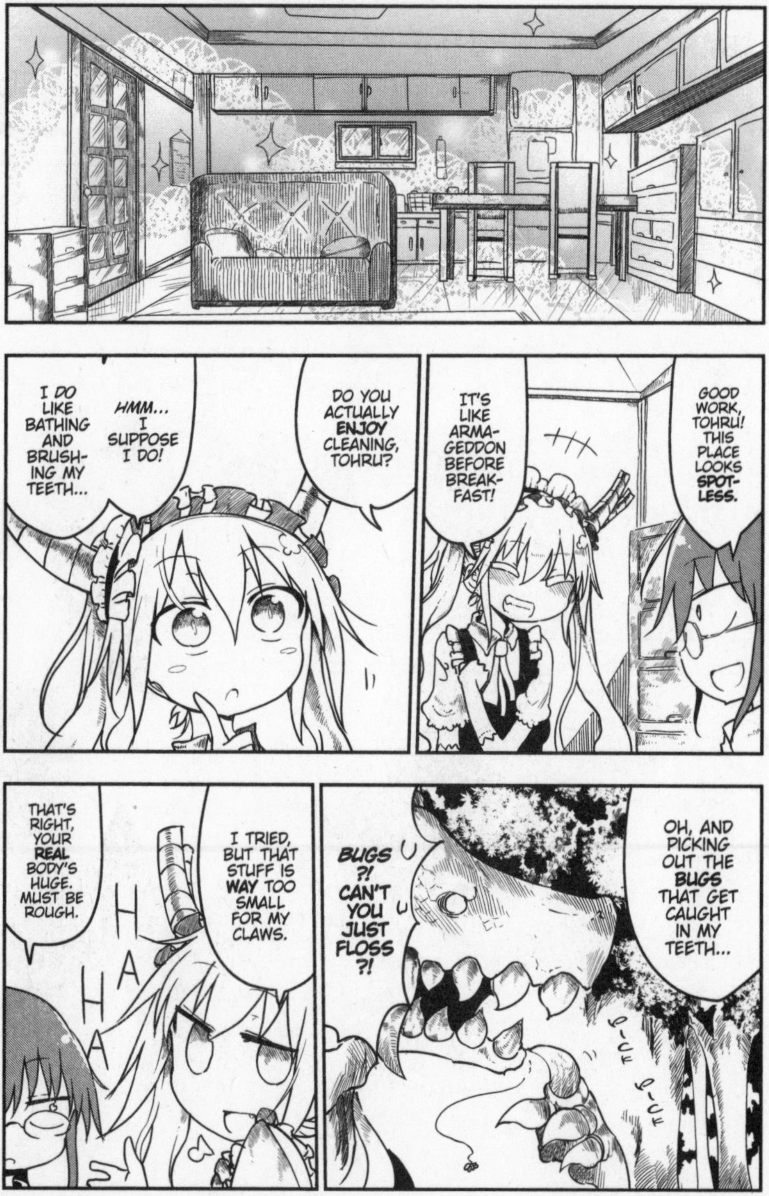
GOOD WORK, TOHRU! THIS PLACE LOOKS SPOTLESS.
IT'S LIKE ARMAGEDDON BEFORE BREAKFAST!
DO YOU ACTUALLY ENJOY CLEANING, TOHRU?
HMM... I SUPPOSE I DO!
I DO LIKE BATHING AND BRUSHING MY TEETH...
OH, AND PICKING OUT THE BUGS THAT GET CAUGHT IN MY TEETH...
BUGS?! CAN'T YOU JUST FLOSS?!
I TRIED, BUT THAT STUFF IS WAY TOO SMALL FOR MY CLAWS.
THAT'S RIGHT, YOUR REAL BODY'S HUGE. MUST BE ROUGH.
HAHAHA

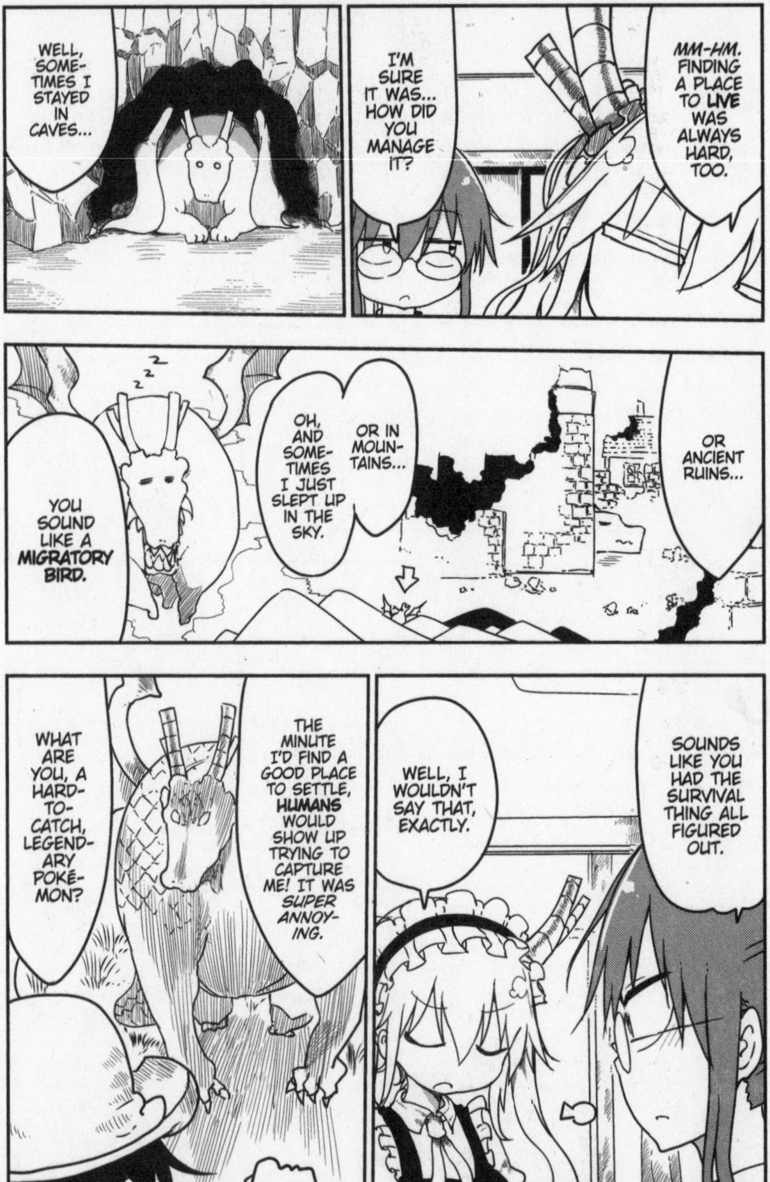
MM-HM. FINDING A PLACE TO LIVE WAS ALWAYS HARD, TOO.
I'M SURE IT WAS... HOW DID YOU MANAGE IT?
WELL, SOMETIMES I STAYED IN CAVES...
OR ANCIENT RUINS...
OR IN MOUNTAINS...
OH, AND SOMETIMES I JUST SLEPT UP IN THE SKY.
YOU SOUND LIKE A MIGRATORY BIRD.
SOUNDS LIKE YOU HAD THE SURVIVAL THING ALL FIGURED OUT.
WELL, I WOULDN'T SAY THAT, EXACTLY.
THE MINUTE I'D FIND A GOOD PLACE TO SETTLE, HUMANS WOULD SHOW UP TRYING TO CAPTURE ME! IT WAS SUPER ANNOYING.
WHAT ARE YOU, A HARD-TO-CATCH, LEGENDARY POKÉMON?

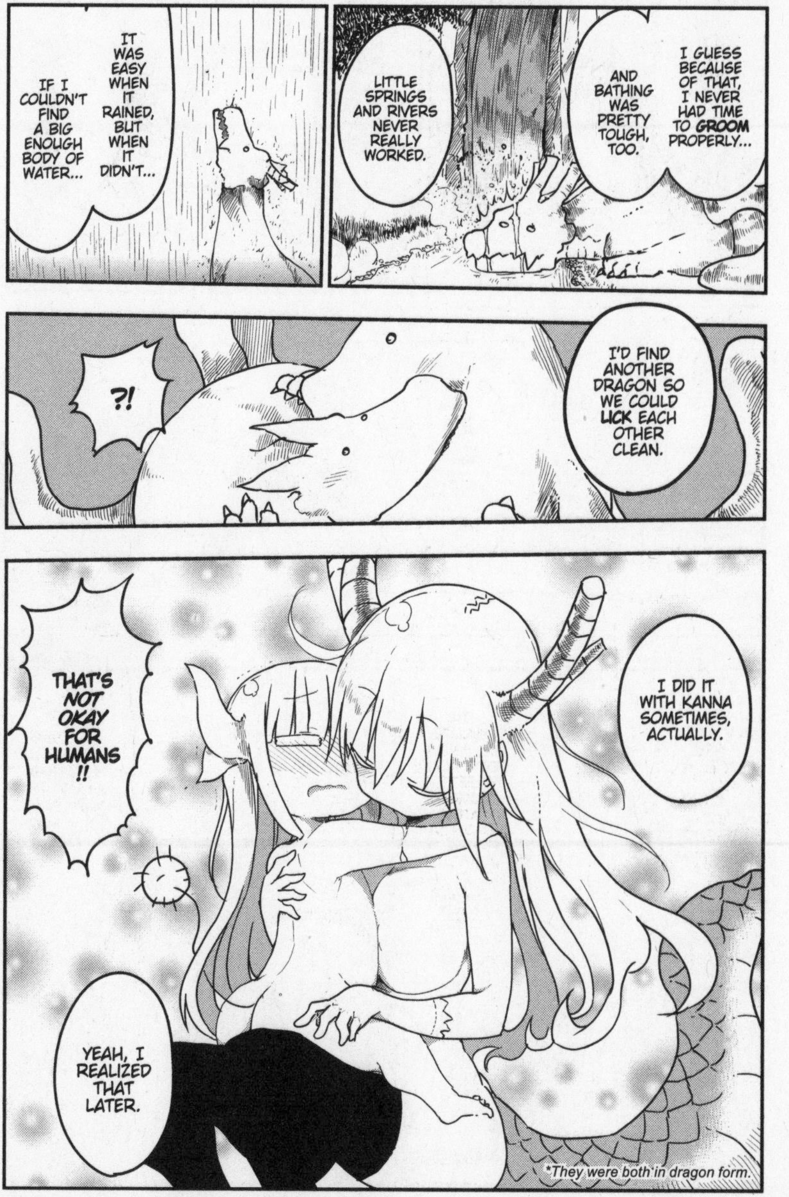
I GUESS BECAUSE OF THAT, I NEVER HAD TIME TO **GROOM** PROPERLY...
AND BATHING WAS PRETTY TOUGH, TOO.
LITTLE SPRINGS AND RIVERS NEVER REALLY WORKED.
IT WAS EASY WHEN IT RAINED, BUT WHEN IT DIDN'T...
IF I COULDN'T FIND A BIG ENOUGH BODY OF WATER...
I'D FIND ANOTHER DRAGON SO WE COULD **LICK** EACH OTHER CLEAN.
?!
I DID IT WITH KANNA SOMETIMES, ACTUALLY.
THAT'S *NOT OKAY* FOR HUMANS!!
YEAH, I REALIZED THAT LATER.
*They were both in dragon form.

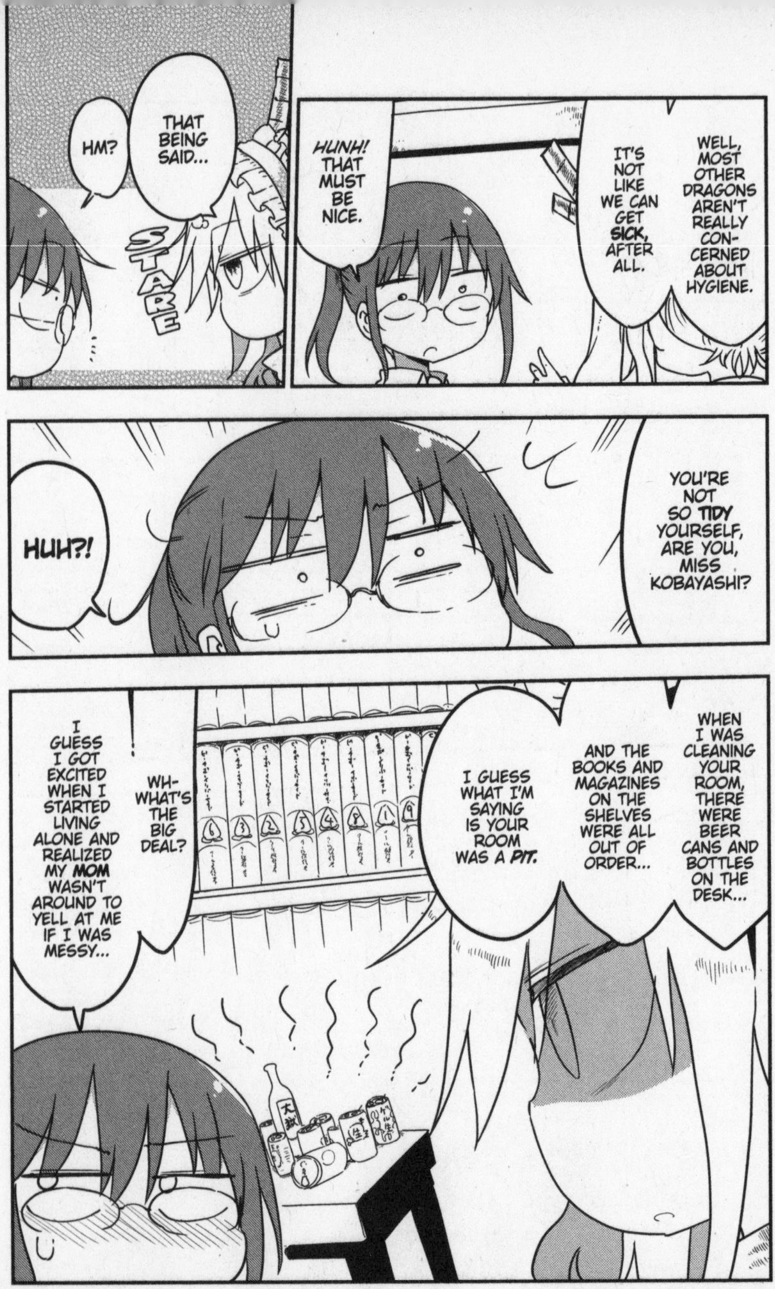
WELL, MOST OTHER DRAGONS AREN'T REALLY CON-CERNED ABOUT HYGIENE.
IT'S NOT LIKE WE CAN GET SICK, AFTER ALL.
HUNH! THAT MUST BE NICE.
THAT BEING SAID...
HM?
STARE
YOU'RE NOT SO TIDY YOURSELF, ARE YOU, MISS KOBAYASHI?
HUH?!
WHEN I WAS CLEANING YOUR ROOM, THERE WERE BEER CANS AND BOTTLES ON THE DESK...
AND THE BOOKS AND MAGAZINES ON THE SHELVES WERE ALL OUT OF ORDER...
I GUESS WHAT I'M SAYING IS YOUR ROOM WAS A PIT.
WH-WHAT'S THE BIG DEAL?
I GUESS I GOT EXCITED WHEN I STARTED LIVING ALONE AND REALIZED MY MOM WASN'T AROUND TO YELL AT ME IF I WAS MESSY...

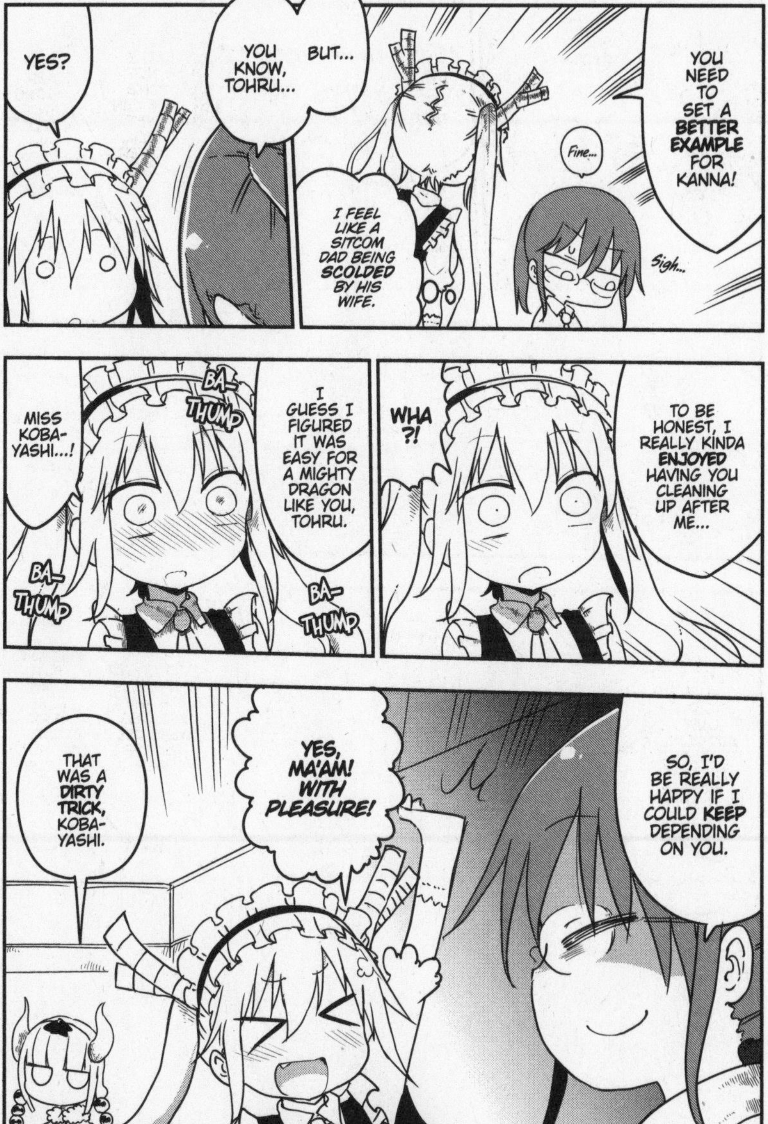
YOU NEED TO SET A BETTER EXAMPLE FOR KANNA!
Sigh...
Fine...
I FEEL LIKE A SITCOM DAD BEING SCOLDED BY HIS WIFE.
YOU KNOW, TOHRU... BUT...
YES?
TO BE HONEST, I REALLY KINDA ENJOYED HAVING YOU CLEANING UP AFTER ME...
WHA ?!
I GUESS I FIGURED IT WAS EASY FOR A MIGHTY DRAGON LIKE YOU, TOHRU.
BA-THUMP
BA-THUMP
BA-THUMP
MISS KOBA-YASHI...!
SO, I'D BE REALLY HAPPY IF I COULD KEEP DEPENDING ON YOU.
YES, MA'AM! WITH PLEASURE!
THAT WAS A DIRTY TRICK, KOBA-YASHI.

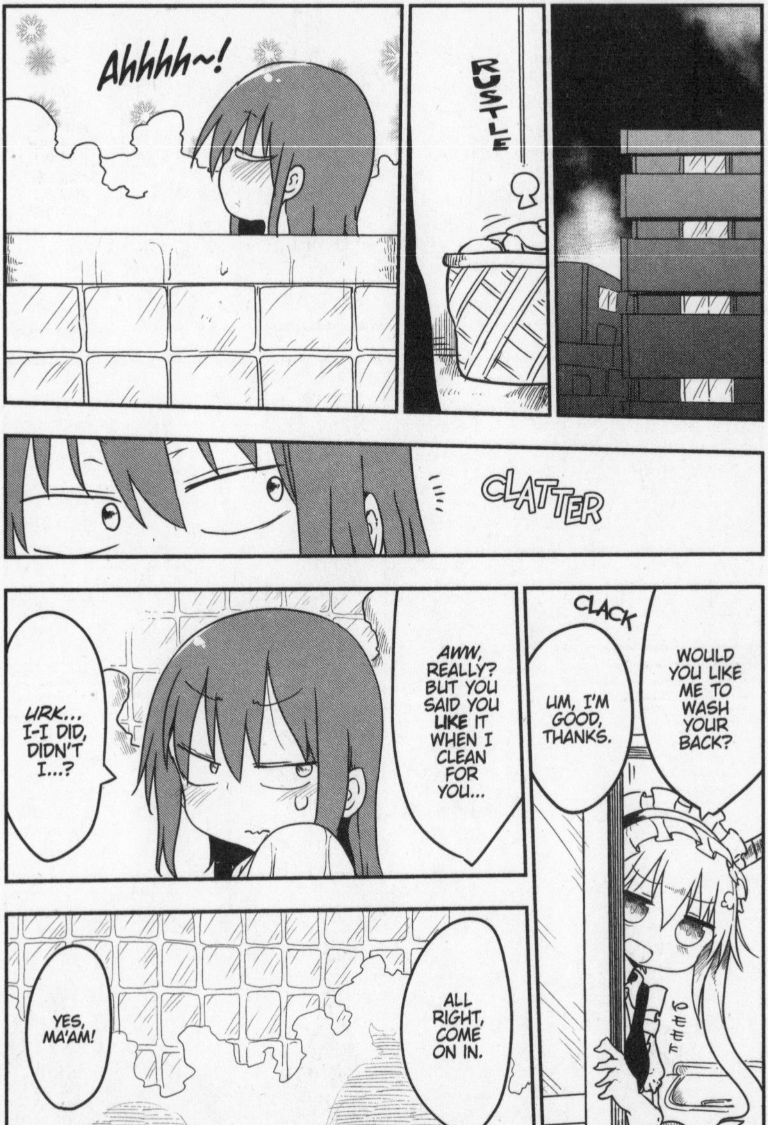
RUSTLE
Ahhhh~!
CLATTER
CLACK
WOULD YOU LIKE ME TO WASH YOUR BACK?
UM, I'M GOOD, THANKS.
AWW, REALLY? BUT YOU SAID YOU LIKE IT WHEN I CLEAN FOR YOU...
URK... I-I DID, DIDN'T I...?
ALL RIGHT, COME ON IN.
YES, MA'AM!

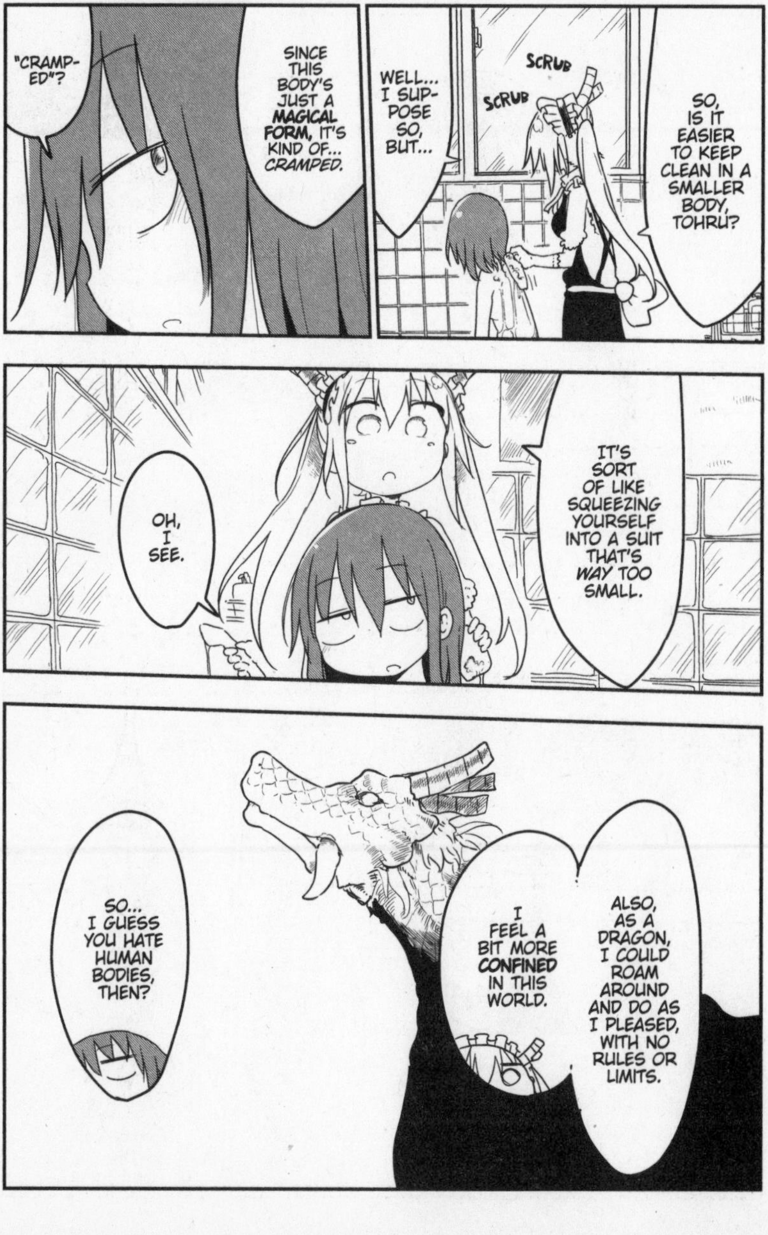
SO, IS IT EASIER TO KEEP CLEAN IN A SMALLER BODY, TOHRU?
SCRUB
SCRUB
WELL... I SUPPOSE SO, BUT...
SINCE THIS BODY'S JUST A **MAGICAL FORM,** IT'S KIND OF... *CRAMPED.*
"CRAMPED"?
IT'S SORT OF LIKE SQUEEZING YOURSELF INTO A SUIT THAT'S *WAY* TOO SMALL.
OH, I SEE.
ALSO, AS A DRAGON, I COULD ROAM AROUND AND DO AS I PLEASED, WITH NO RULES OR LIMITS.
I FEEL A BIT MORE **CONFINED** IN THIS WORLD.
SO... I GUESS YOU HATE HUMAN BODIES, THEN?

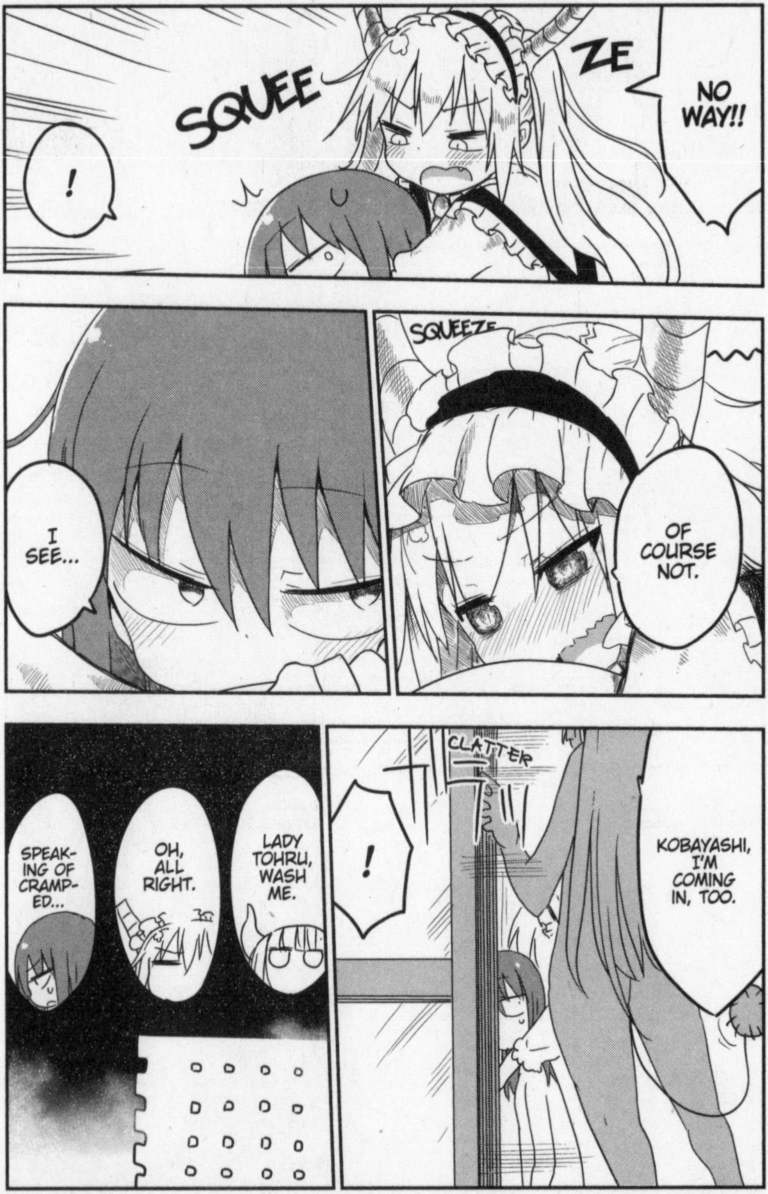
NO WAY!!
SQUEE ZE
!
SQUEEZE
OF COURSE NOT.
I SEE...
CLATTER
KOBAYASHI, I'M COMING IN, TOO.
!
LADY TOHRU, WASH ME.
OH, ALL RIGHT.
SPEAK-ING OF CRAMP-ED...

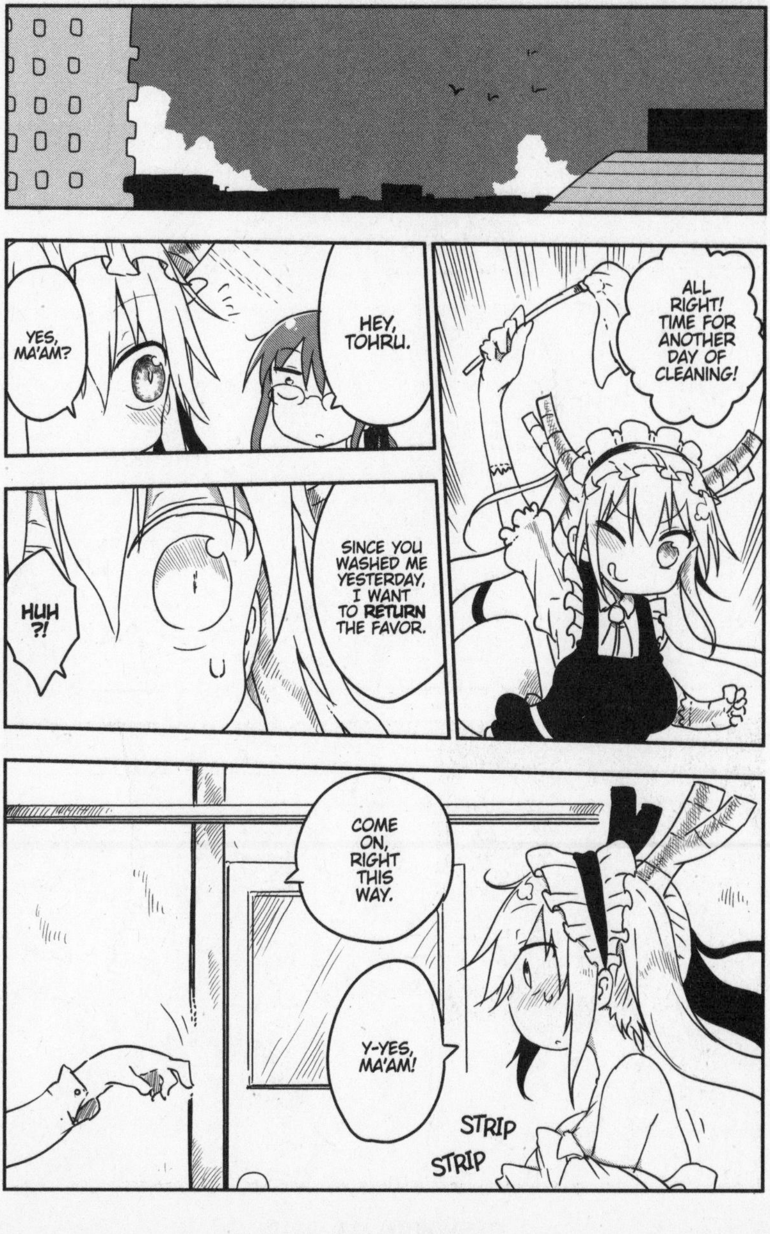
ALL RIGHT! TIME FOR ANOTHER DAY OF CLEANING!
HEY, TOHRU.
YES, MA'AM?
SINCE YOU WASHED ME YESTERDAY, I WANT TO **RETURN** THE FAVOR.
HUH?!
COME ON, RIGHT THIS WAY.
Y-YES, MA'AM!
STRIP
STRIP

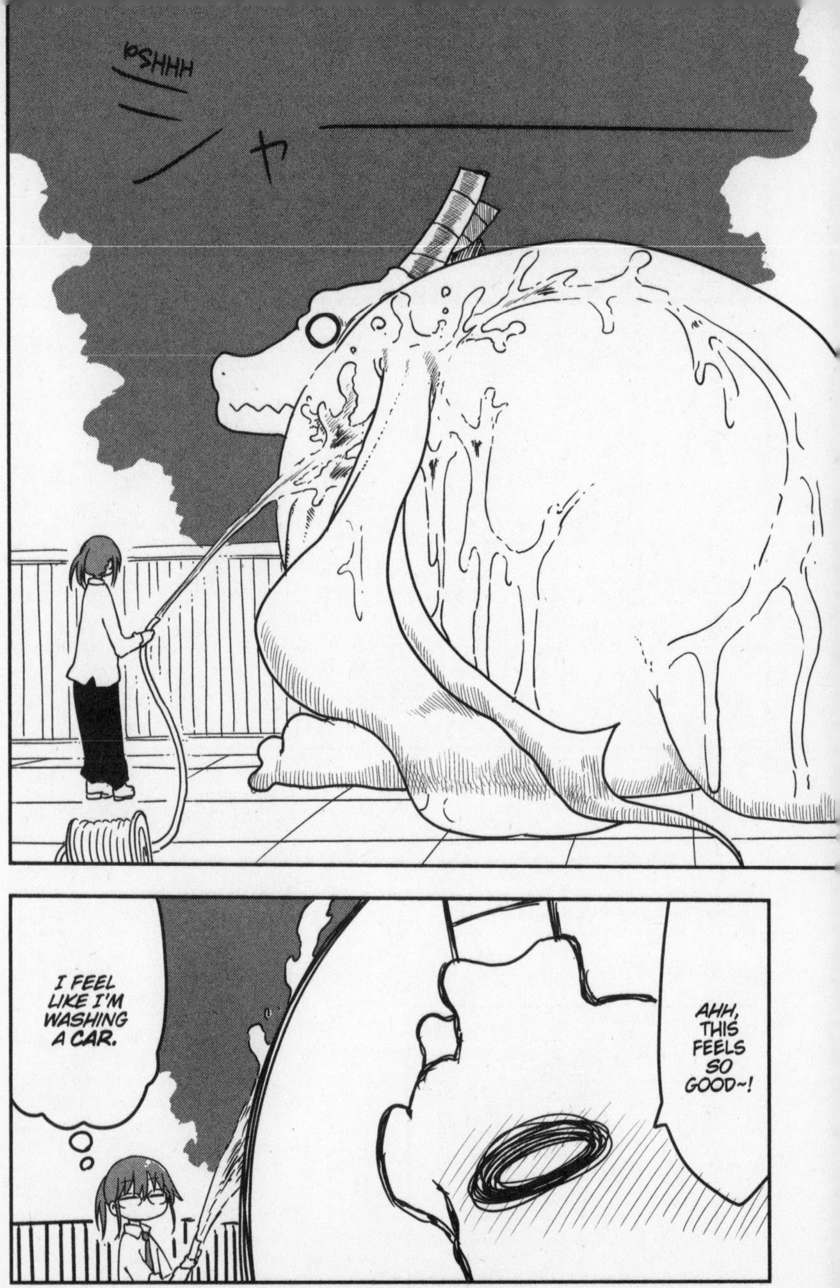
SHHH
AHH, THIS FEELS SO GOOD~!
I FEEL LIKE I'M WASHING A CAR.

CHAPTER 11/END

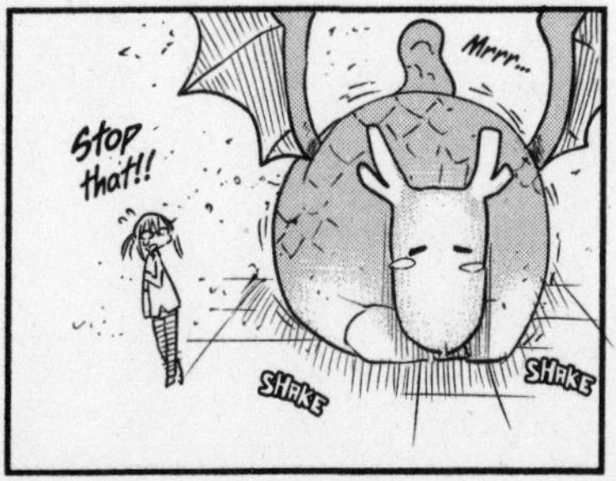
Mrrr...
Stop that!!
SHAKE
SHAKE

Miss Kobayashi's
Dragon Maid

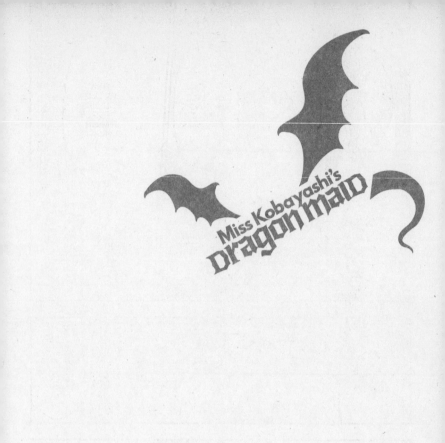

CHAPTER 12

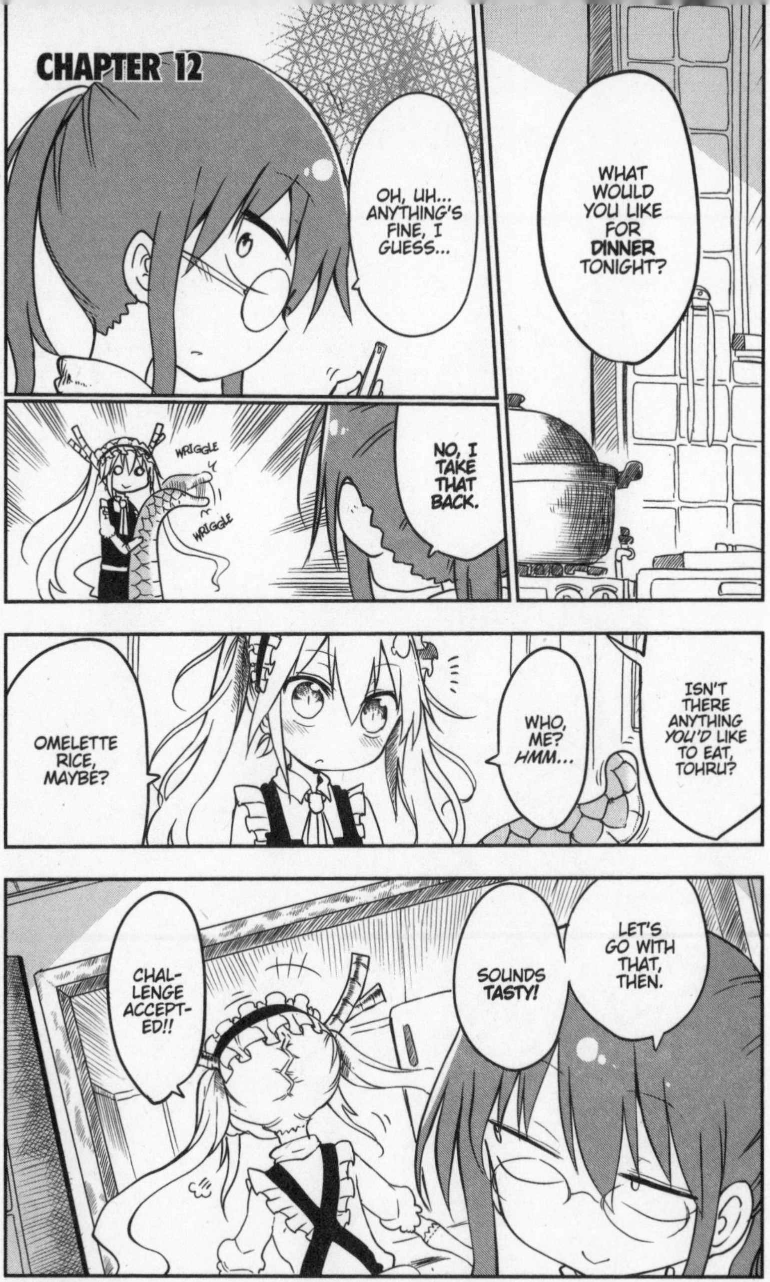
WHAT WOULD YOU LIKE FOR DINNER TONIGHT?
OH, UH... ANYTHING'S FINE, I GUESS...
NO, I TAKE THAT BACK.
WRIGGLE
WRIGGLE
ISN'T THERE ANYTHING YOU'D LIKE TO EAT, TOHRU?
WHO, ME? HMM...
OMELETTE RICE, MAYBE?
LET'S GO WITH THAT, THEN.
SOUNDS TASTY!
CHAL-LENGE ACCEPT-ED!!

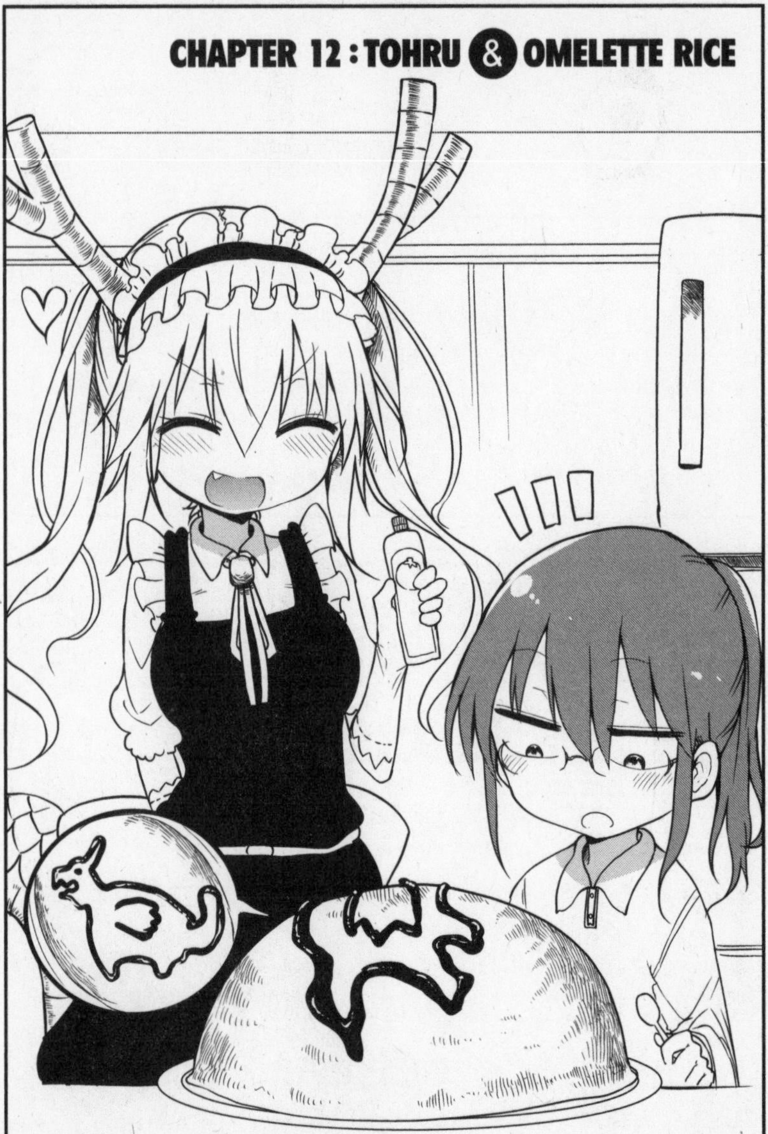
CHAPTER 12 : TOHRU & OMELETTE RICE

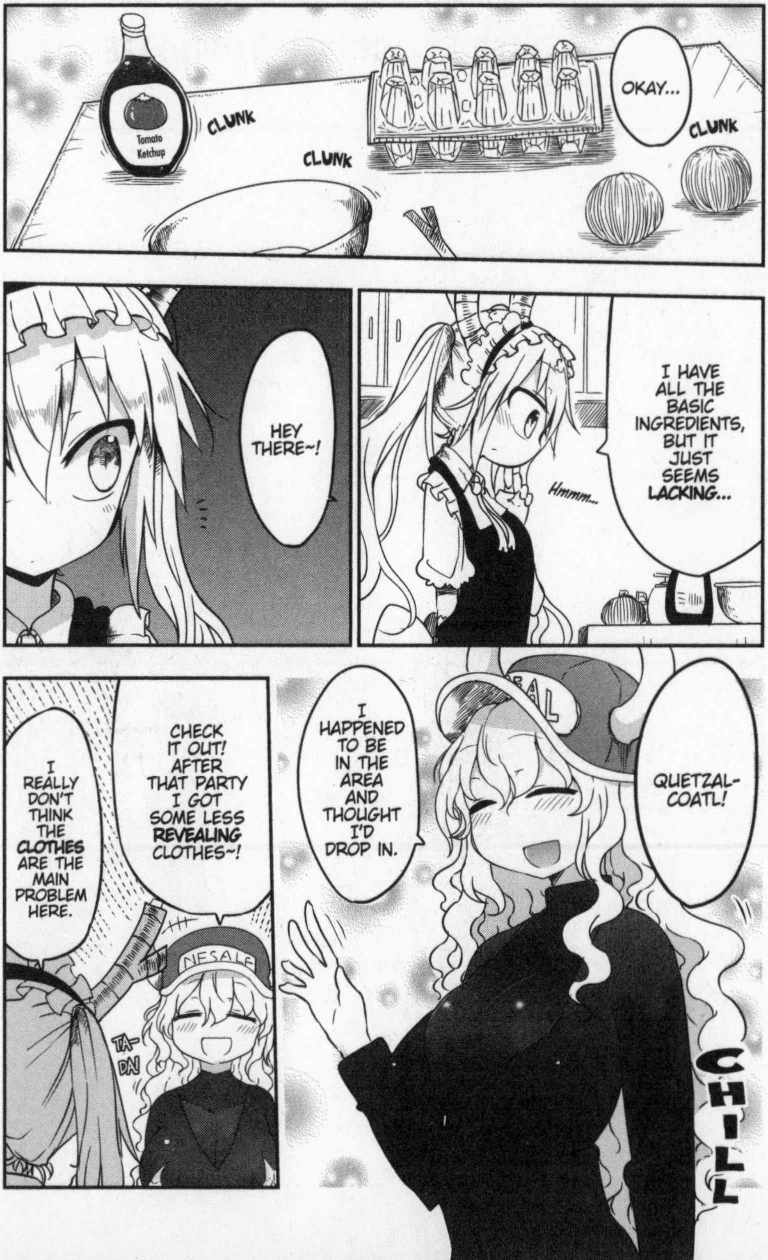
OKAY...
CLUNK
CLUNK
CLUNK
Tomato Ketchup
I HAVE ALL THE BASIC INGREDIENTS, BUT IT JUST SEEMS LACKING...
Hmmm...
HEY THERE~!
QUETZAL-COATL!
I HAPPENED TO BE IN THE AREA AND THOUGHT I'D DROP IN.
CHILL
CHECK IT OUT! AFTER THAT PARTY I GOT SOME LESS REVEALING CLOTHES~!
TA-DA!
I REALLY DON'T THINK THE CLOTHES ARE THE MAIN PROBLEM HERE.

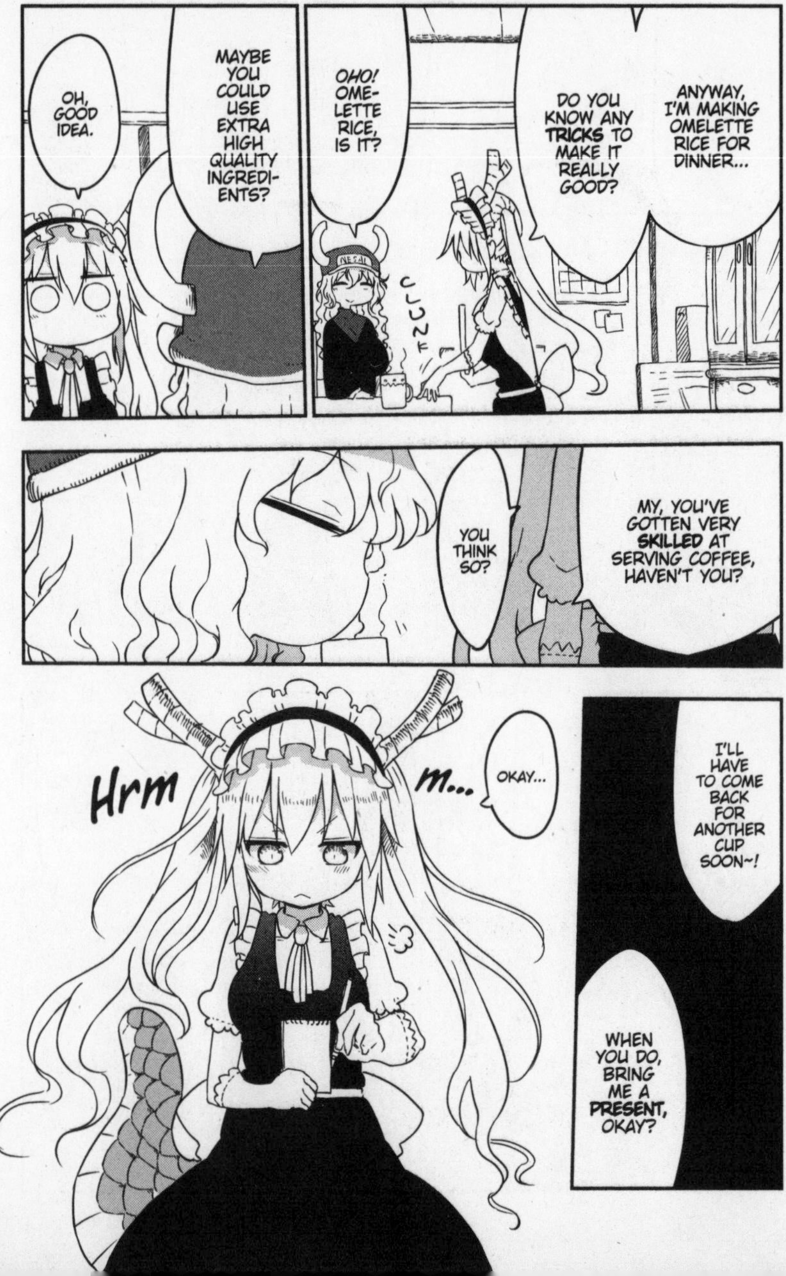
ANYWAY, I'M MAKING OMELETTE RICE FOR DINNER...
DO YOU KNOW ANY **TRICKS** TO MAKE IT REALLY GOOD?
OHO! OME-LETTE RICE, IS IT?
CLUNK
MAYBE YOU COULD USE EXTRA HIGH QUALITY INGREDI-ENTS?
OH, GOOD IDEA.
MY, YOU'VE GOTTEN VERY **SKILLED** AT SERVING COFFEE, HAVEN'T YOU?
YOU THINK SO?
I'LL HAVE TO COME BACK FOR ANOTHER CUP SOON~!
WHEN YOU DO, BRING ME A **PRESENT**, OKAY?
OKAY...
Hrm m...

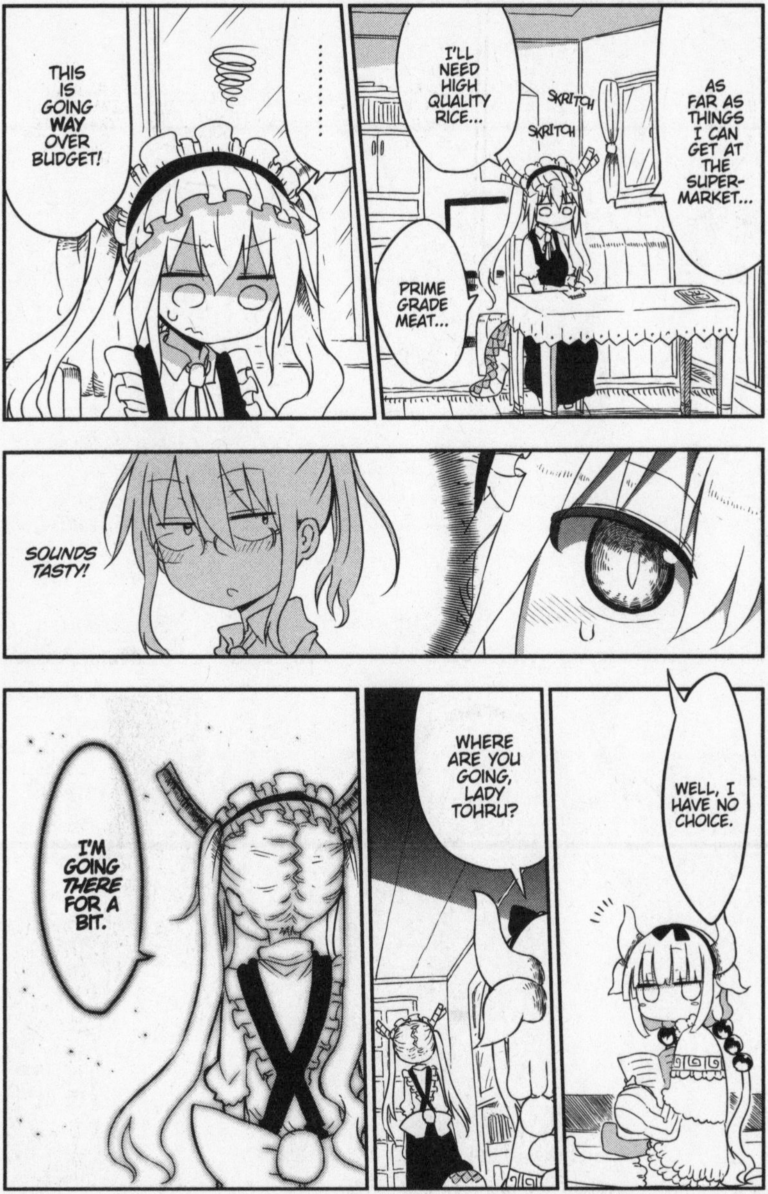
AS FAR AS THINGS I CAN GET AT THE SUPER-MARKET...
I'LL NEED HIGH QUALITY RICE...
SKRITCH
SKRITCH
PRIME GRADE MEAT...
......
THIS IS GOING WAY OVER BUDGET!
SOUNDS TASTY!
WELL, I HAVE NO CHOICE.
WHERE ARE YOU GOING, LADY TOHRU?
I'M GOING *THERE* FOR A BIT.

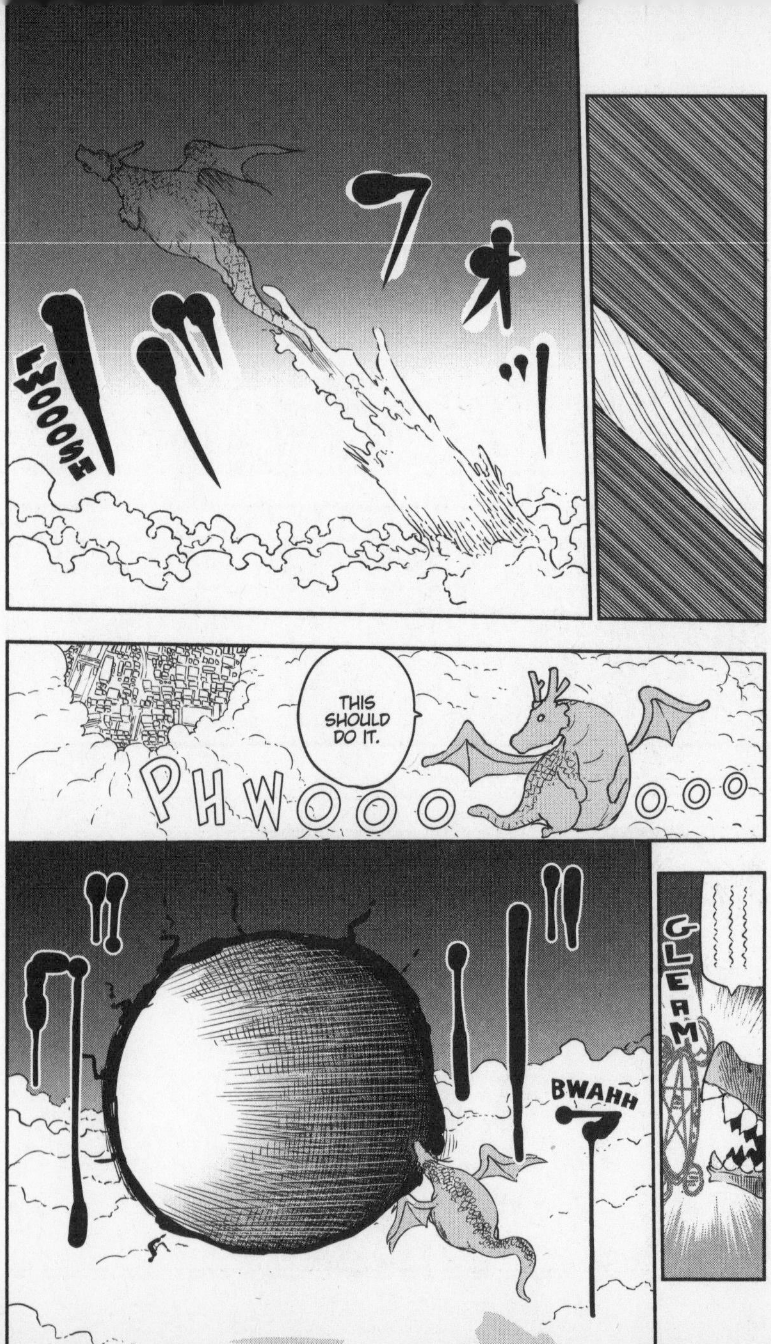
WHOOSH
THIS SHOULD DO IT.
PHWOOOOOOO
GLEAM
BWAHH

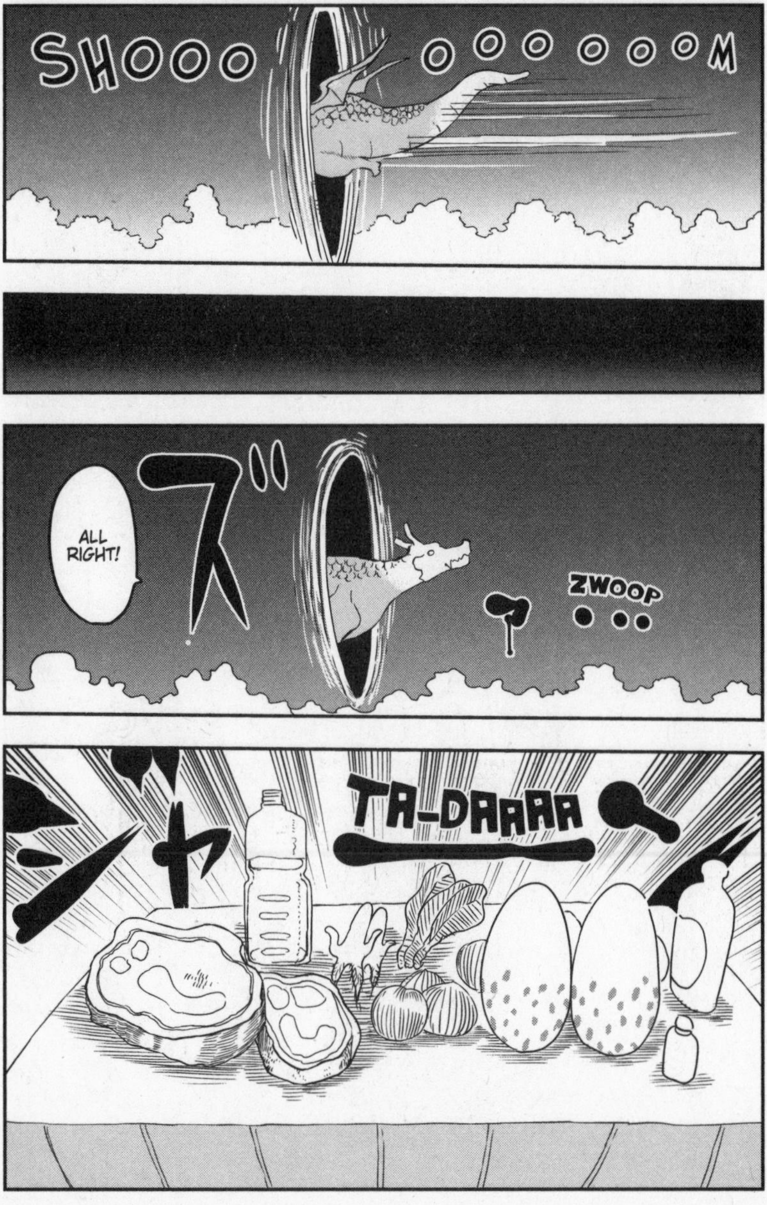
SHOOOOOOOOOM
ZWOOP • • •
ALL RIGHT!
TA-DAAAA

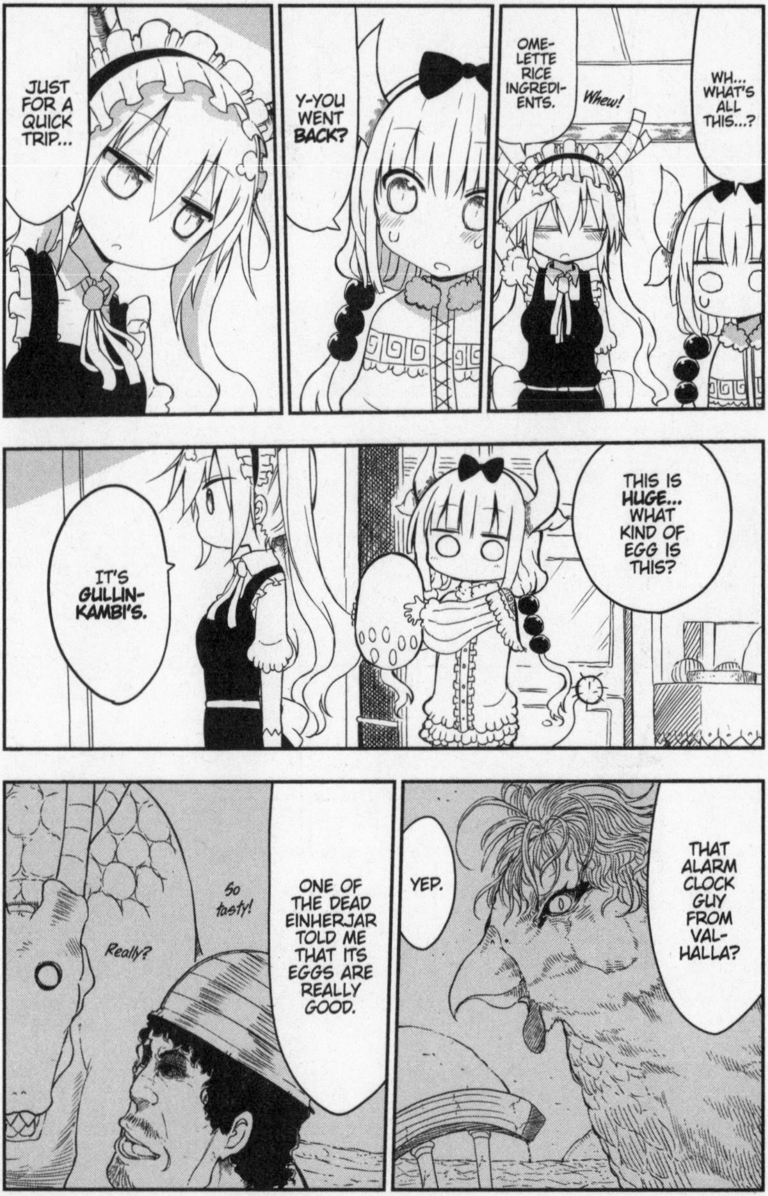

WH... WHAT'S ALL THIS...?
OMELETTE RICE INGREDIENTS.
Whew!
Y-YOU WENT BACK?
JUST FOR A QUICK TRIP...
THIS IS HUGE... WHAT KIND OF EGG IS THIS?
IT'S GULLINKAMBI'S.
THAT ALARM CLOCK GUY FROM VALHALLA?
YEP.
ONE OF THE DEAD EINHERJAR TOLD ME THAT ITS EGGS ARE REALLY GOOD.
So tasty!
Really?

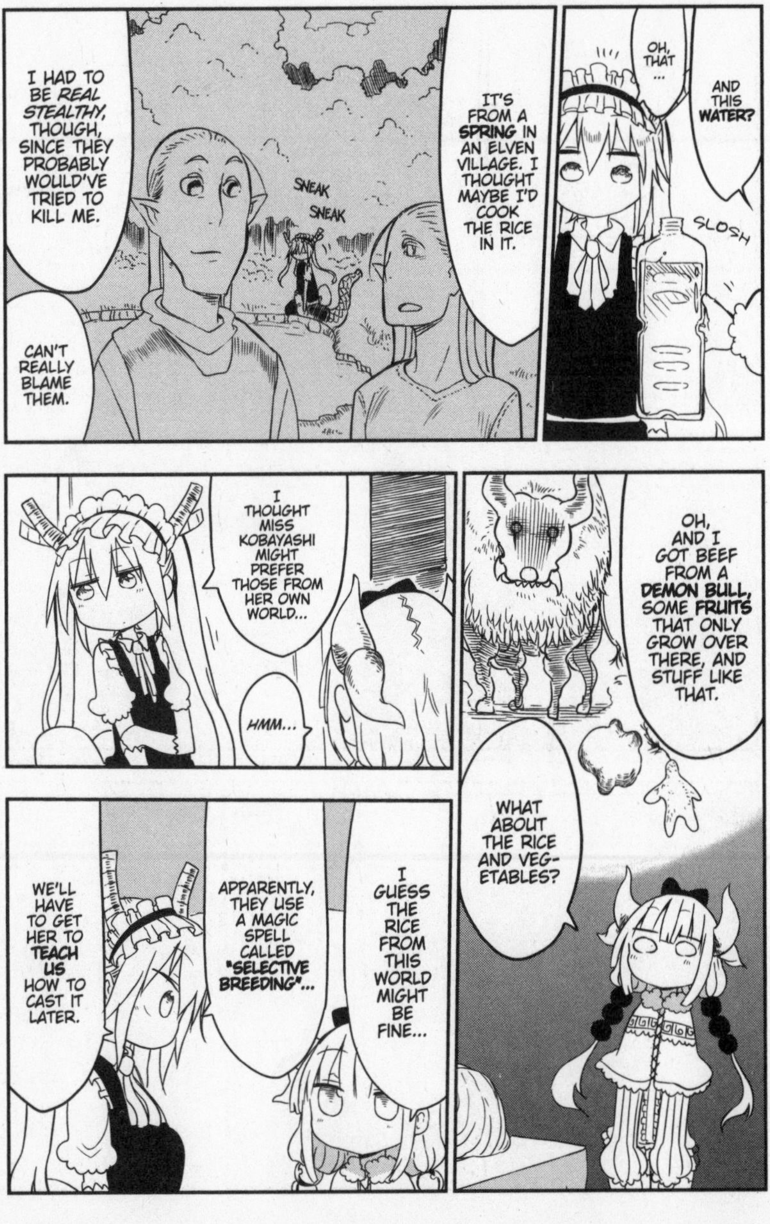
AND THIS **WATER?**
OH, THAT ...
SLOSH
IT'S FROM A **SPRING** IN AN ELVEN VILLAGE. I THOUGHT MAYBE I'D COOK THE RICE IN IT.
I HAD TO BE *REAL STEALTHY,* THOUGH, SINCE THEY PROBABLY WOULD'VE TRIED TO KILL ME.
SNEAK
SNEAK
CAN'T REALLY BLAME THEM.
OH, AND I GOT BEEF FROM A **DEMON BULL,** SOME **FRUITS** THAT ONLY GROW OVER THERE, AND STUFF LIKE THAT.
WHAT ABOUT THE RICE AND VEG-ETABLES?
I THOUGHT MISS KOBAYASHI MIGHT PREFER THOSE FROM HER OWN WORLD...
HMM...
I GUESS THE RICE FROM THIS WORLD MIGHT BE FINE...
APPARENTLY, THEY USE A MAGIC SPELL CALLED **"SELECTIVE BREEDING"...**
WE'LL HAVE TO GET HER TO **TEACH US** HOW TO CAST IT LATER.

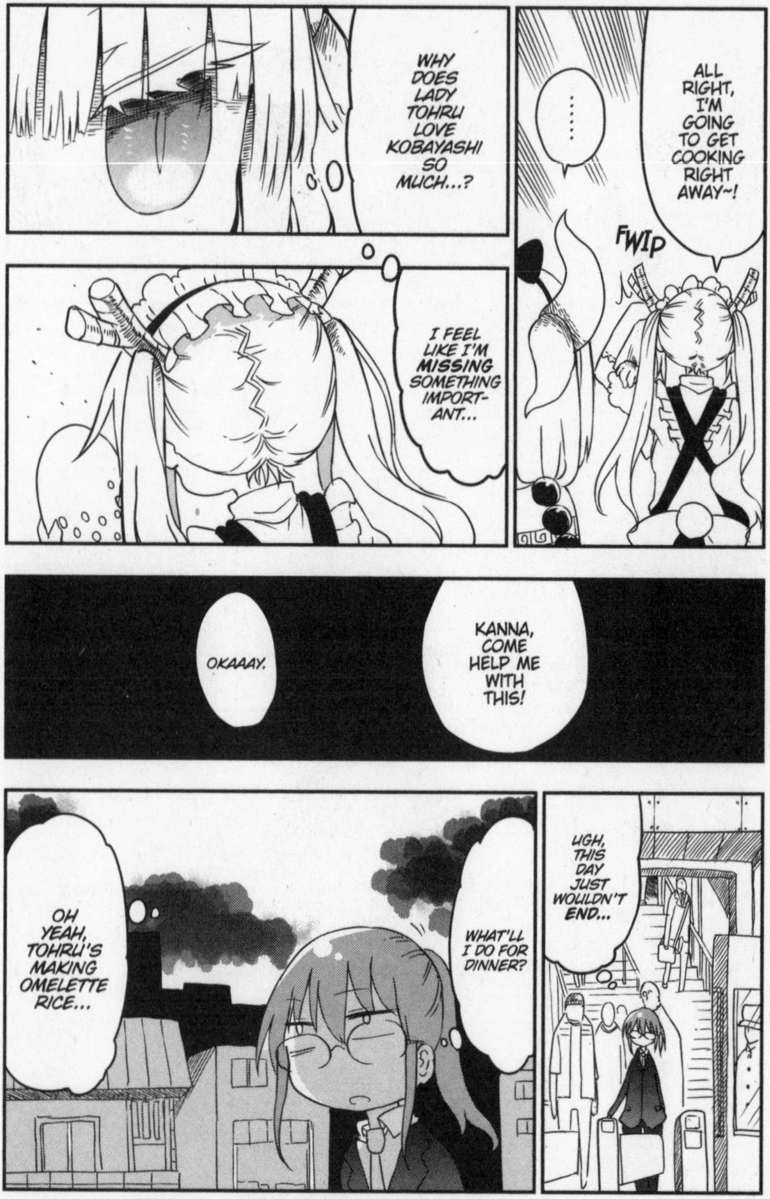
......
ALL RIGHT, I'M GOING TO GET COOKING RIGHT AWAY~!
FWIP
WHY DOES LADY TOHRU LOVE KOBAYASHI SO MUCH...?
I FEEL LIKE I'M MISSING SOMETHING IMPORTANT...
KANNA, COME HELP ME WITH THIS!
OKAAAY.
UGH, THIS DAY JUST WOULDN'T END...
WHAT'LL I DO FOR DINNER?
OH YEAH, TOHRU'S MAKING OMELETTE RICE...

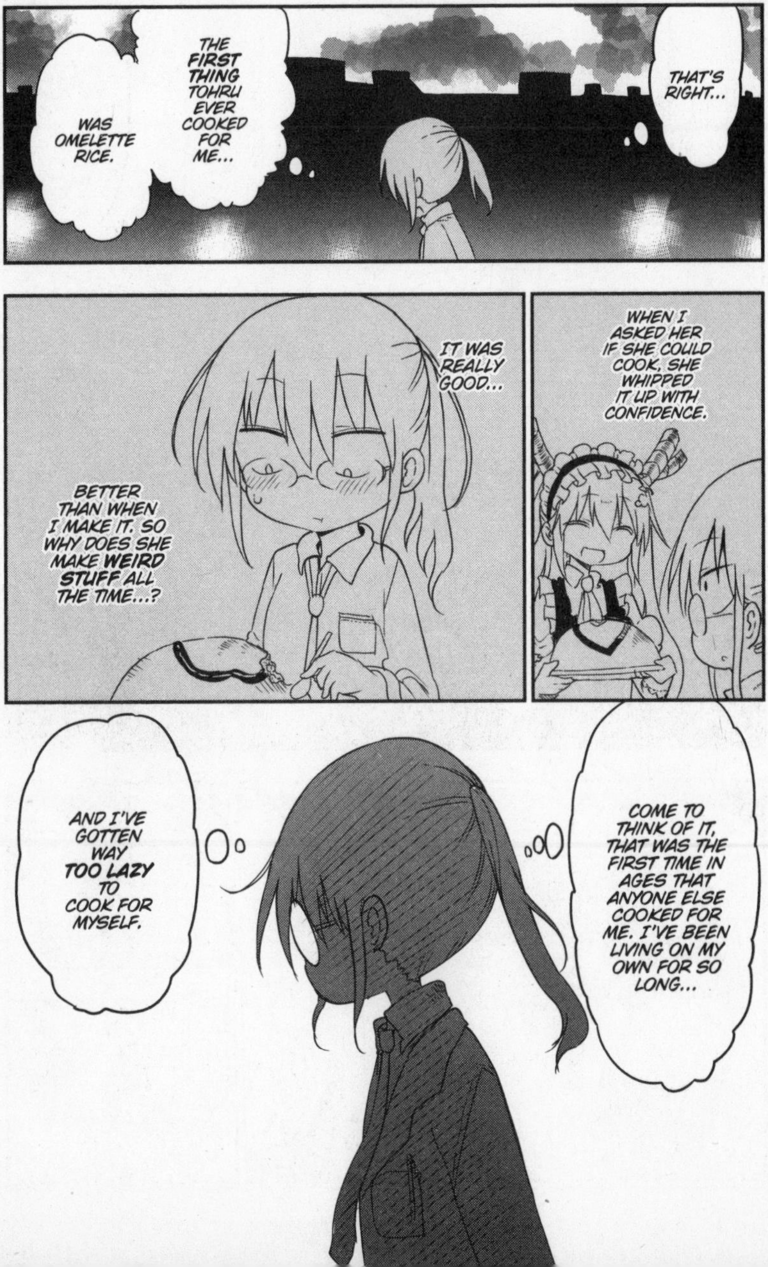
THAT'S RIGHT...
THE FIRST THING TOHRU EVER COOKED FOR ME...
WAS OMELETTE RICE.
WHEN I ASKED HER IF SHE COULD COOK, SHE WHIPPED IT UP WITH CONFIDENCE.
IT WAS REALLY GOOD...
BETTER THAN WHEN I MAKE IT. SO WHY DOES SHE MAKE WEIRD STUFF ALL THE TIME...?
COME TO THINK OF IT, THAT WAS THE FIRST TIME IN AGES THAT ANYONE ELSE COOKED FOR ME. I'VE BEEN LIVING ON MY OWN FOR SO LONG...
AND I'VE GOTTEN WAY TOO LAZY TO COOK FOR MYSELF.

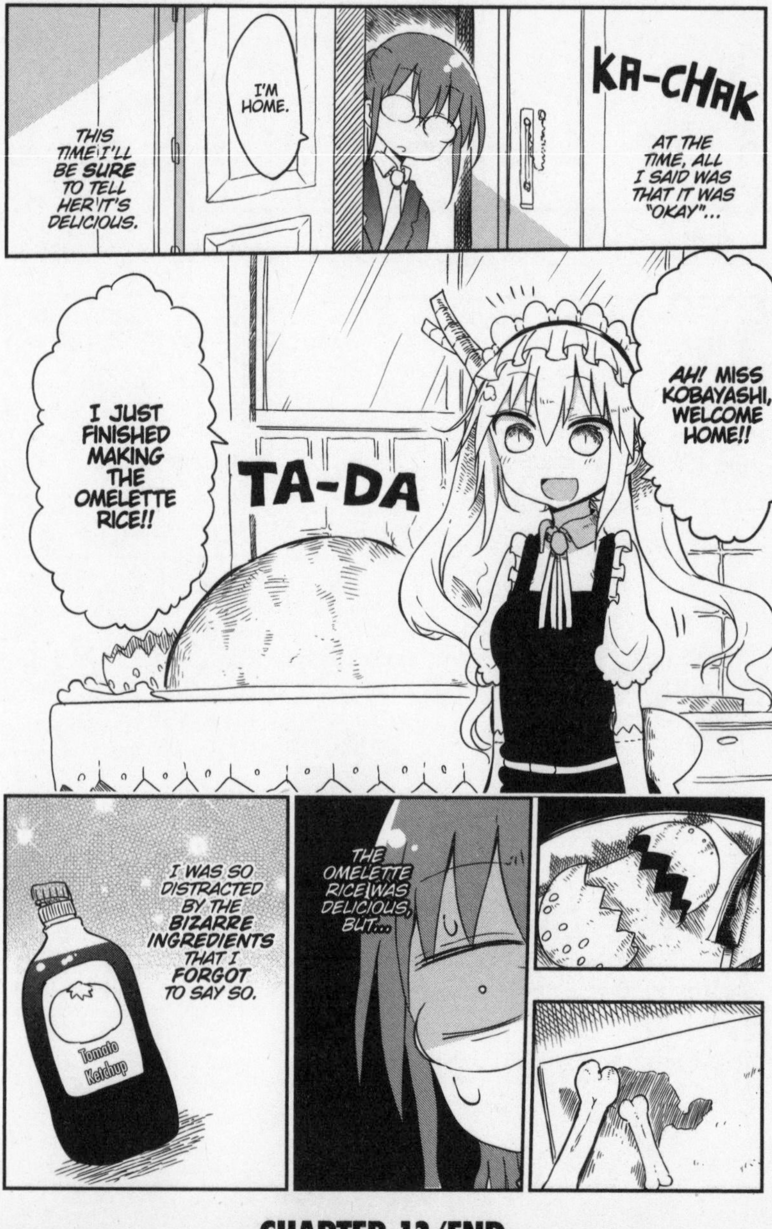
KA-CHAK
AT THE TIME, ALL I SAID WAS THAT IT WAS "OKAY"...
I'M HOME.
THIS TIME I'LL BE SURE TO TELL HER IT'S DELICIOUS.
AH! MISS KOBAYASHI, WELCOME HOME!!
TA-DA
I JUST FINISHED MAKING THE OMELETTE RICE!!
THE OMELETTE RICE WAS DELICIOUS, BUT...
I WAS SO DISTRACTED BY THE BIZARRE INGREDIENTS THAT I FORGOT TO SAY SO.
Tomato Ketchup

CHAPTER 12/END

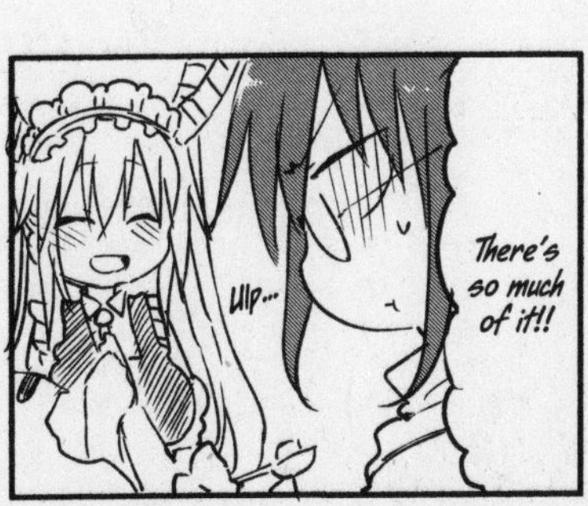
There's so much of it!!
Ulp...

Miss Kobayashi's
Dragon Maid

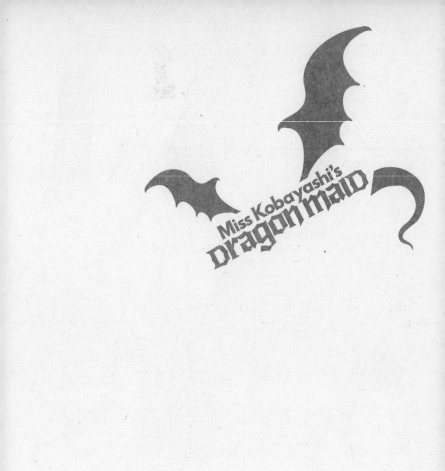

CHAPTER 13 : KANNA & SCHOOL

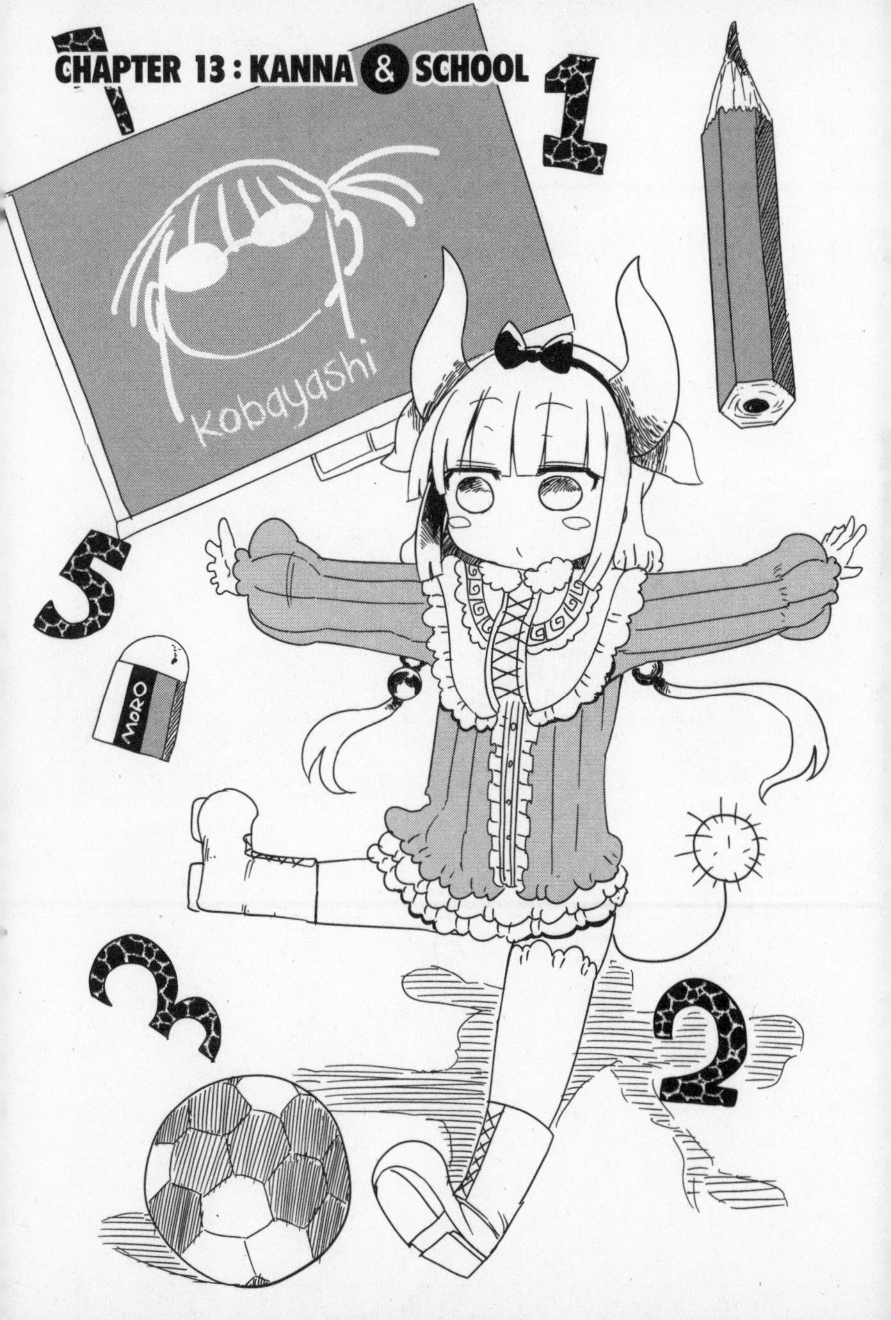
Kobayashi
MORO

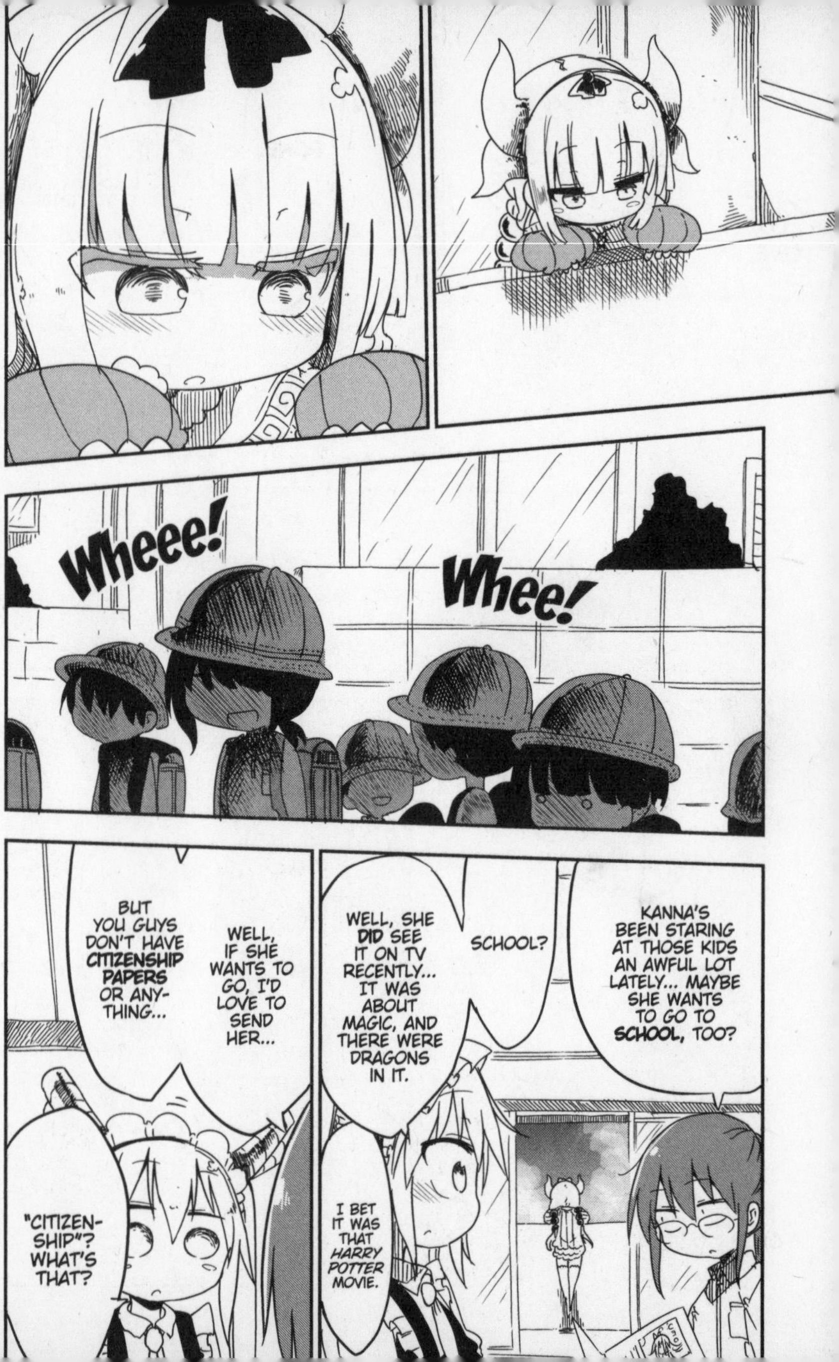
Whee!
Wheeee!
KANNA'S BEEN STARING AT THOSE KIDS AN AWFUL LOT LATELY... MAYBE SHE WANTS TO GO TO **SCHOOL**, TOO?
SCHOOL?
WELL, SHE **DID** SEE IT ON TV RECENTLY... IT WAS ABOUT MAGIC, AND THERE WERE DRAGONS IN IT.
I BET IT WAS THAT *HARRY POTTER* MOVIE.
WELL, IF SHE WANTS TO GO, I'D LOVE TO SEND HER...
BUT YOU GUYS DON'T HAVE **CITIZENSHIP PAPERS** OR ANY-THING...
"CITIZEN-SHIP"? WHAT'S THAT?

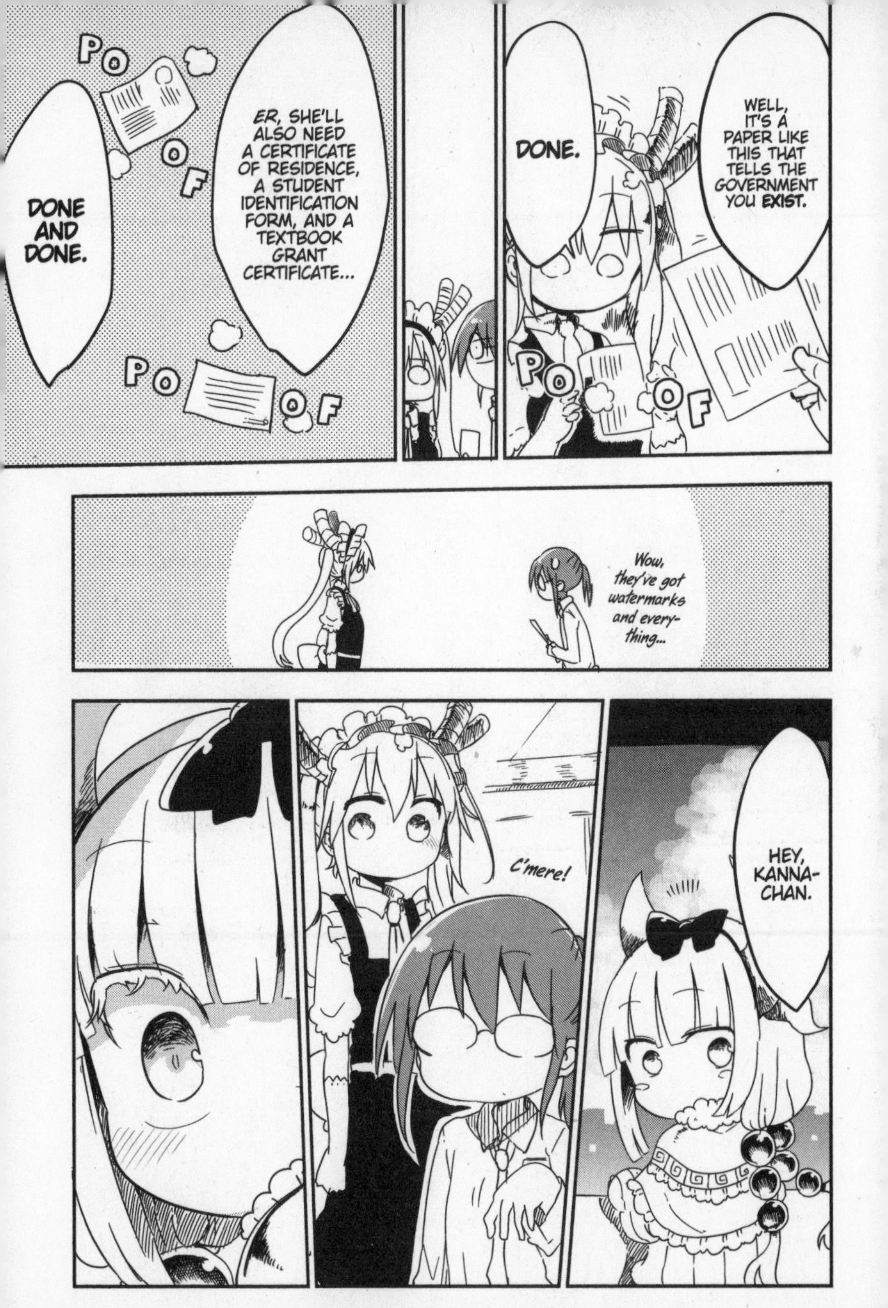
WELL, IT'S A PAPER LIKE THIS THAT TELLS THE GOVERNMENT YOU **EXIST.**
DONE.
POOF
ER, SHE'LL ALSO NEED A CERTIFICATE OF RESIDENCE, A STUDENT IDENTIFICATION FORM, AND A TEXTBOOK GRANT CERTIFICATE...
POOF
DONE AND DONE.
POOF
Wow, they've got watermarks and everything...
HEY, KANNA-CHAN.
C'mere!

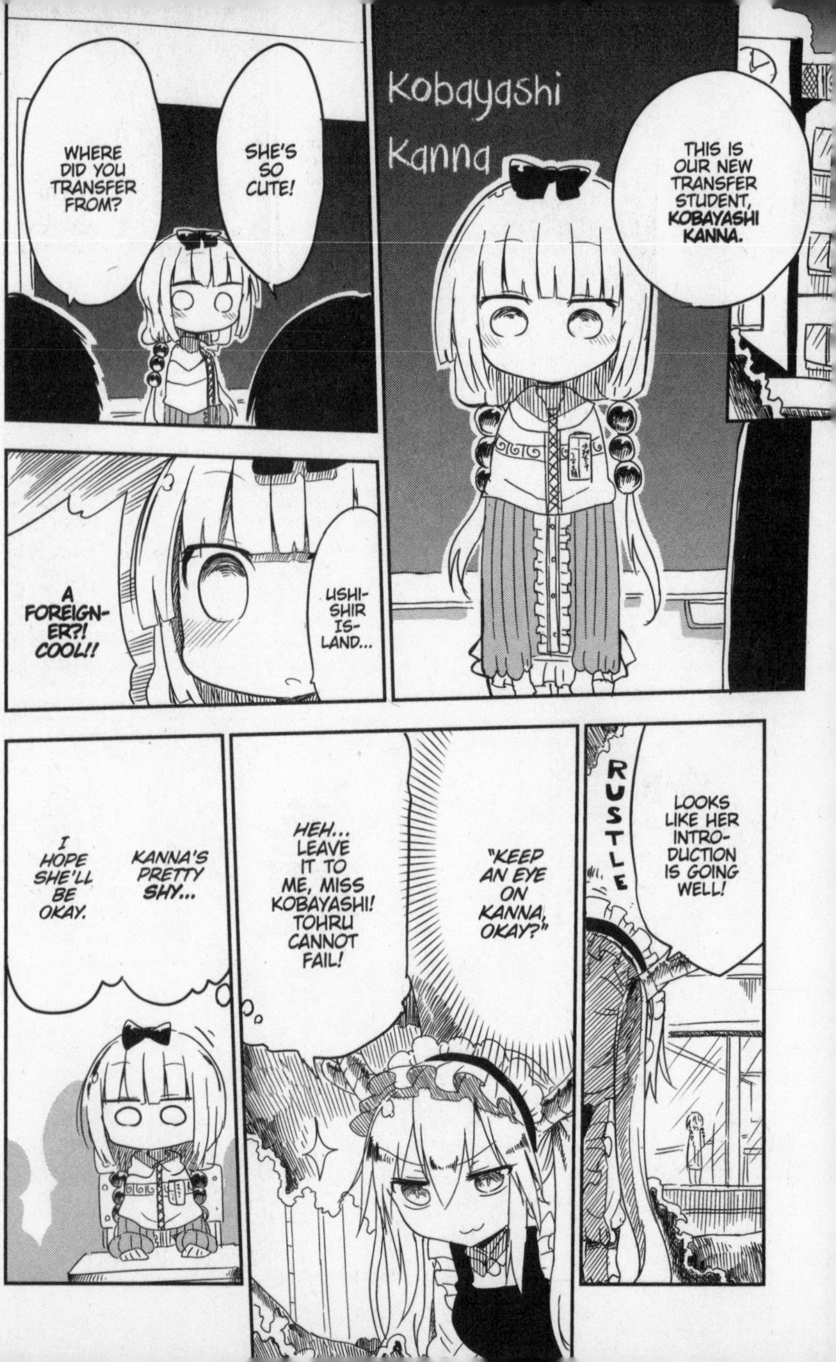
THIS IS OUR NEW TRANSFER STUDENT, KOBAYASHI KANNA.
Kobayashi Kanna
SHE'S SO CUTE!
WHERE DID YOU TRANSFER FROM?
USHI-SHIR IS-LAND...
A FOREIGN-ER?! COOL!!
LOOKS LIKE HER INTRO-DUCTION IS GOING WELL!
RUSTLE
"KEEP AN EYE ON KANNA, OKAY?"
HEH... LEAVE IT TO ME, MISS KOBAYASHI! TOHRU CANNOT FAIL!
KANNA'S PRETTY SHY...
I HOPE SHE'LL BE OKAY.

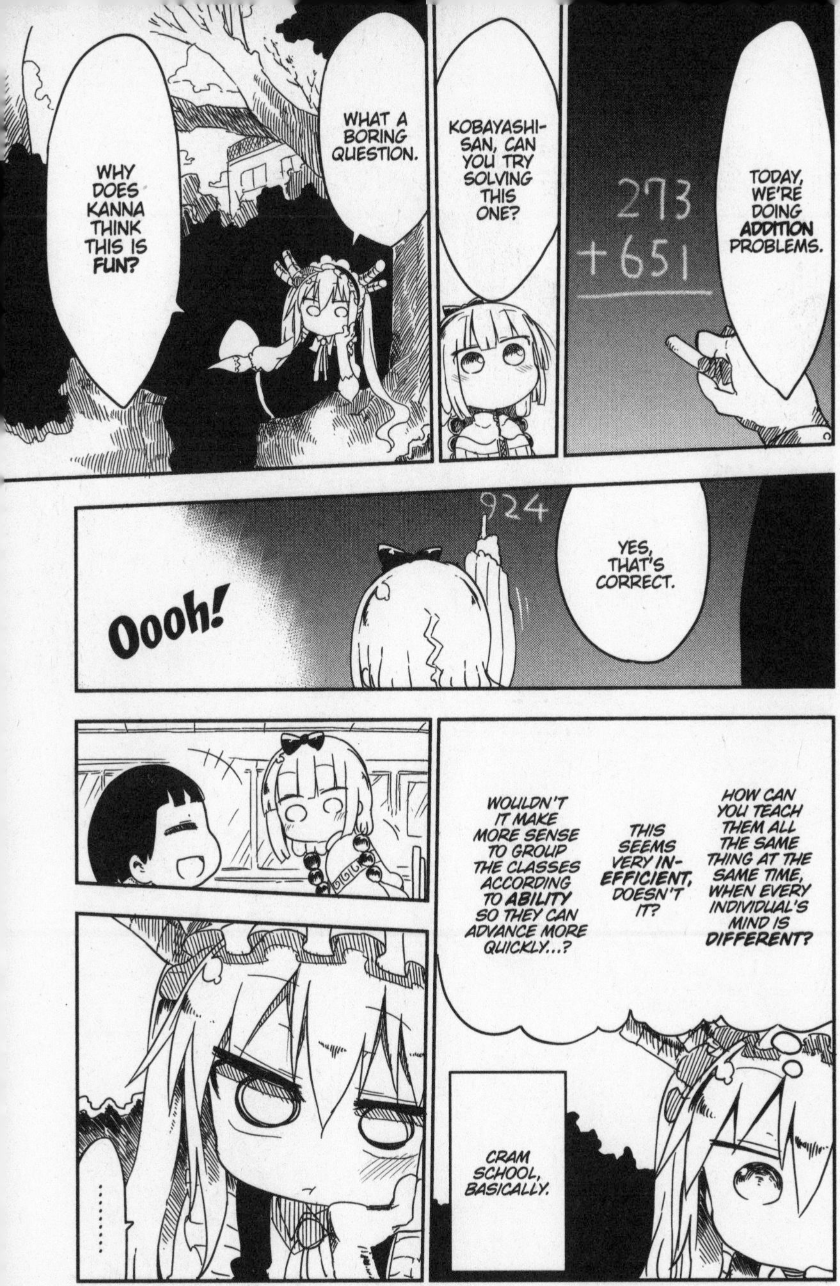
TODAY, WE'RE DOING ADDITION PROBLEMS.
273
+651
KOBAYASHI-SAN, CAN YOU TRY SOLVING THIS ONE?
WHAT A BORING QUESTION.
WHY DOES KANNA THINK THIS IS FUN?
924
YES, THAT'S CORRECT.
Oooh!
HOW CAN YOU TEACH THEM ALL THE SAME THING AT THE SAME TIME, WHEN EVERY INDIVIDUAL'S MIND IS DIFFERENT?
THIS SEEMS VERY IN-EFFICIENT, DOESN'T IT?
WOULDN'T IT MAKE MORE SENSE TO GROUP THE CLASSES ACCORDING TO ABILITY SO THEY CAN ADVANCE MORE QUICKLY...?
CRAM SCHOOL, BASICALLY.
......

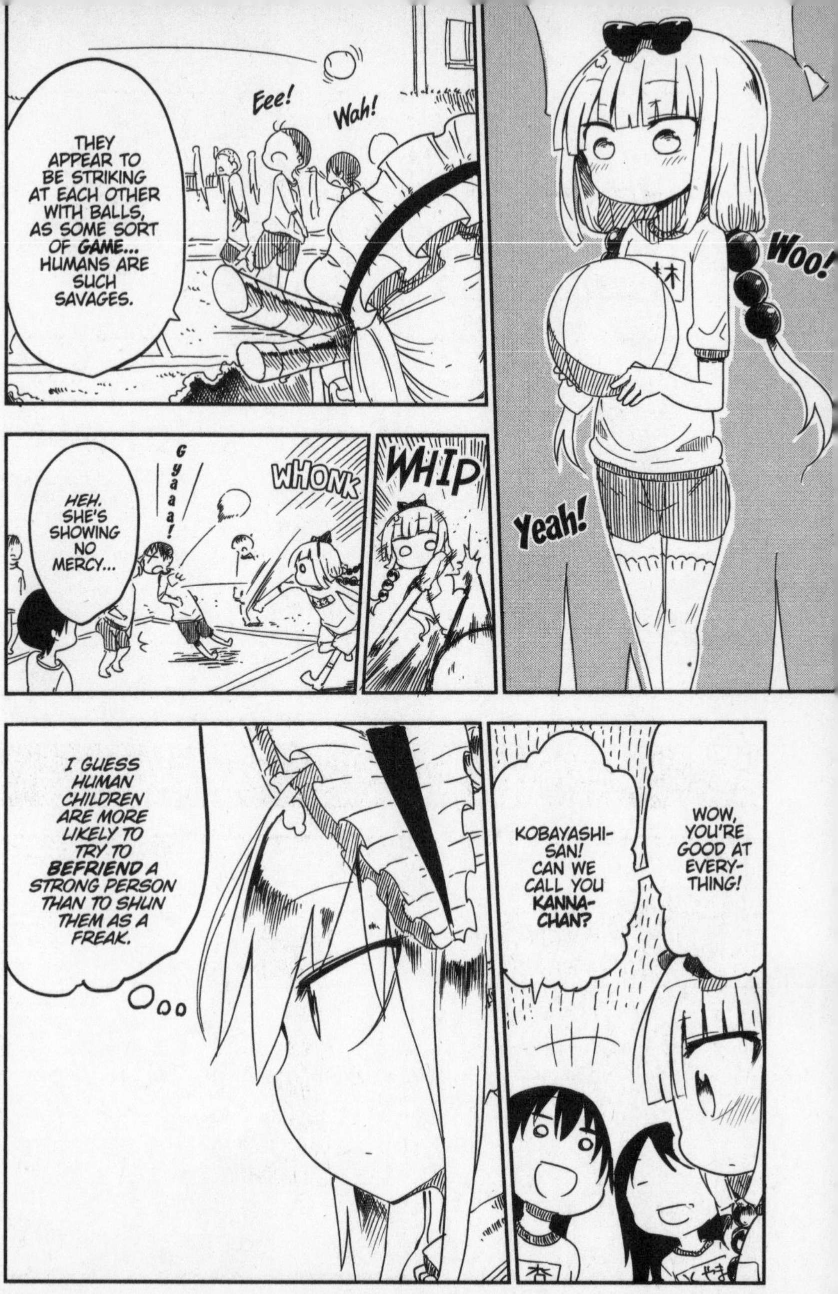
Woo!
Yeah!
Wah!
Eee!
THEY APPEAR TO BE STRIKING AT EACH OTHER WITH BALLS, AS SOME SORT OF **GAME**... HUMANS ARE SUCH SAVAGES.
WHIP
WHONK
Gyaaaa!
HEH. SHE'S SHOWING NO MERCY...
WOW, YOU'RE GOOD AT EVERY-THING!
KOBAYASHI-SAN! CAN WE CALL YOU **KANNA-CHAN**?
I GUESS HUMAN CHILDREN ARE MORE LIKELY TO TRY TO **BEFRIEND** A STRONG PERSON THAN TO SHUN THEM AS A FREAK.

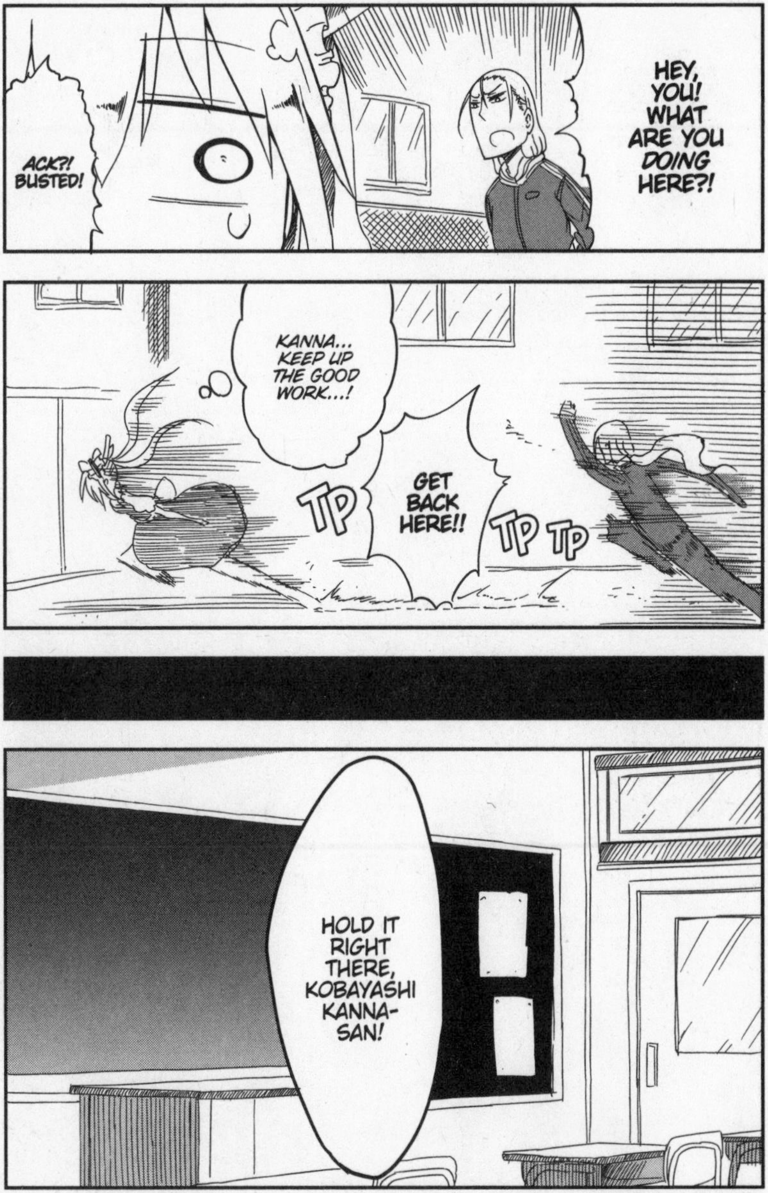
HEY, YOU! WHAT ARE YOU DOING HERE?!
ACK?! BUSTED!
TP TP
GET BACK HERE!!
KANNA... KEEP UP THE GOOD WORK...!
TP
HOLD IT RIGHT THERE, KOBAYASHI KANNA-SAN!

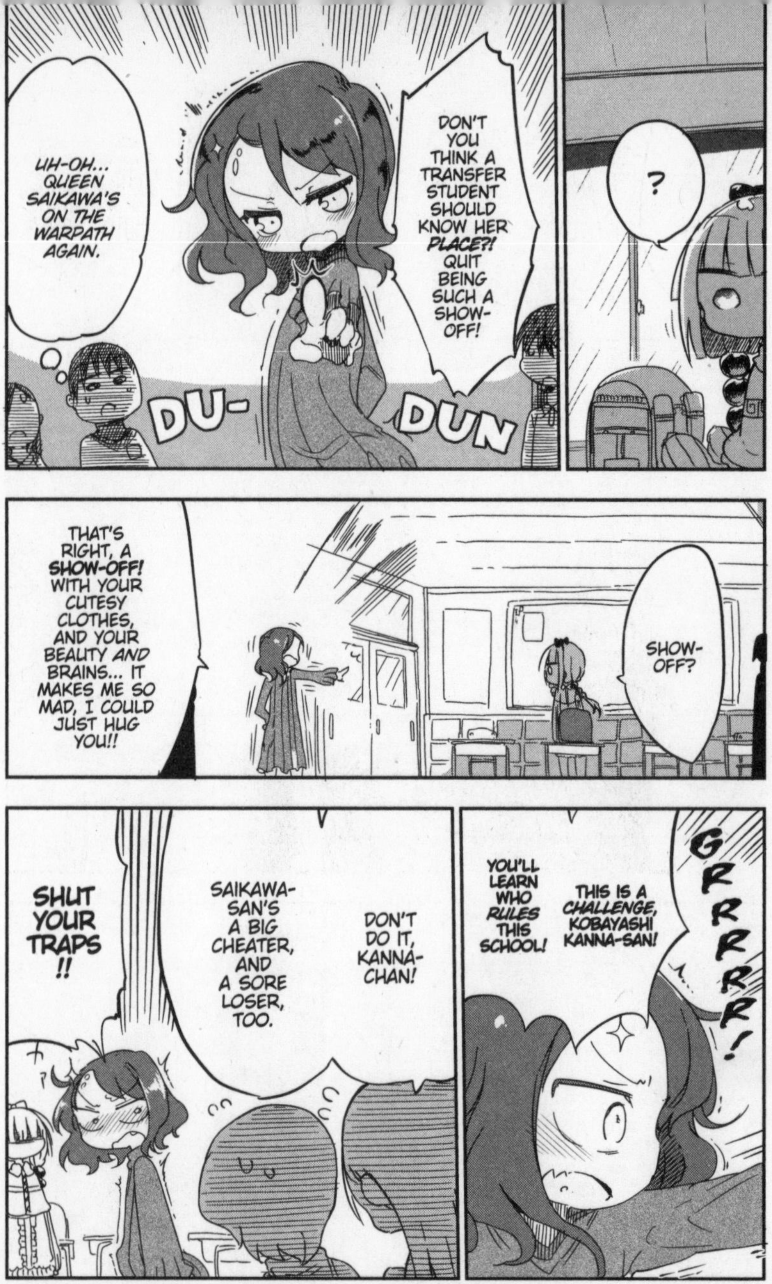

?
DON'T YOU THINK A TRANSFER STUDENT SHOULD KNOW HER PLACE?! QUIT BEING SUCH A SHOW-OFF!
DU-DUN
UH-OH... QUEEN SAIKAWA'S ON THE WARPATH AGAIN.
SHOW-OFF?
THAT'S RIGHT, A SHOW-OFF! WITH YOUR CUTESY CLOTHES, AND YOUR BEAUTY AND BRAINS... IT MAKES ME SO MAD, I COULD JUST HUG YOU!!
GRRRRR!
THIS IS A CHALLENGE, KOBAYASHI KANNA-SAN!
YOU'LL LEARN WHO RULES THIS SCHOOL!
DON'T DO IT, KANNA-CHAN!
SAIKAWA-SAN'S A BIG CHEATER, AND A SORE LOSER, TOO.
SHUT YOUR TRAPS!!

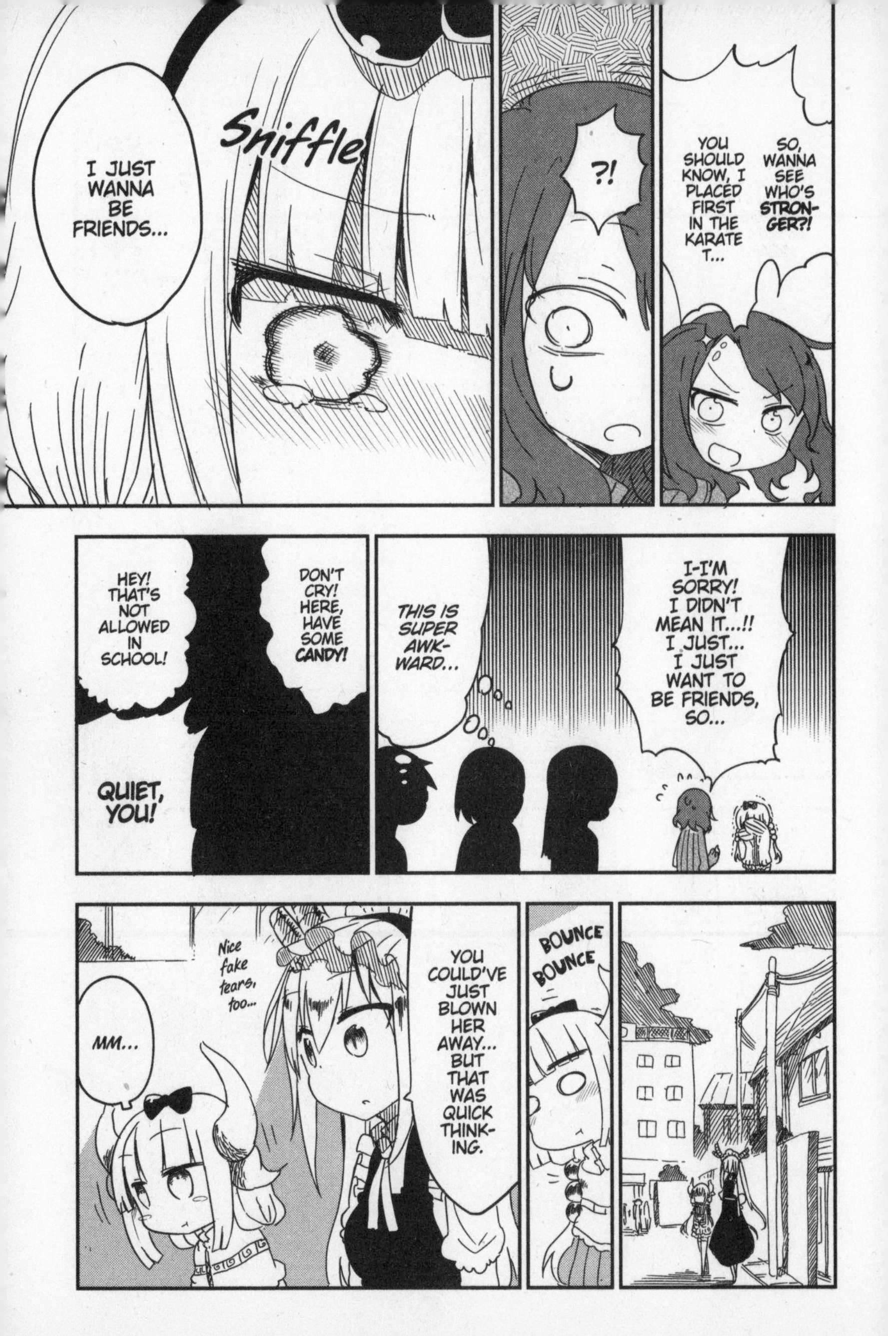
SO, WANNA SEE WHO'S STRONGER?!
YOU SHOULD KNOW, I PLACED FIRST IN THE KARATE T...
?!
Sniffle
I JUST WANNA BE FRIENDS...
I-I'M SORRY! I DIDN'T MEAN IT...!! I JUST... I JUST WANT TO BE FRIENDS, SO...
THIS IS SUPER AWKWARD...
DON'T CRY! HERE, HAVE SOME CANDY!
HEY! THAT'S NOT ALLOWED IN SCHOOL!
QUIET, YOU!
BOUNCE
BOUNCE
YOU COULD'VE JUST BLOWN HER AWAY... BUT THAT WAS QUICK THINKING.
Nice fake tears, too...
MM...

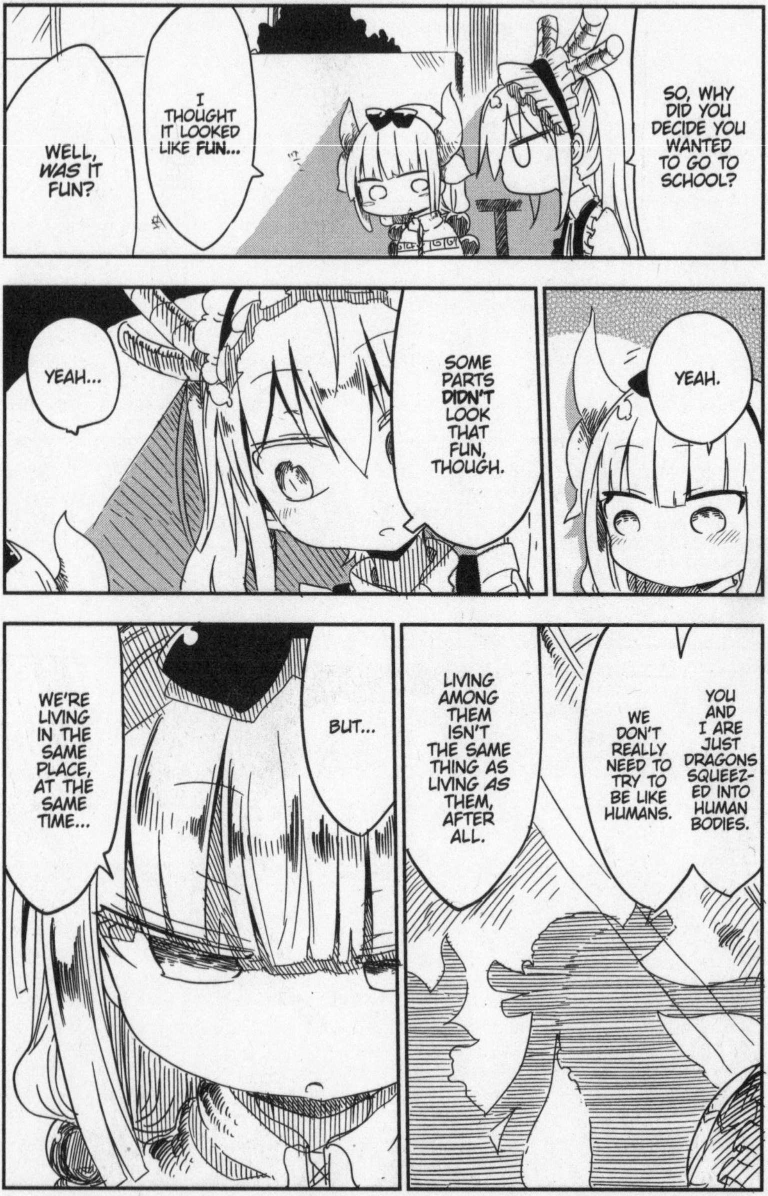
SO, WHY DID YOU DECIDE YOU WANTED TO GO TO SCHOOL?
I THOUGHT IT LOOKED LIKE FUN...
WELL, WAS IT FUN?
YEAH.
SOME PARTS DIDN'T LOOK THAT FUN, THOUGH.
YEAH...
YOU AND I ARE JUST DRAGONS SQUEEZED INTO HUMAN BODIES.
WE DON'T REALLY NEED TO TRY TO BE LIKE HUMANS.
LIVING AMONG THEM ISN'T THE SAME THING AS LIVING AS THEM, AFTER ALL.
BUT...
WE'RE LIVING IN THE SAME PLACE, AT THE SAME TIME...

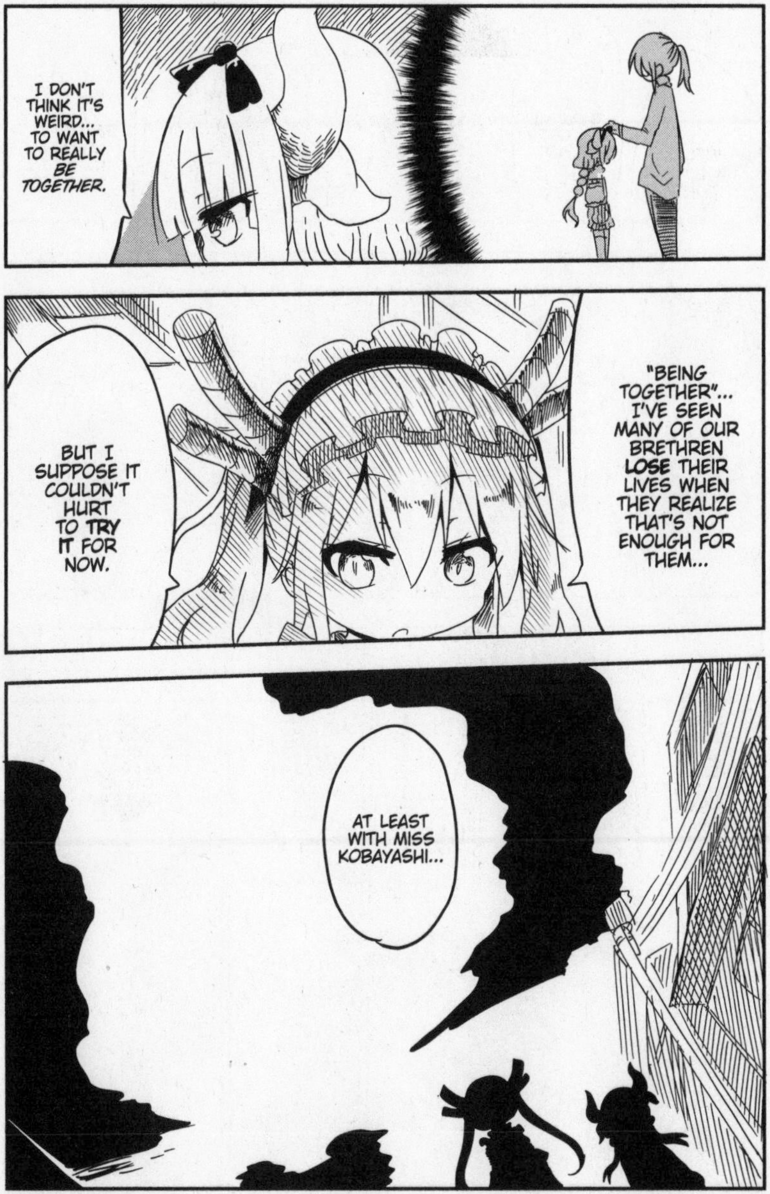
I DON'T THINK IT'S WEIRD... TO WANT TO REALLY BE TOGETHER.
"BEING TOGETHER"... I'VE SEEN MANY OF OUR BRETHREN LOSE THEIR LIVES WHEN THEY REALIZE THAT'S NOT ENOUGH FOR THEM...
BUT I SUPPOSE IT COULDN'T HURT TO TRY IT FOR NOW.
AT LEAST WITH MISS KOBAYASHI...

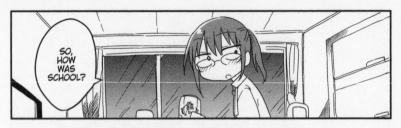

SO, HOW WAS SCHOOL?
IT WAS FUN.
OH, GOOD.
HERE, THIS IS FOR YOU.
RUSTLE
?
TO CEL-EBRATE YOUR STARTING SCHOOL.
RATTLE
YOU CAN PUT IT ON YOUR BACK-PACK.
SQUEEZE
HEY! WHERE'S MY GIFT?! WHAT ABOUT ME, MISS KOBAYASHI?!
HERE, HAVE A CAN OF COFFEE.
YAAAAAY!!

CHAPTER 13/END

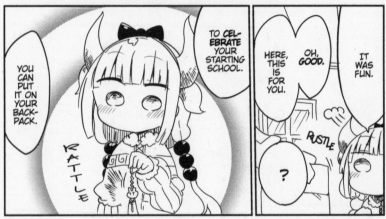

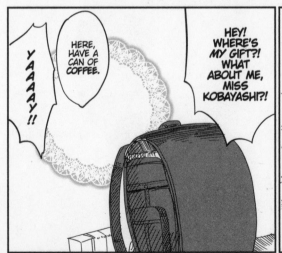

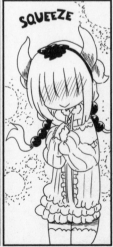

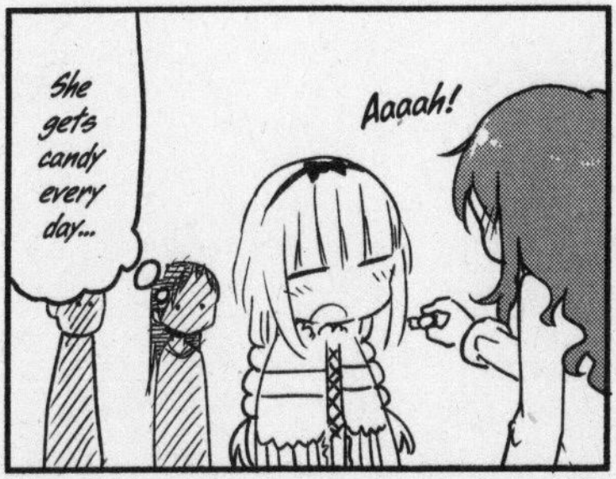
She gets candy every day...
Aaaah!

Miss Kobayashi's Dragon Maid

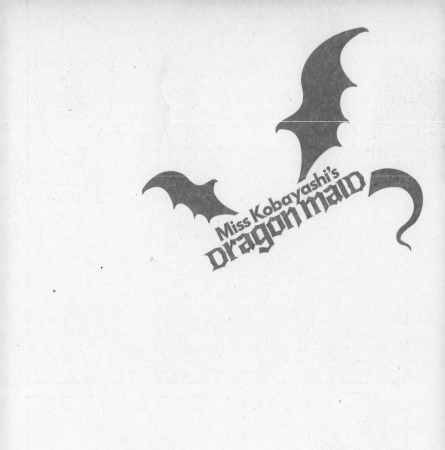

CHAPTER 14

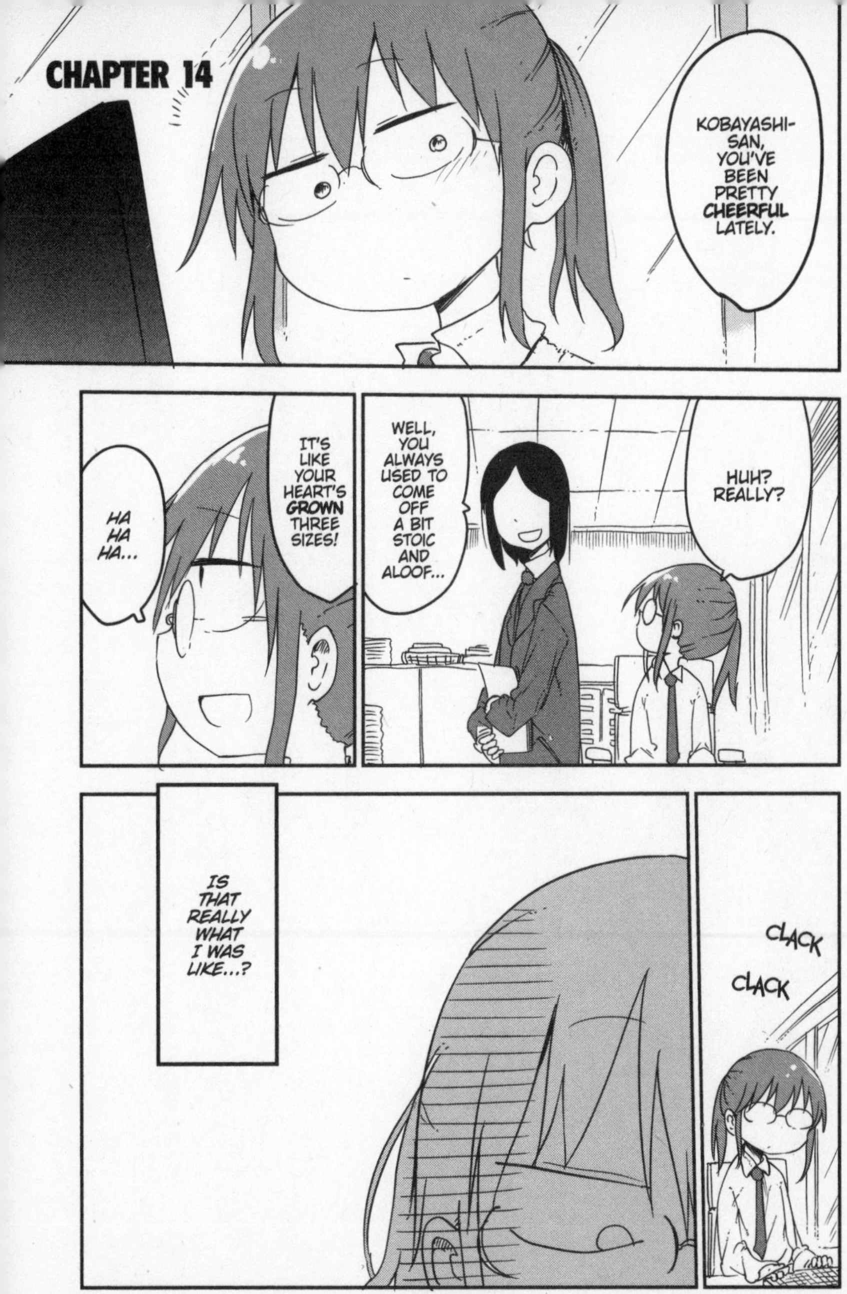
KOBAYASHI-SAN, YOU'VE BEEN PRETTY **CHEERFUL** LATELY.
HUH? REALLY?
WELL, YOU ALWAYS USED TO COME OFF A BIT STOIC AND ALOOF...
IT'S LIKE YOUR HEART'S **GROWN** THREE SIZES!
HA HA HA...
CLACK
CLACK
IS THAT REALLY WHAT I WAS LIKE...?

CHAPTER 14 : TOHRU & OFFICE WORK

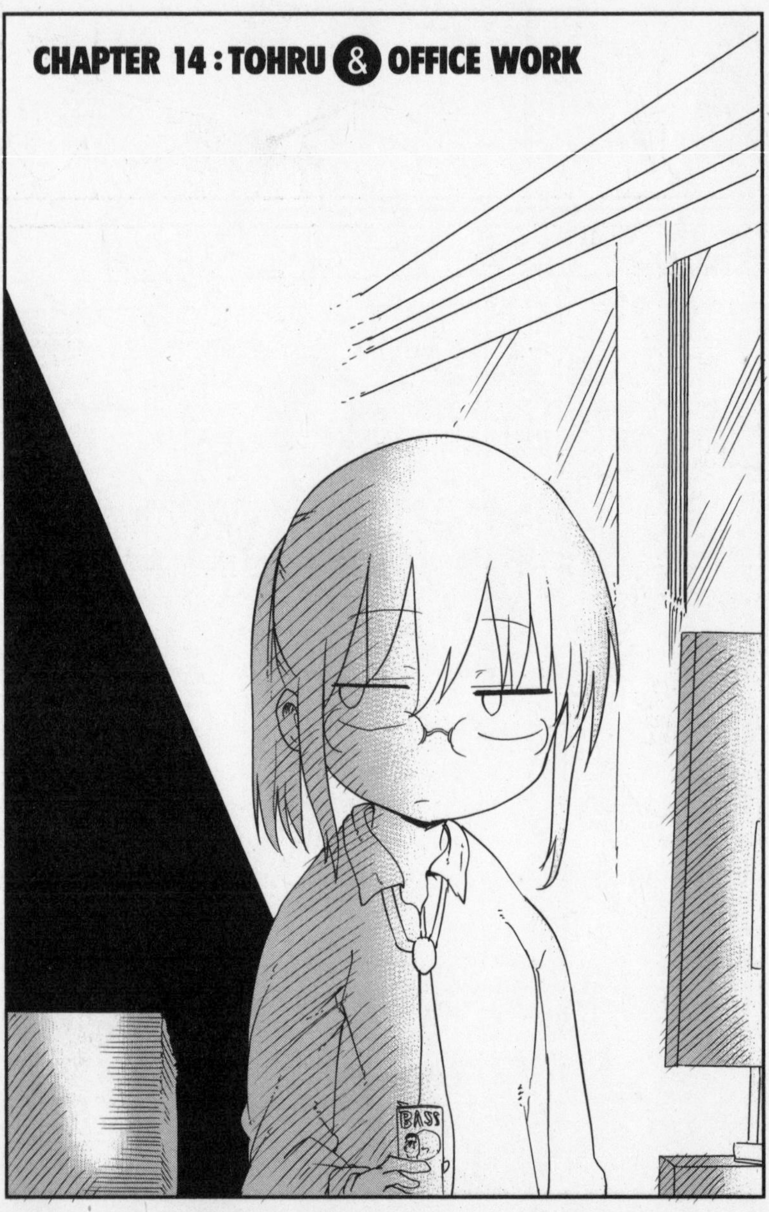
BASS

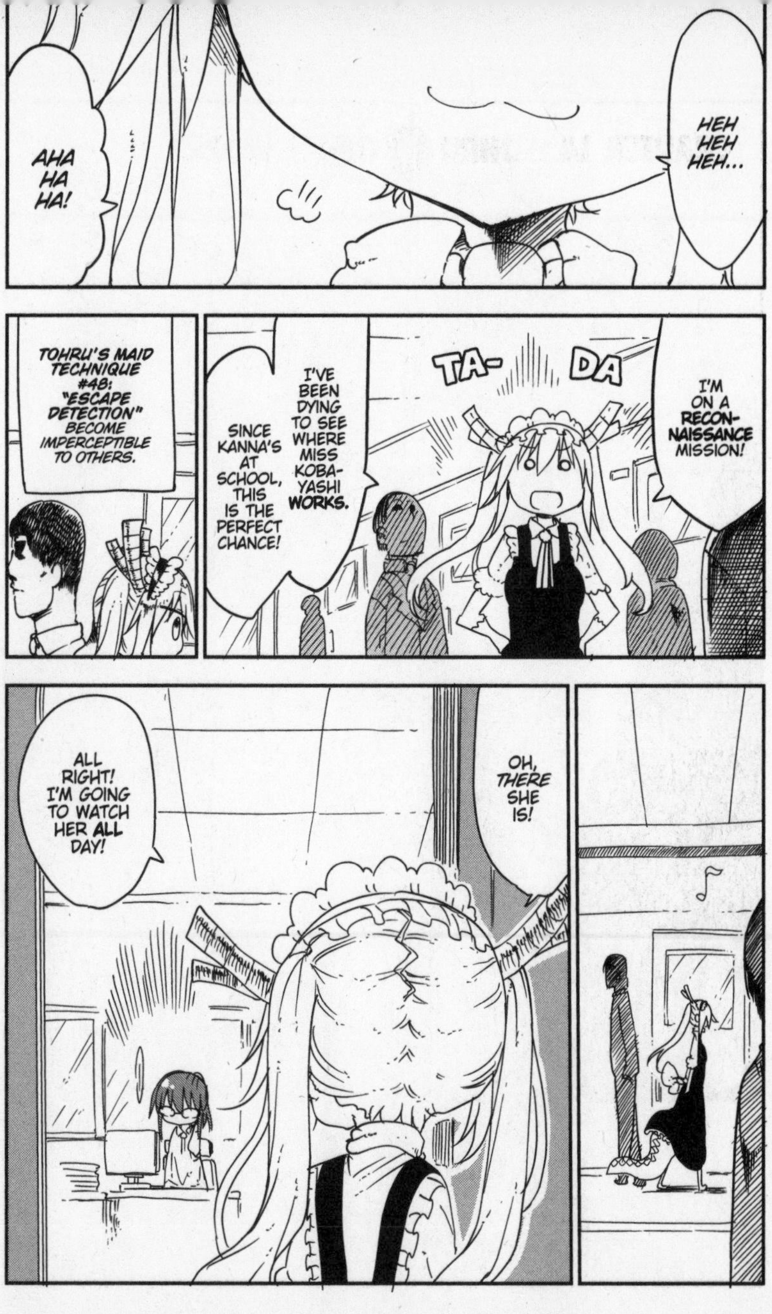

HEH HEH HEH...
AHA HA HA!
TA- DA
I'M ON A RECONNAISSANCE MISSION!
I'VE BEEN DYING TO SEE WHERE MISS KOBAYASHI WORKS.
SINCE KANNA'S AT SCHOOL, THIS IS THE PERFECT CHANCE!
TOHRU'S MAID TECHNIQUE #48: "ESCAPE DETECTION" BECOME IMPERCEPTIBLE TO OTHERS.
OH, THERE SHE IS!
ALL RIGHT! I'M GOING TO WATCH HER ALL DAY!

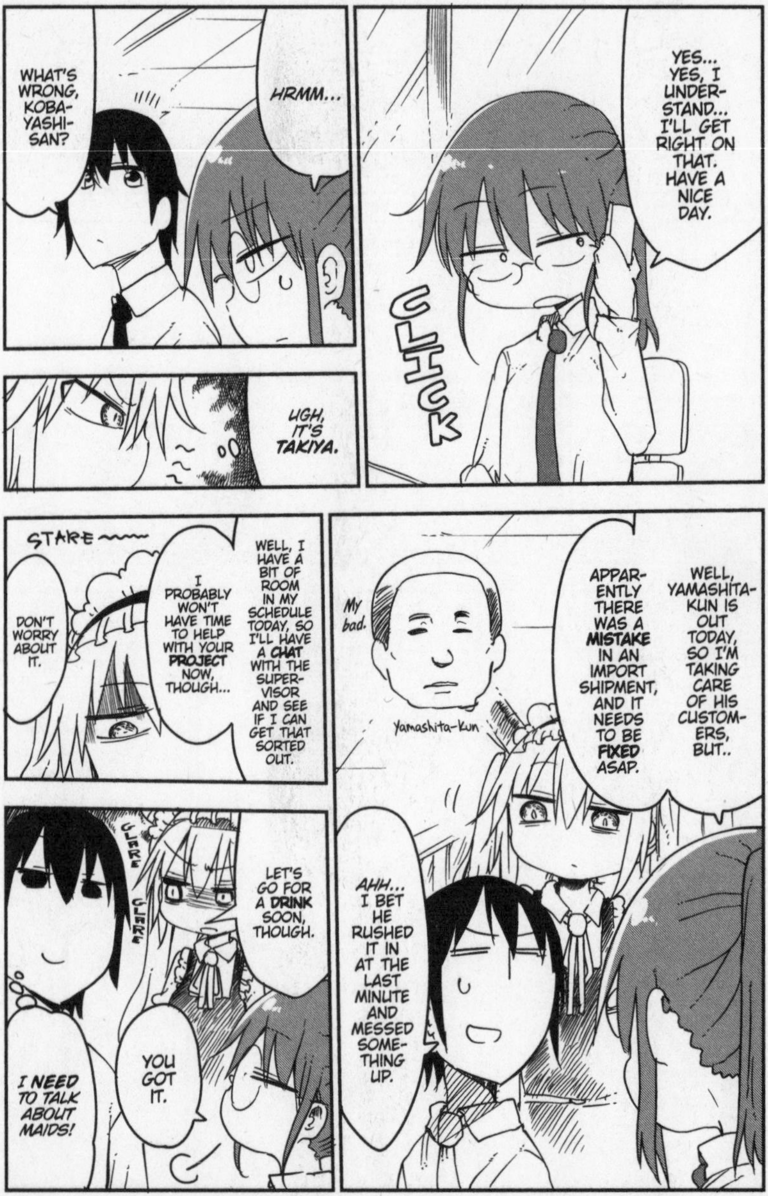
YES... YES, I UNDER-STAND... I'LL GET RIGHT ON THAT. HAVE A NICE DAY.
CLICK
HRMM...
WHAT'S WRONG, KOBA-YASHI-SAN?
UGH, IT'S TAKIYA.
WELL, YAMASHITA-KUN IS OUT TODAY, SO I'M TAKING CARE OF HIS CUSTOM-ERS, BUT..
APPAR-ENTLY THERE WAS A MISTAKE IN AN IMPORT SHIPMENT, AND IT NEEDS TO BE FIXED ASAP.
My bad.
Yamashita-Kun
AHH... I BET HE RUSHED IT IN AT THE LAST MINUTE AND MESSED SOME-THING UP.
WELL, I HAVE A BIT OF ROOM IN MY SCHEDULE TODAY, SO I'LL HAVE A CHAT WITH THE SUPER-VISOR AND SEE IF I CAN GET THAT SORTED OUT.
I PROBABLY WON'T HAVE TIME TO HELP WITH YOUR PROJECT NOW, THOUGH...
STARE~~~
DON'T WORRY ABOUT IT.
LET'S GO FOR A DRINK SOON, THOUGH.
GLARE
GLARE
YOU GOT IT.
I NEED TO TALK ABOUT MAIDS!

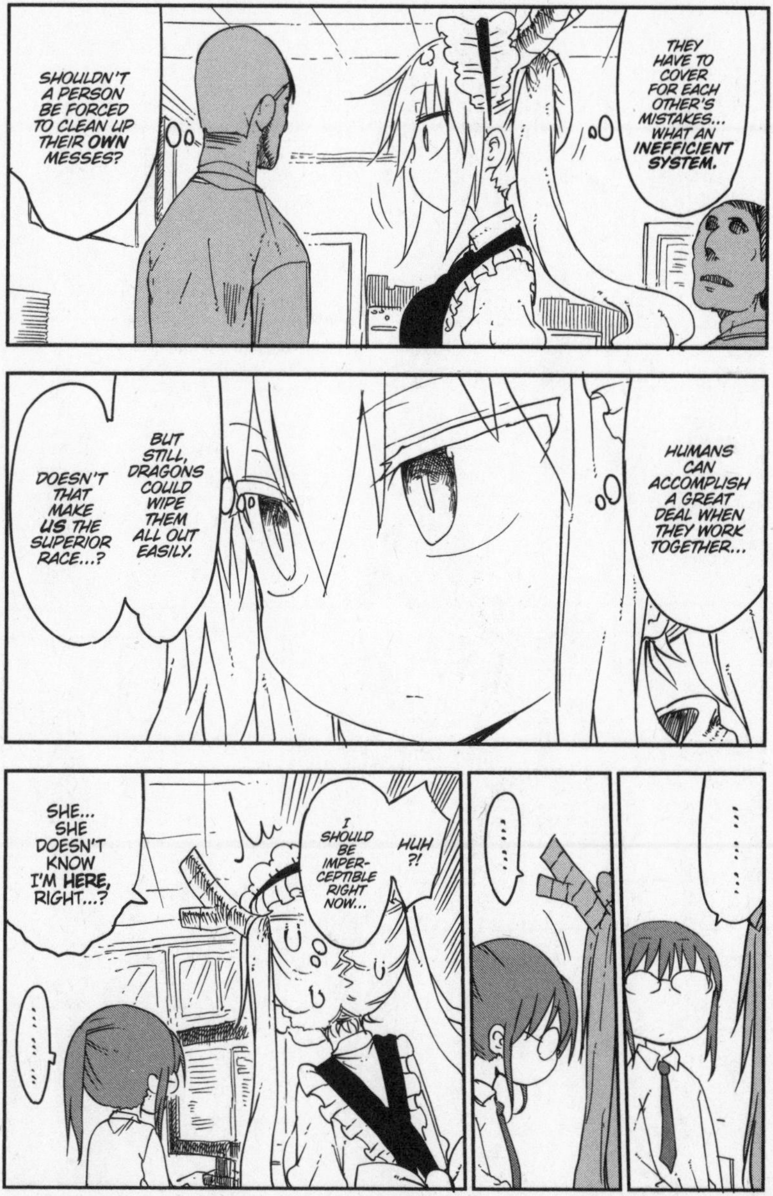
THEY HAVE TO COVER FOR EACH OTHER'S MISTAKES... WHAT AN INEFFICIENT SYSTEM.
SHOULDN'T A PERSON BE FORCED TO CLEAN UP THEIR OWN MESSES?
HUMANS CAN ACCOMPLISH A GREAT DEAL WHEN THEY WORK TOGETHER...
BUT STILL, DRAGONS COULD WIPE THEM ALL OUT EASILY.
DOESN'T THAT MAKE US THE SUPERIOR RACE...?
......
......
HUH?!
I SHOULD BE IMPERCEPTIBLE RIGHT NOW...
SHE... SHE DOESN'T KNOW I'M HERE, RIGHT...?
......

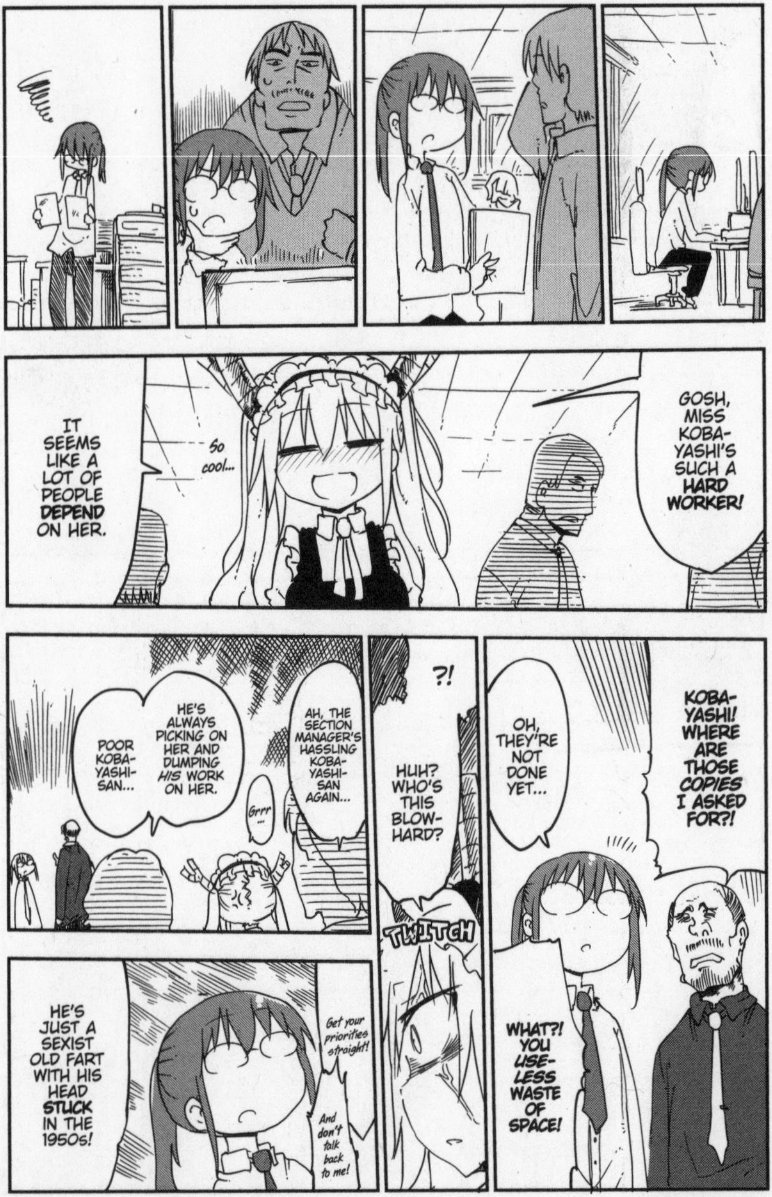
GOSH, MISS KOBA-YASHI'S SUCH A HARD WORKER!
So cool...
IT SEEMS LIKE A LOT OF PEOPLE DEPEND ON HER.
KOBA-YASHI! WHERE ARE THOSE COPIES I ASKED FOR?!
OH, THEY'RE NOT DONE YET...
WHAT?! YOU USE-LESS WASTE OF SPACE!
?!
HUH? WHO'S THIS BLOW-HARD?
TWITCH
AH, THE SECTION MANAGER'S HASSLING KOBA-YASHI-SAN AGAIN...
Grrr...
HE'S ALWAYS PICKING ON HER AND DUMPING HIS WORK ON HER.
POOR KOBA-YASHI-SAN...
Get your priorities straight!
And don't talk back to me!
HE'S JUST A SEXIST OLD FART WITH HIS HEAD STUCK IN THE 1950s!

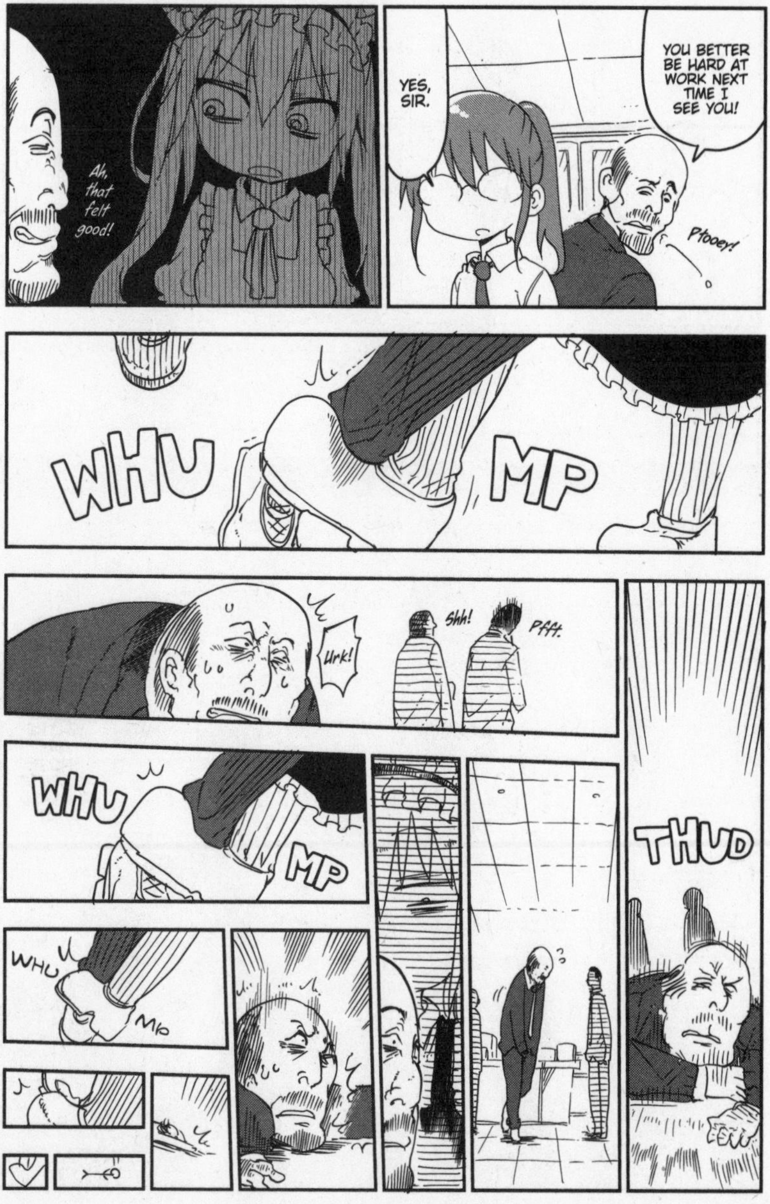
YOU BETTER BE HARD AT WORK NEXT TIME I SEE YOU!
Ptooey!
YES, SIR.
Ah, that felt good!
WHUMP
THUD
Shh!
Pfft.
Urk!
WHUMP
WHUMp

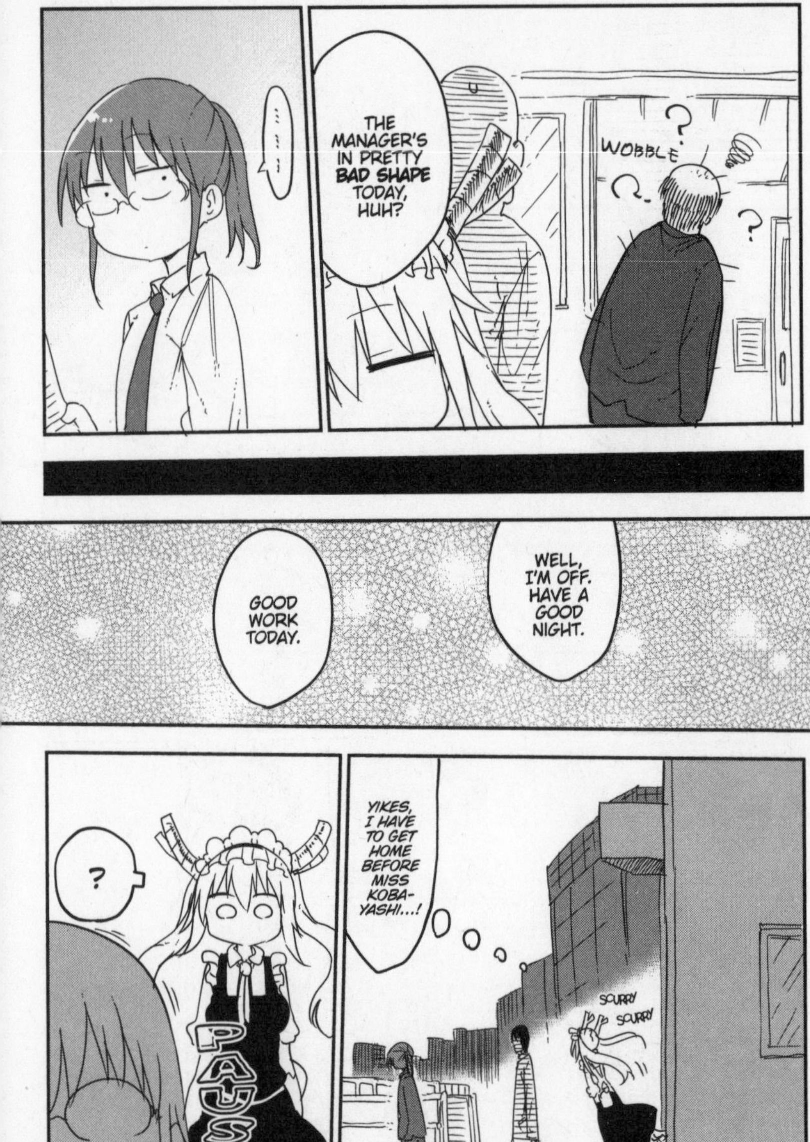
WOBBLE
THE MANAGER'S IN PRETTY **BAD SHAPE** TODAY, HUH?
……
WELL, I'M OFF. HAVE A GOOD NIGHT.
GOOD WORK TODAY.
YIKES, I HAVE TO GET HOME BEFORE MISS KOBA-YASHI...!
SCURRY SCURRY
?
PAUSE

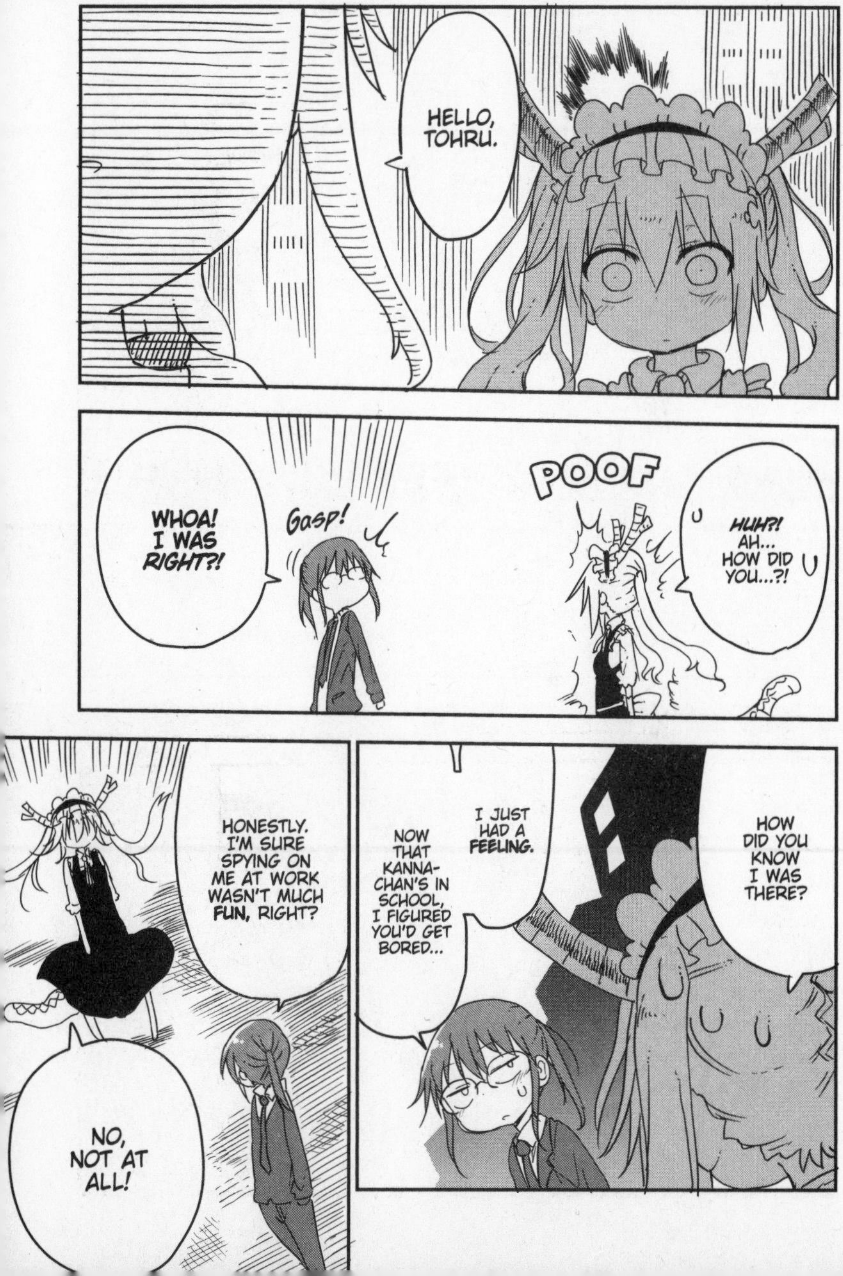
HELLO, TOHRU.
POOF
HUH?! AH... HOW DID YOU...?!
Gasp!
WHOA! I WAS RIGHT?!
HOW DID YOU KNOW I WAS THERE?
I JUST HAD A FEELING.
NOW THAT KANNA-CHAN'S IN SCHOOL, I FIGURED YOU'D GET BORED...
HONESTLY. I'M SURE SPYING ON ME AT WORK WASN'T MUCH FUN, RIGHT?
NO, NOT AT ALL!

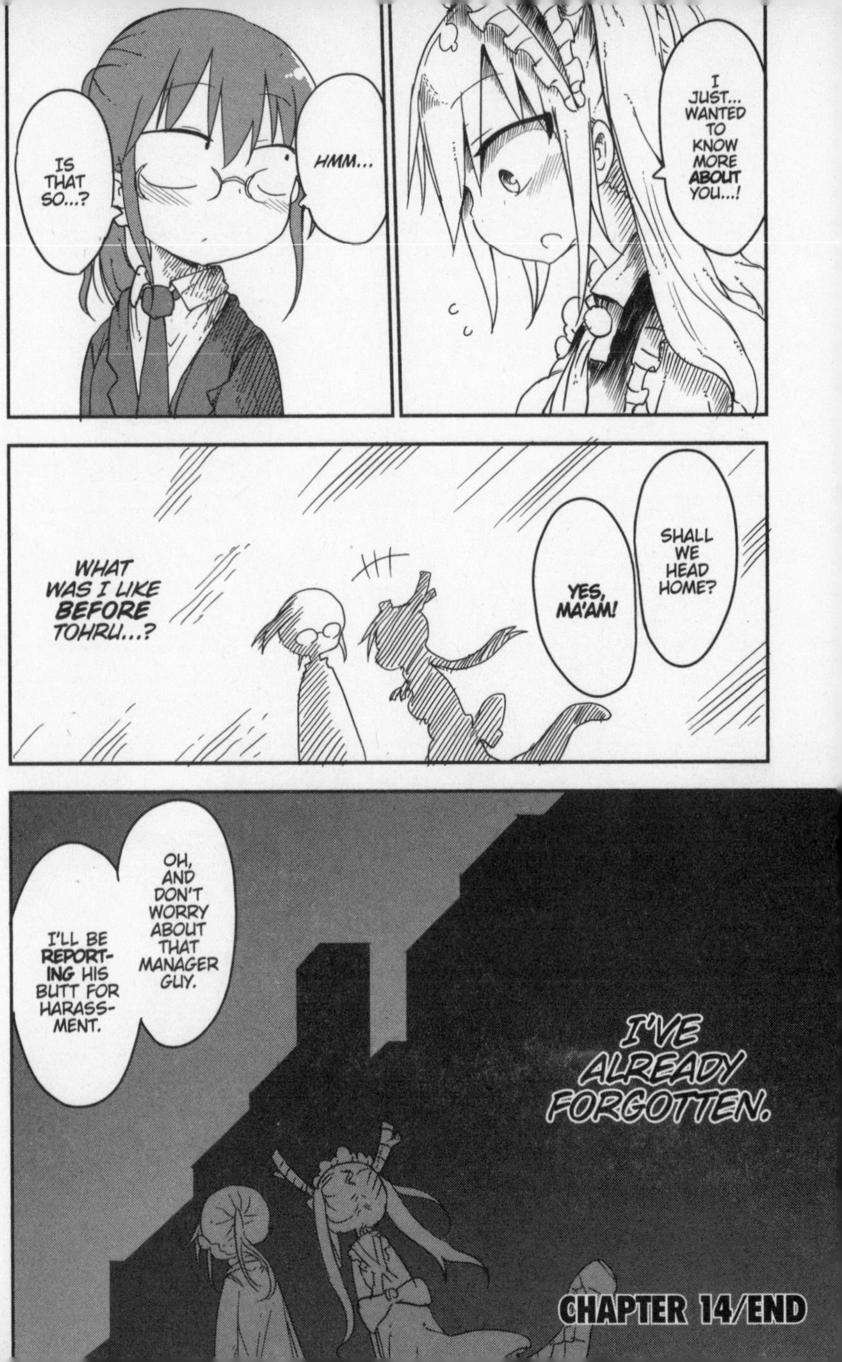
I JUST... WANTED TO KNOW MORE ABOUT YOU...!
HMM...
IS THAT SO...?
SHALL WE HEAD HOME?
YES, MA'AM!
WHAT WAS I LIKE BEFORE TOHRU...?
OH, AND DON'T WORRY ABOUT THAT MANAGER GUY.
I'LL BE REPORTING HIS BUTT FOR HARASSMENT.
I'VE ALREADY FORGOTTEN.
CHAPTER 14/END

I heard the section manager got fired for harass-ment!
Apparently, someone caught him on tape and sent it to the CEO...
I wonder who did it?
Pfft!

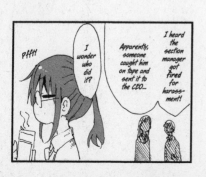

Miss Kobayashi's Dragon Maid

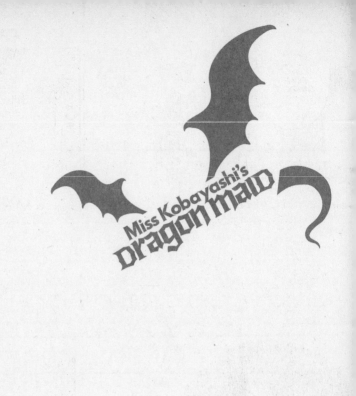

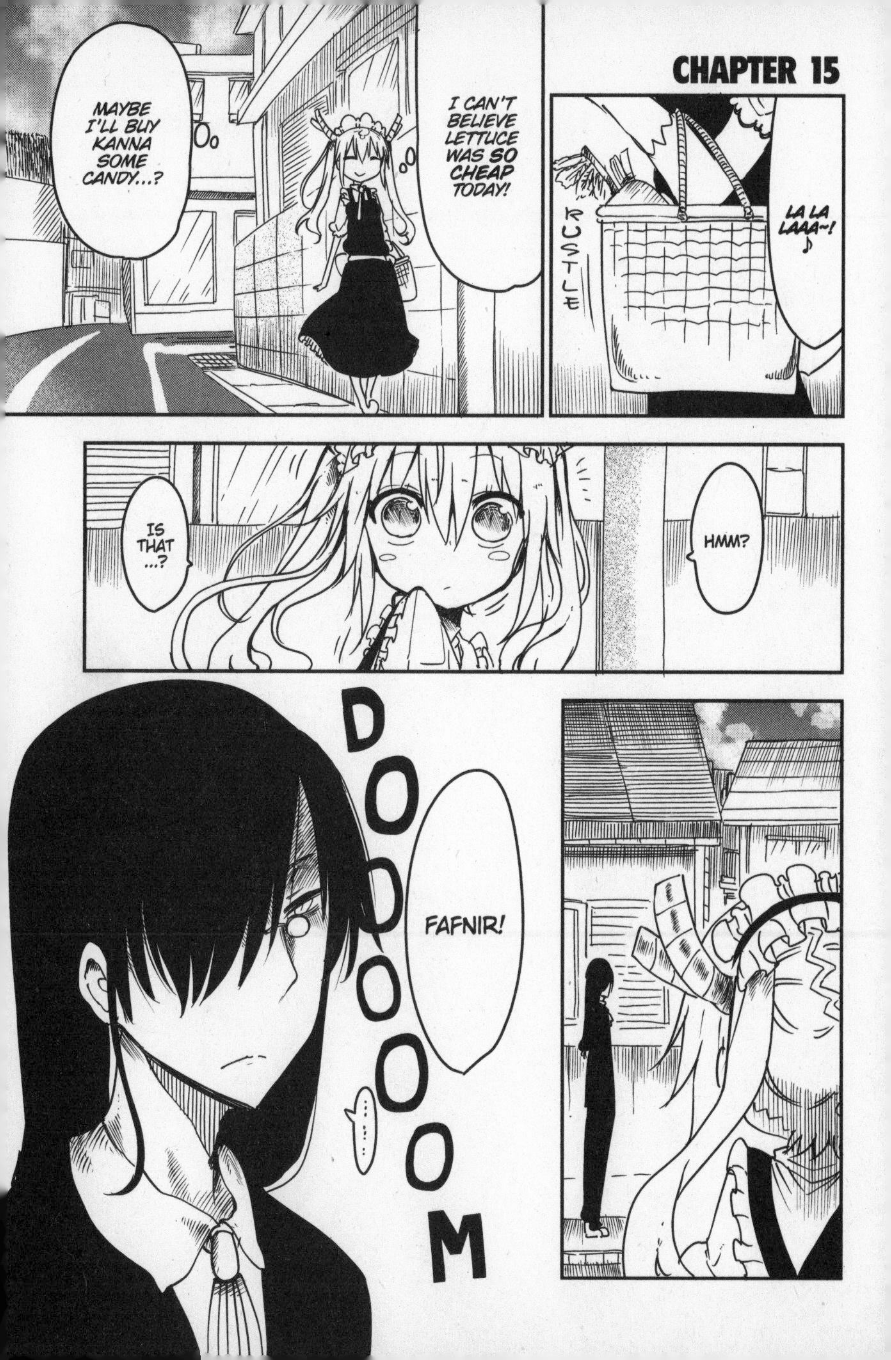
CHAPTER 15
LA LA LAAA~! ♪
RUSTLE
I CAN'T BELIEVE LETTUCE WAS SO CHEAP TODAY!
MAYBE I'LL BUY KANNA SOME CANDY...?
HMM?
IS THAT ...?
FAFNIR!
DOOOOOM
...

CHAPTER 15: TOHRU & HOUSE-HUNTING

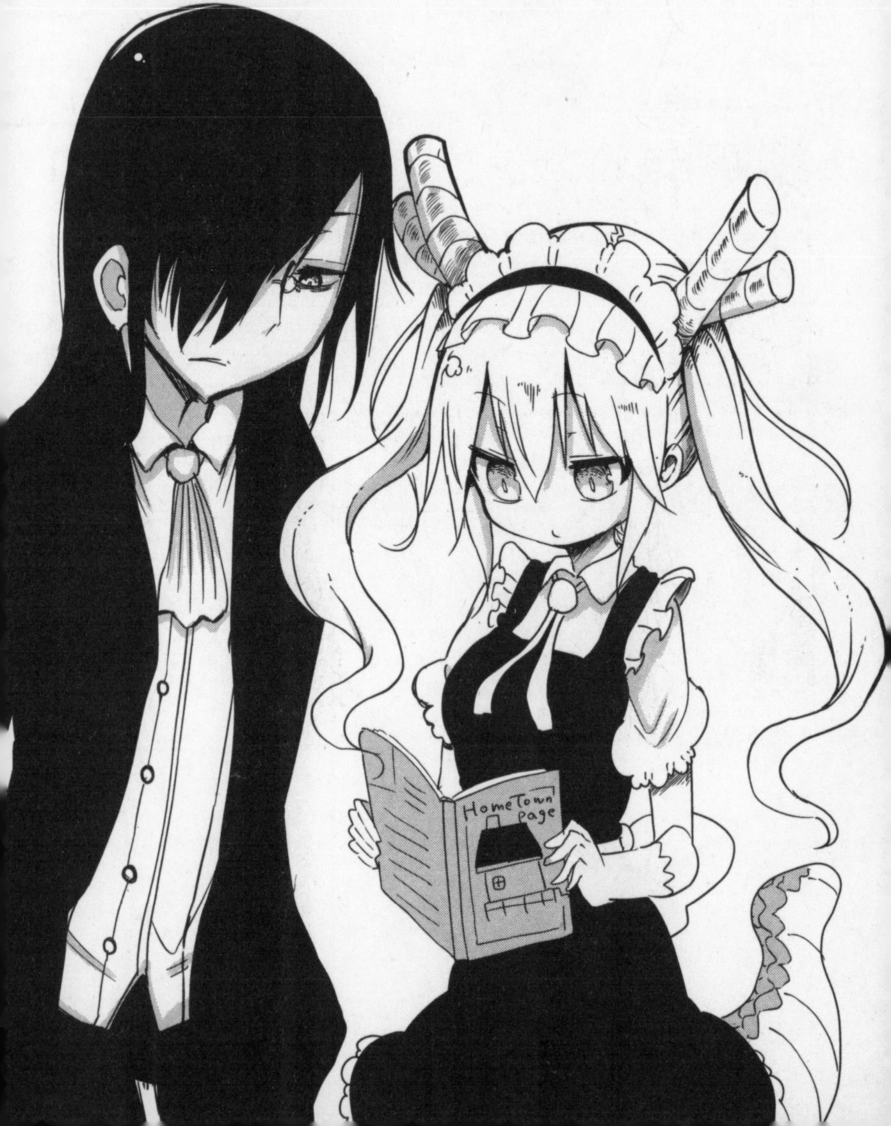
HomeTown Page

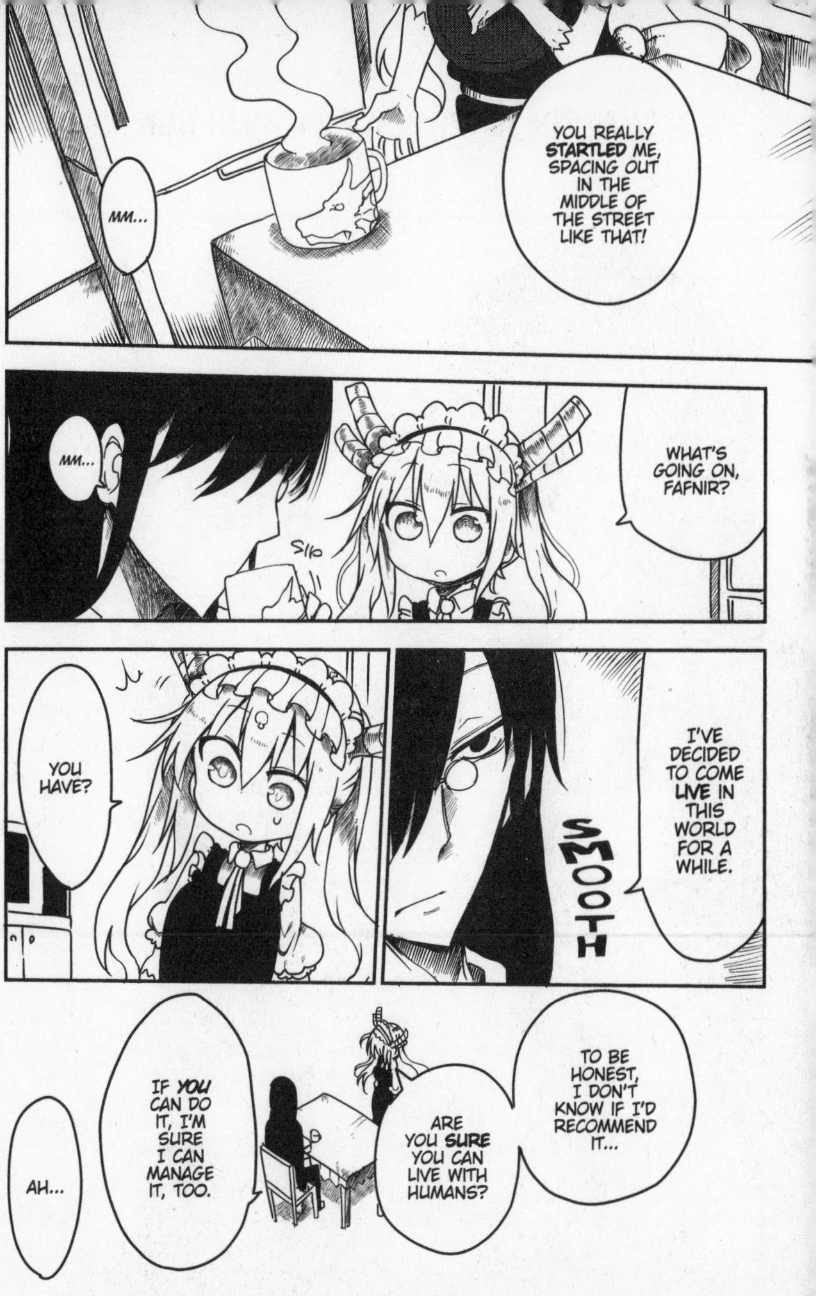
YOU REALLY STARTLED ME, SPACING OUT IN THE MIDDLE OF THE STREET LIKE THAT!
MM...
WHAT'S GOING ON, FAFNIR?
MM...
SIP
I'VE DECIDED TO COME LIVE IN THIS WORLD FOR A WHILE.
SMOOTH
YOU HAVE?
TO BE HONEST, I DON'T KNOW IF I'D RECOMMEND IT...
ARE YOU SURE YOU CAN LIVE WITH HUMANS?
IF YOU CAN DO IT, I'M SURE I CAN MANAGE IT, TOO.
AH...

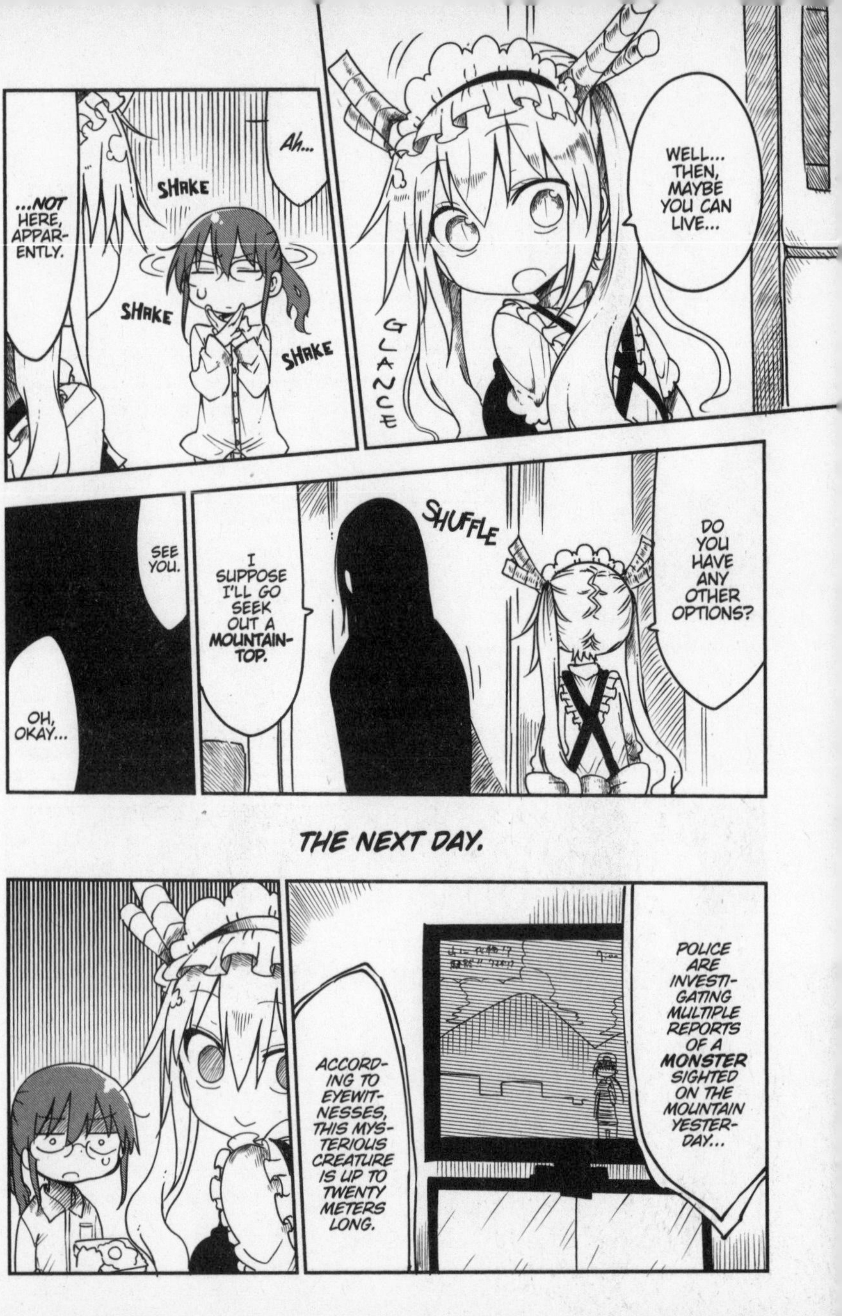
WELL... THEN, MAYBE YOU CAN LIVE...
GLANCE
Ah...
SHAKE
...NOT HERE, APPARENTLY.
SHAKE
SHAKE
DO YOU HAVE ANY OTHER OPTIONS?
SHUFFLE
I SUPPOSE I'LL GO SEEK OUT A MOUNTAINTOP.
SEE YOU.
OH, OKAY...
THE NEXT DAY.
POLICE ARE INVESTIGATING MULTIPLE REPORTS OF A MONSTER SIGHTED ON THE MOUNTAIN YESTERDAY...
ACCORDING TO EYEWITNESSES, THIS MYSTERIOUS CREATURE IS UP TO TWENTY METERS LONG.

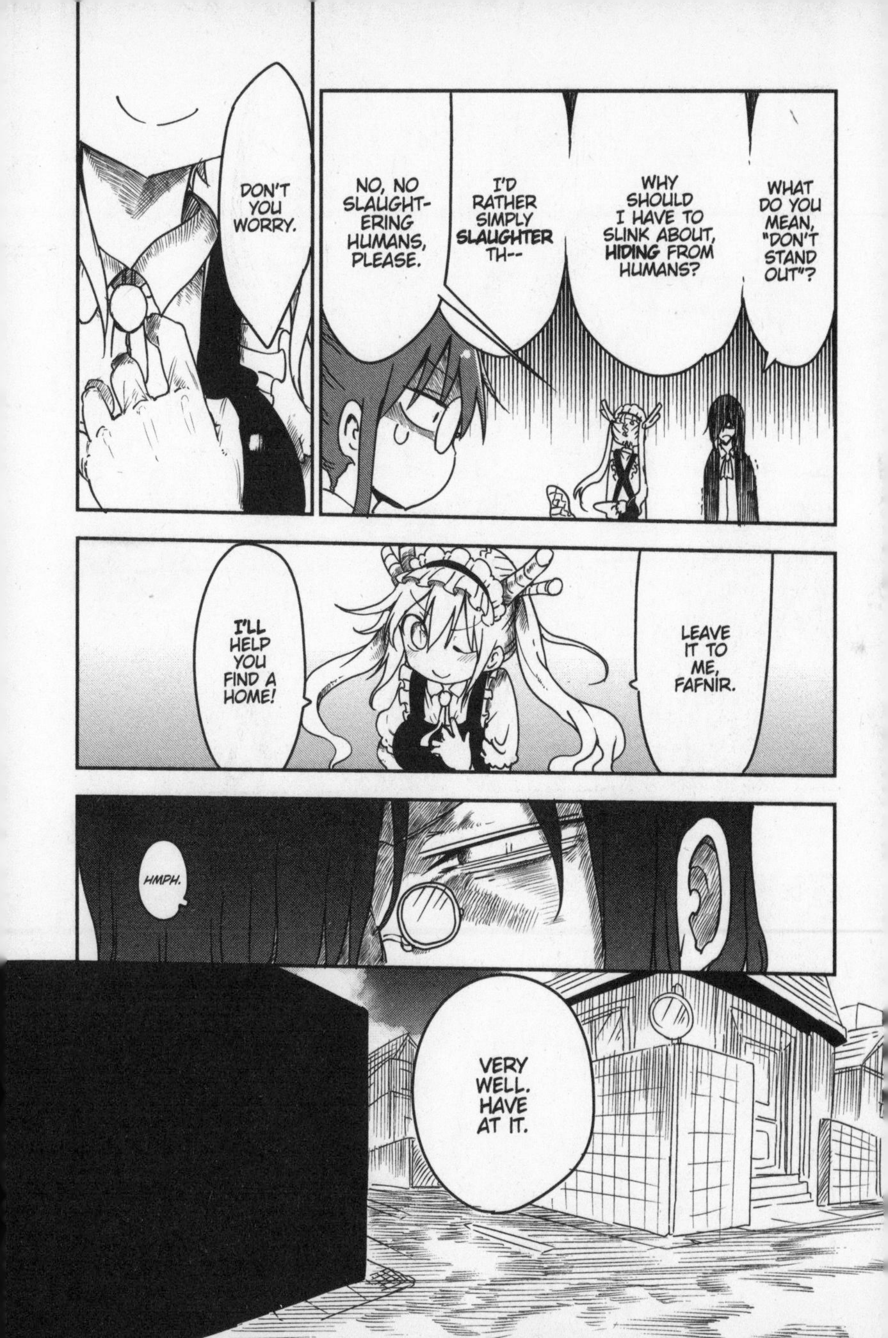
WHAT DO YOU MEAN, "DON'T STAND OUT"?
WHY SHOULD I HAVE TO SLINK ABOUT, **HIDING** FROM HUMANS?
I'D RATHER SIMPLY **SLAUGHTER** TH--
NO, NO SLAUGHTERING HUMANS, PLEASE.
DON'T YOU WORRY.
LEAVE IT TO ME, FAFNIR.
I'LL HELP YOU FIND A HOME!
HMPH.
VERY WELL. HAVE AT IT.

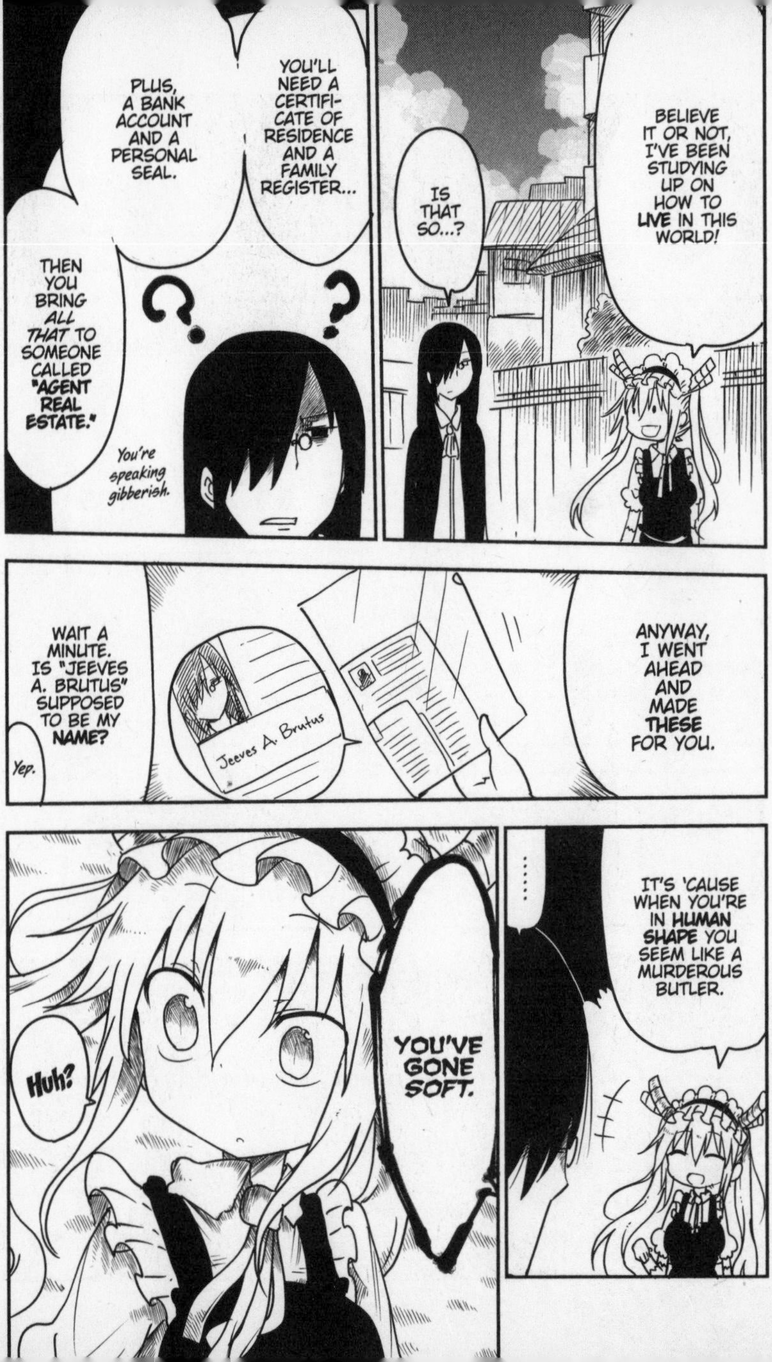
BELIEVE IT OR NOT, I'VE BEEN STUDYING UP ON HOW TO LIVE IN THIS WORLD!
IS THAT SO...?
YOU'LL NEED A CERTIFICATE OF RESIDENCE AND A FAMILY REGISTER...
PLUS, A BANK ACCOUNT AND A PERSONAL SEAL.
THEN YOU BRING ALL THAT TO SOMEONE CALLED "AGENT REAL ESTATE."
You're speaking gibberish.
ANYWAY, I WENT AHEAD AND MADE THESE FOR YOU.
Jeeves A. Brutus
WAIT A MINUTE. IS "JEEVES A. BRUTUS" SUPPOSED TO BE MY NAME?
Yep.
IT'S 'CAUSE WHEN YOU'RE IN HUMAN SHAPE YOU SEEM LIKE A MURDEROUS BUTLER.
......
YOU'VE GONE SOFT.
Huh?

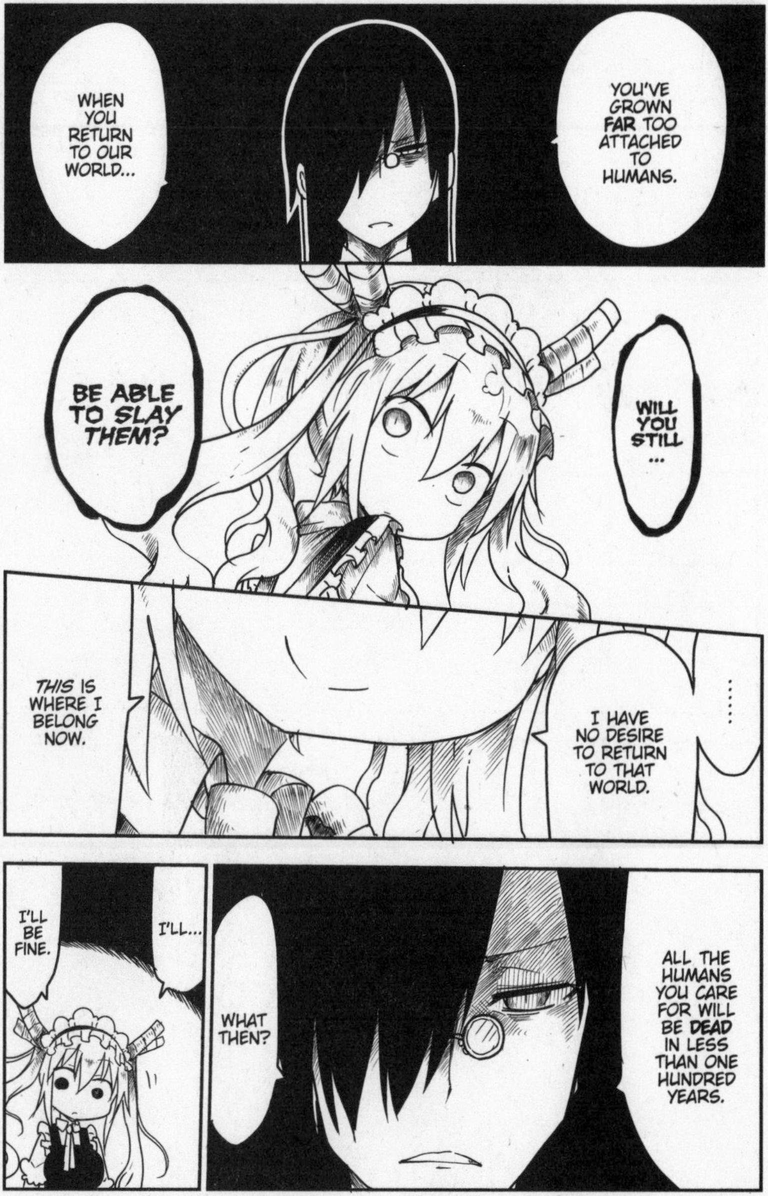
YOU'VE GROWN **FAR** TOO ATTACHED TO HUMANS.
WHEN YOU RETURN TO OUR WORLD...
WILL YOU STILL ...
BE ABLE TO *SLAY* THEM?
......
I HAVE NO DESIRE TO RETURN TO THAT WORLD.
THIS IS WHERE I BELONG NOW.
ALL THE HUMANS YOU CARE FOR WILL BE **DEAD** IN LESS THAN ONE HUNDRED YEARS.
WHAT THEN?
I'LL...
I'LL BE FINE.

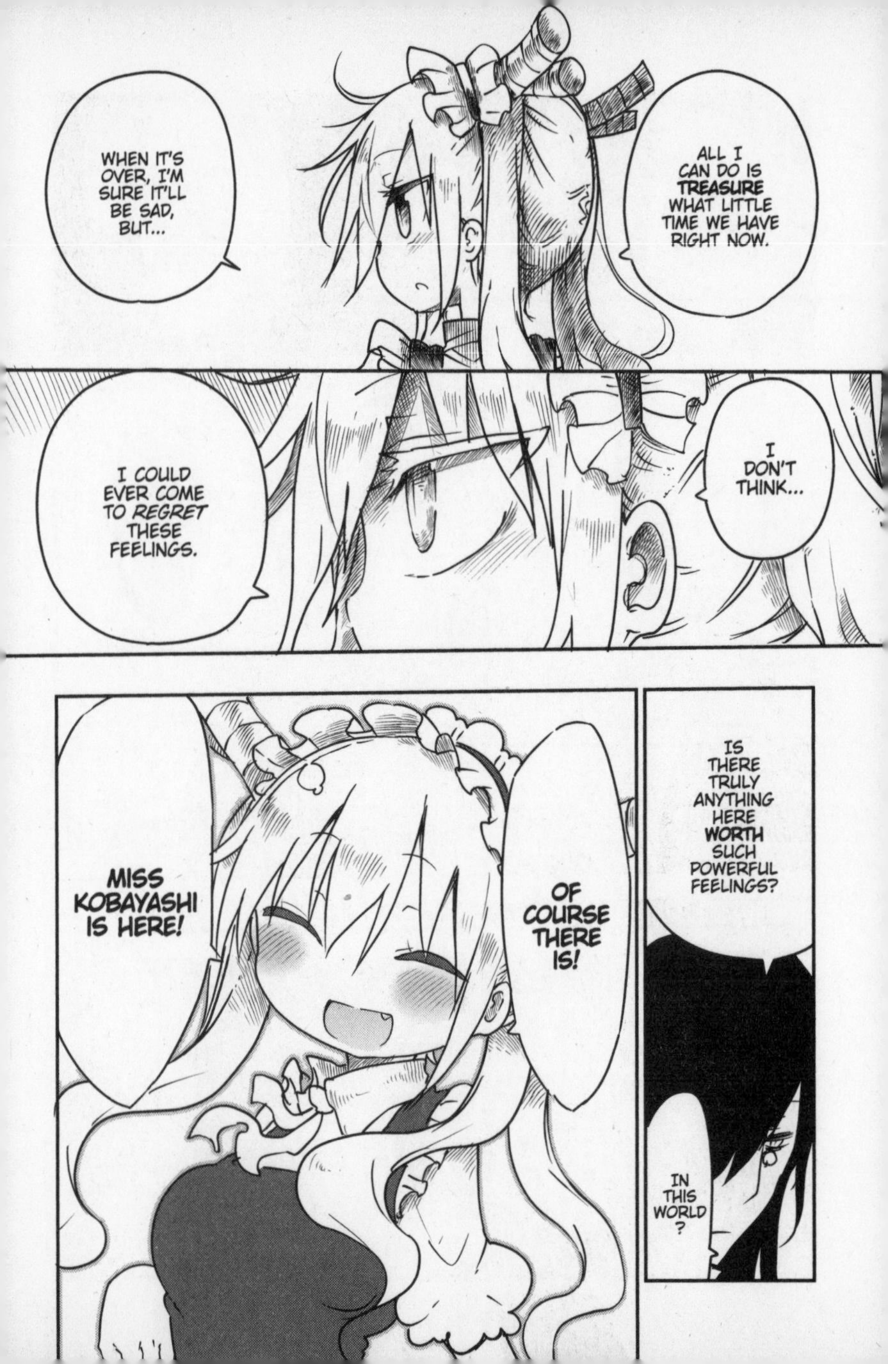
ALL I CAN DO IS **TREASURE** WHAT LITTLE TIME WE HAVE RIGHT NOW.
WHEN IT'S OVER, I'M SURE IT'LL BE SAD, BUT...
I DON'T THINK...
I COULD EVER COME TO *REGRET* THESE FEELINGS.
IS THERE TRULY ANYTHING HERE **WORTH** SUCH POWERFUL FEELINGS?
IN THIS WORLD?
OF COURSE THERE IS!
MISS KOBAYASHI IS HERE!

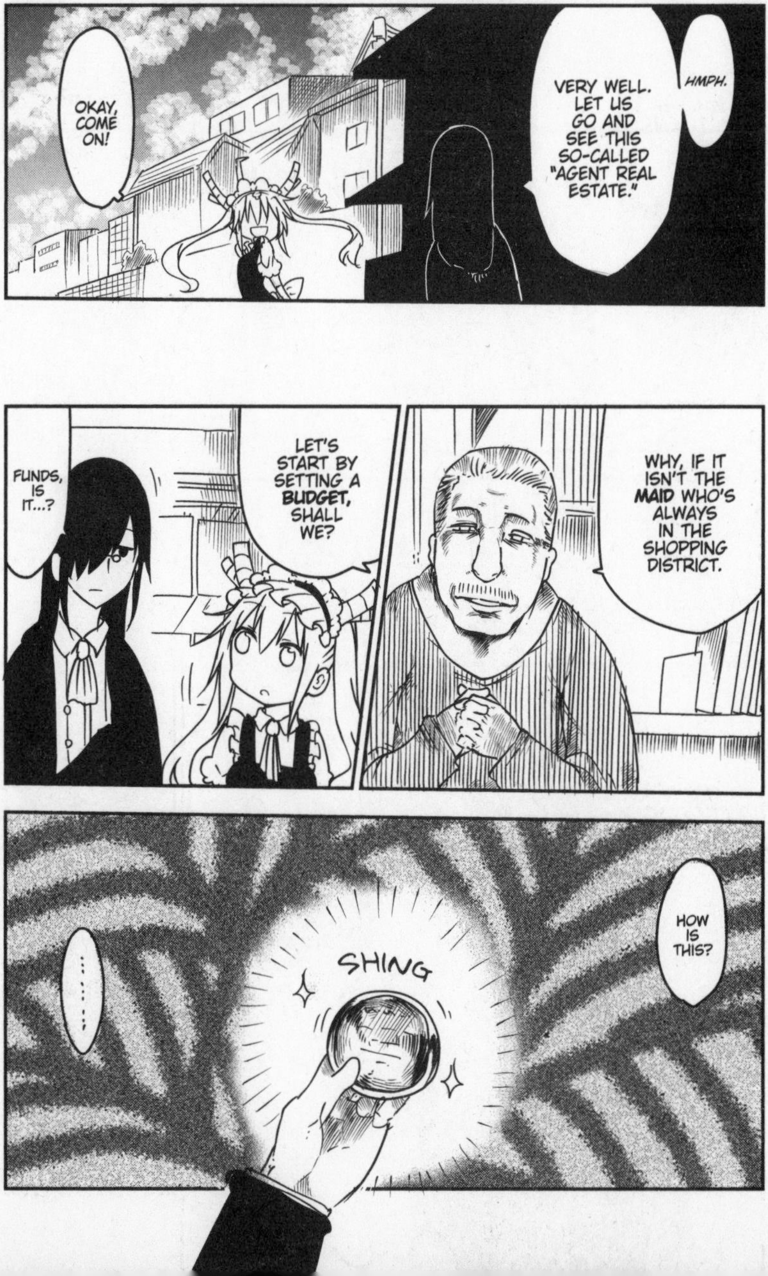
HMPH.
VERY WELL. LET US GO AND SEE THIS SO-CALLED "AGENT REAL ESTATE."
OKAY, COME ON!
WHY, IF IT ISN'T THE **MAID** WHO'S ALWAYS IN THE SHOPPING DISTRICT.
LET'S START BY SETTING A **BUDGET**, SHALL WE?
FUNDS, IS IT...?
HOW IS THIS?
SHING
......

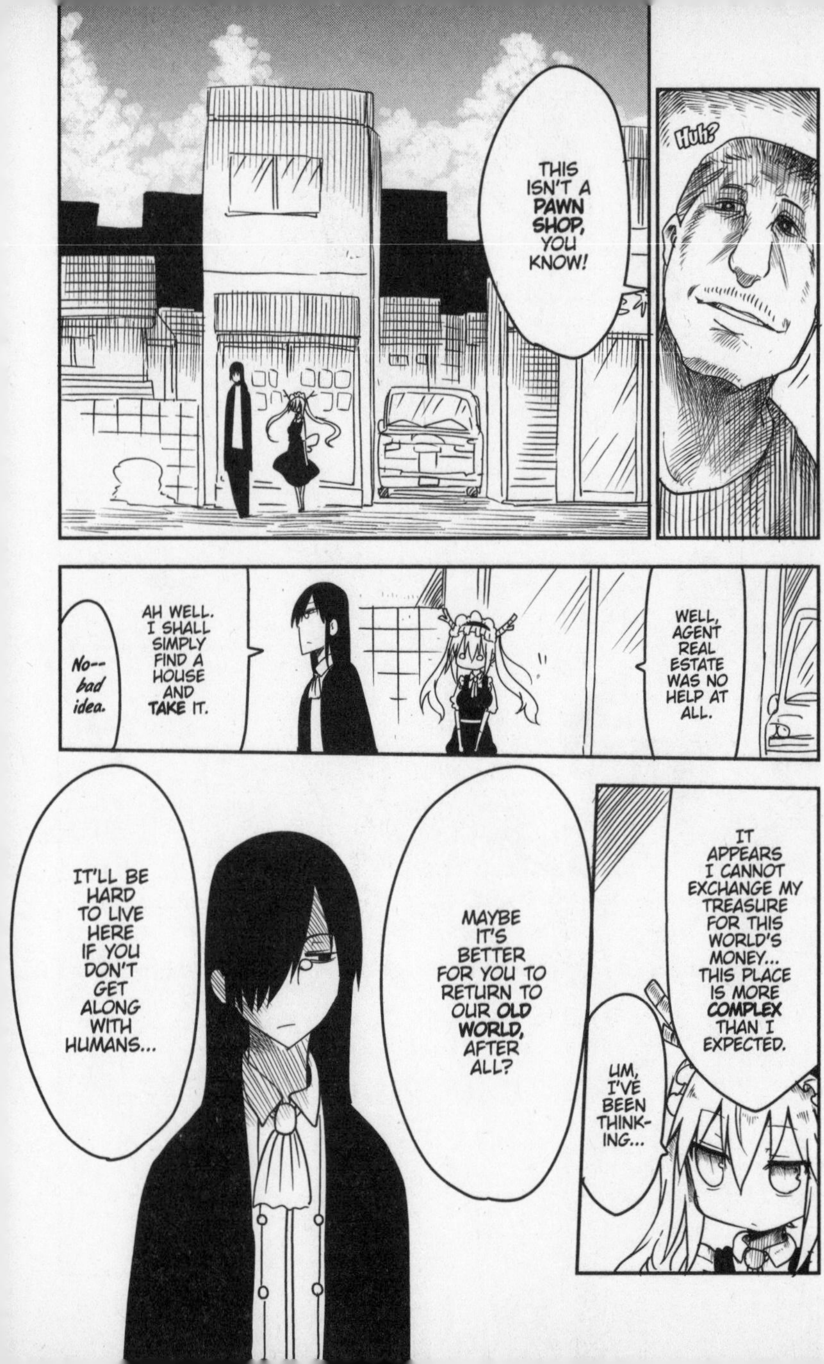
Huh?
THIS ISN'T A PAWN SHOP, YOU KNOW!
WELL, AGENT REAL ESTATE WAS NO HELP AT ALL.
AH WELL. I SHALL SIMPLY FIND A HOUSE AND TAKE IT.
No-- bad idea.
IT APPEARS I CANNOT EXCHANGE MY TREASURE FOR THIS WORLD'S MONEY... THIS PLACE IS MORE COMPLEX THAN I EXPECTED.
UM, I'VE BEEN THINKING...
MAYBE IT'S BETTER FOR YOU TO RETURN TO OUR OLD WORLD, AFTER ALL?
IT'LL BE HARD TO LIVE HERE IF YOU DON'T GET ALONG WITH HUMANS...

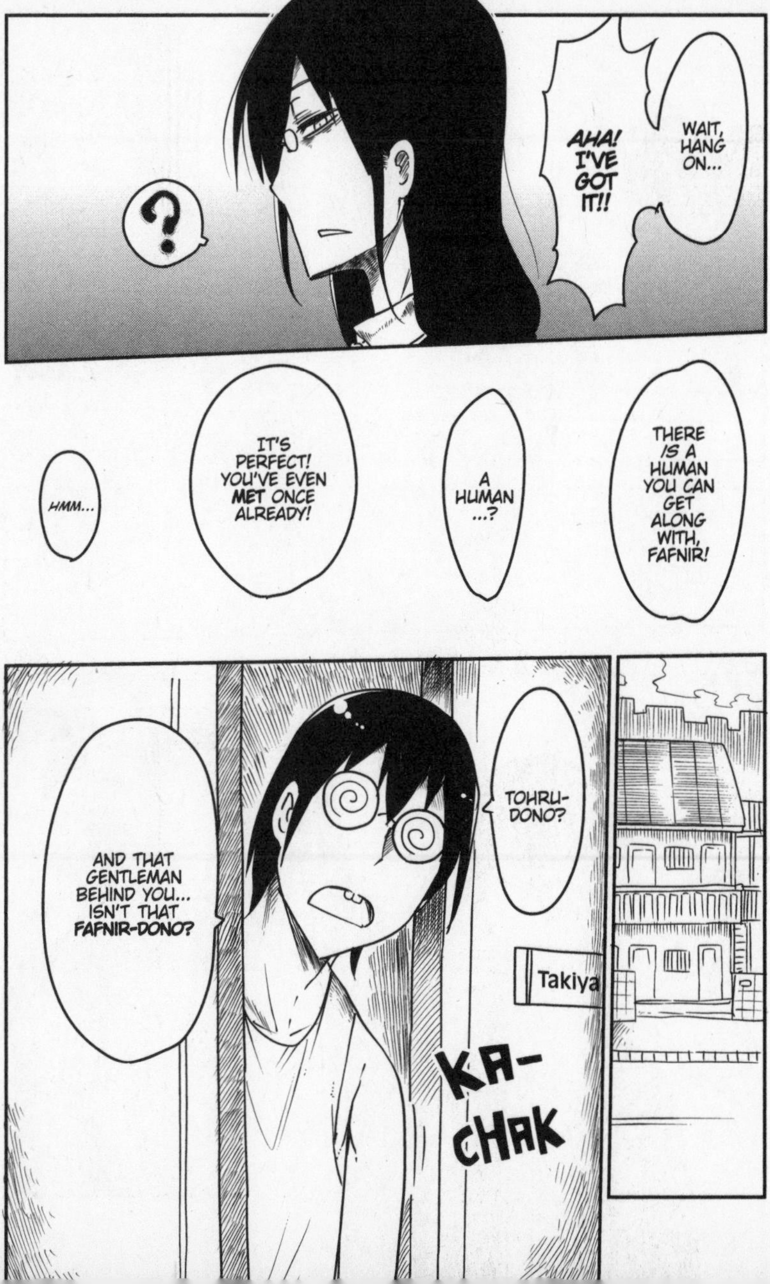
WAIT, HANG ON...
AHA! I'VE GOT IT!!
?
THERE IS A HUMAN YOU CAN GET ALONG WITH, FAFNIR!
A HUMAN ...?
IT'S PERFECT! YOU'VE EVEN MET ONCE ALREADY!
HMM...
TOHRU-DONO?
Takiya
KA-CHAK
AND THAT GENTLEMAN BEHIND YOU... ISN'T THAT FAFNIR-DONO?

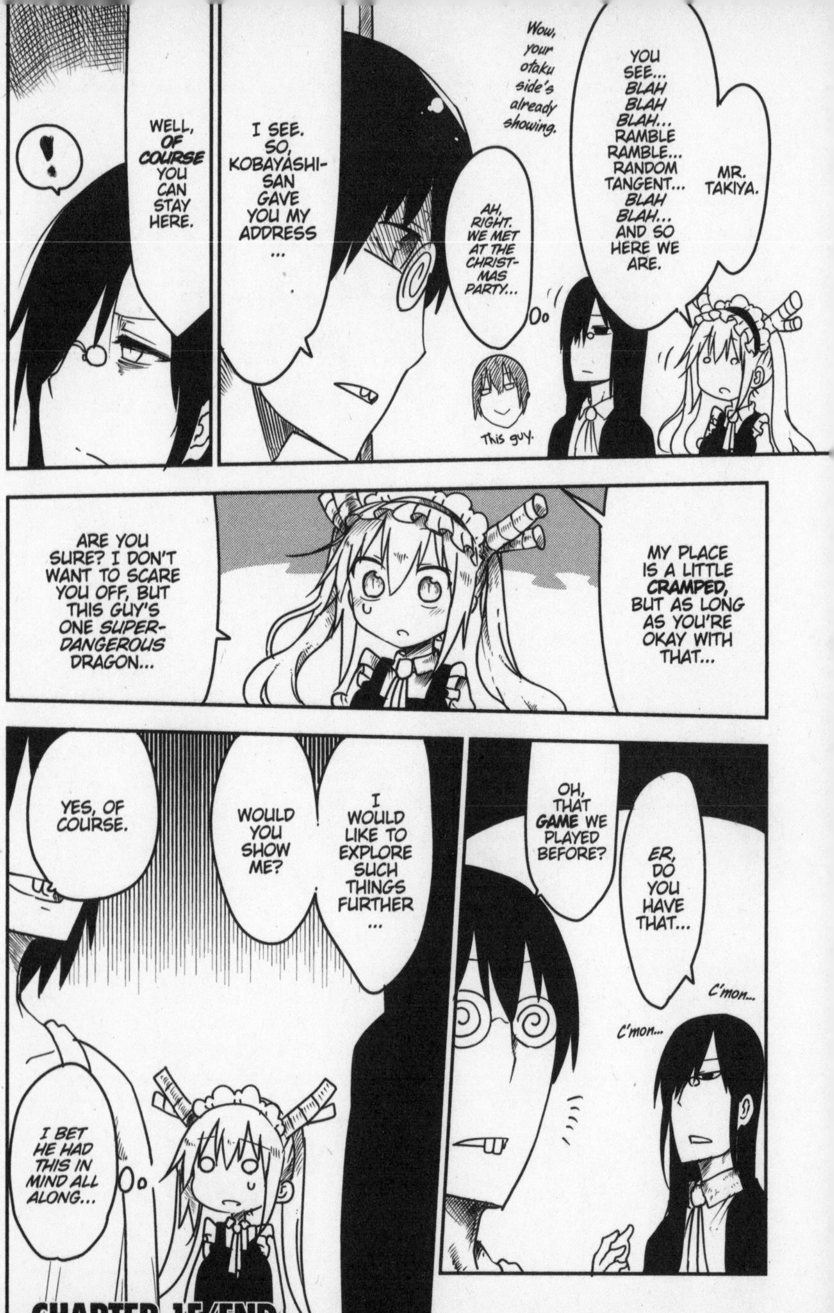
MR. TAKIYA.
YOU SEE... BLAH BLAH BLAH... RAMBLE RAMBLE... RANDOM TANGENT... BLAH BLAH... AND SO HERE WE ARE.
Wow, your otaku side's already showing.
AH, RIGHT. WE MET AT THE CHRISTMAS PARTY...
This guy.
I SEE. SO, KOBAYASHI-SAN GAVE YOU MY ADDRESS...
WELL, OF COURSE YOU CAN STAY HERE.
!
MY PLACE IS A LITTLE CRAMPED, BUT AS LONG AS YOU'RE OKAY WITH THAT...
ARE YOU SURE? I DON'T WANT TO SCARE YOU OFF, BUT THIS GUY'S ONE SUPER-DANGEROUS DRAGON...
ER, DO YOU HAVE THAT...
OH, THAT GAME WE PLAYED BEFORE?
C'mon...
C'mon...
I WOULD LIKE TO EXPLORE SUCH THINGS FURTHER...
WOULD YOU SHOW ME?
YES, OF COURSE.
I BET HE HAD THIS IN MIND ALL ALONG...

CHAPTER 15/END

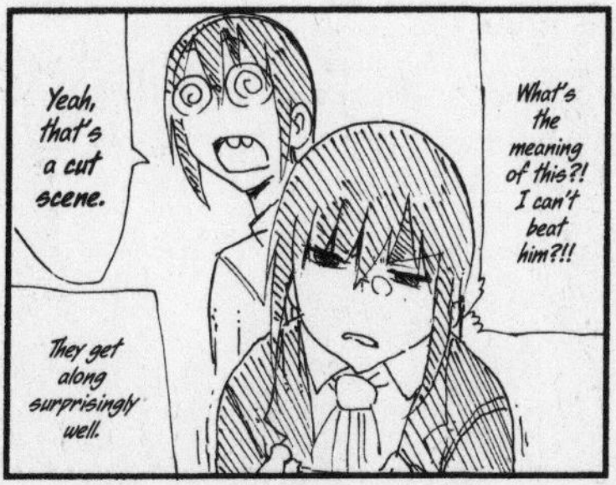
What's the meaning of this?! I can't beat him?!!
Yeah, that's a cut scene.
They get along surprisingly well.

Miss Kobayashi's Dragon Maid

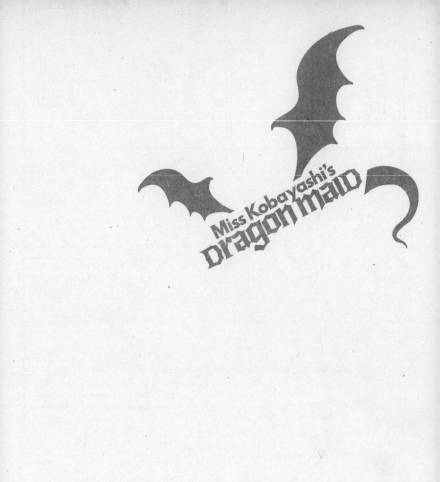

CHAPTER 16

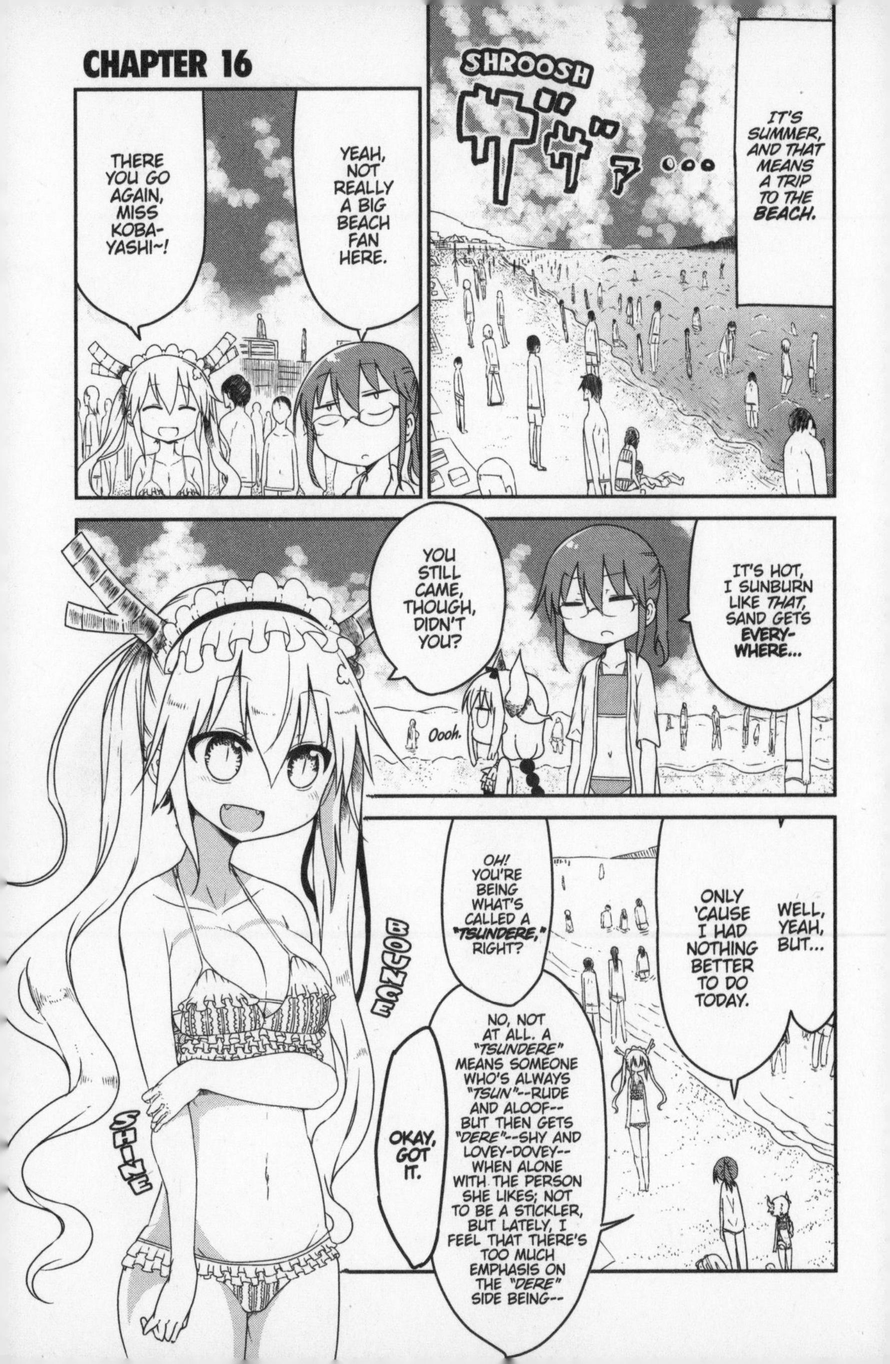
SHROOSH
ザザァ…
IT'S SUMMER, AND THAT MEANS A TRIP TO THE *BEACH.*
YEAH, NOT REALLY A BIG BEACH FAN HERE.
THERE YOU GO AGAIN, MISS KOBA-YASHI~!
IT'S HOT, I SUNBURN LIKE *THAT,* SAND GETS **EVERY-WHERE...**
YOU STILL CAME, THOUGH, DIDN'T YOU?
Oooh.
WELL, YEAH, BUT...
ONLY 'CAUSE I HAD NOTHING BETTER TO DO TODAY.
OH! YOU'RE BEING WHAT'S CALLED A "TSUNDERE," RIGHT?
NO, NOT AT ALL. A *"TSUNDERE"* MEANS SOMEONE WHO'S ALWAYS *"TSUN"*--RUDE AND ALOOF--BUT THEN GETS *"DERE"*--SHY AND LOVEY-DOVEY--WHEN ALONE WITH THE PERSON SHE LIKES; NOT TO BE A STICKLER, BUT LATELY, I FEEL THAT THERE'S TOO MUCH EMPHASIS ON THE *"DERE"* SIDE BEING--
OKAY, GOT IT.
BOUNCE
SHINE

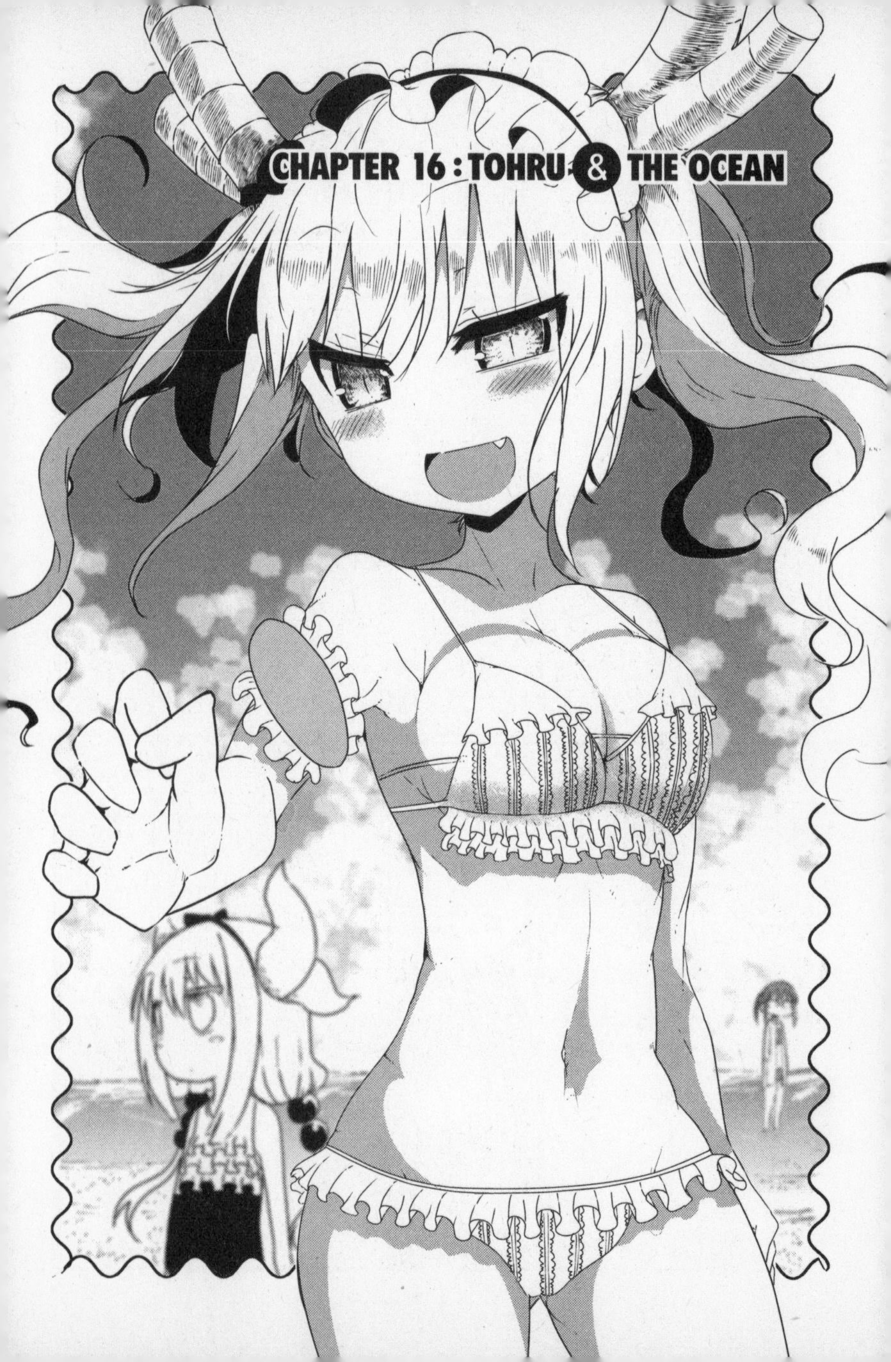
CHAPTER 16 : TOHRU & THE OCEAN

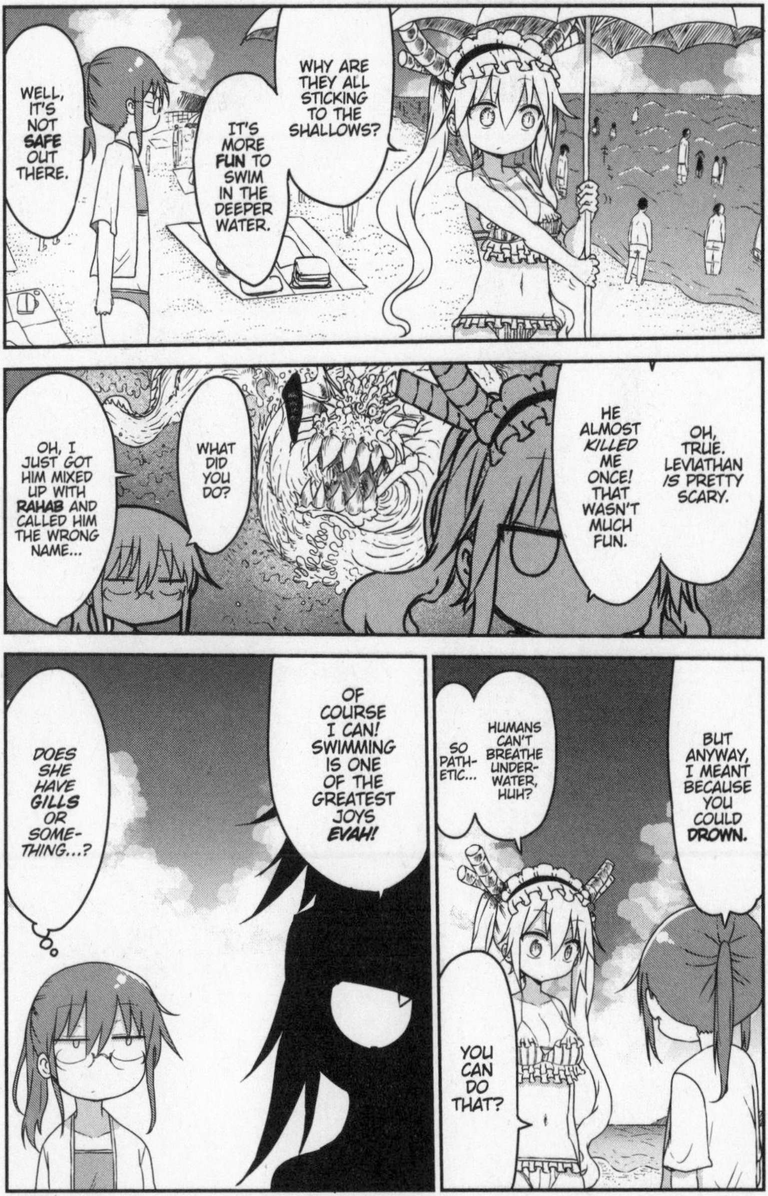
WHY ARE THEY ALL STICKING TO THE SHALLOWS?
IT'S MORE FUN TO SWIM IN THE DEEPER WATER.
WELL, IT'S NOT SAFE OUT THERE.
OH, TRUE. LEVIATHAN IS PRETTY SCARY.
HE ALMOST KILLED ME ONCE! THAT WASN'T MUCH FUN.
WHAT DID YOU DO?
OH, I JUST GOT HIM MIXED UP WITH RAHAB AND CALLED HIM THE WRONG NAME...
BUT ANYWAY, I MEANT BECAUSE YOU COULD DROWN.
HUMANS CAN'T BREATHE UNDER-WATER, HUH?
SO PATH-ETIC...
YOU CAN DO THAT?
OF COURSE I CAN! SWIMMING IS ONE OF THE GREATEST JOYS EVAH!
DOES SHE HAVE GILLS OR SOME-THING...?

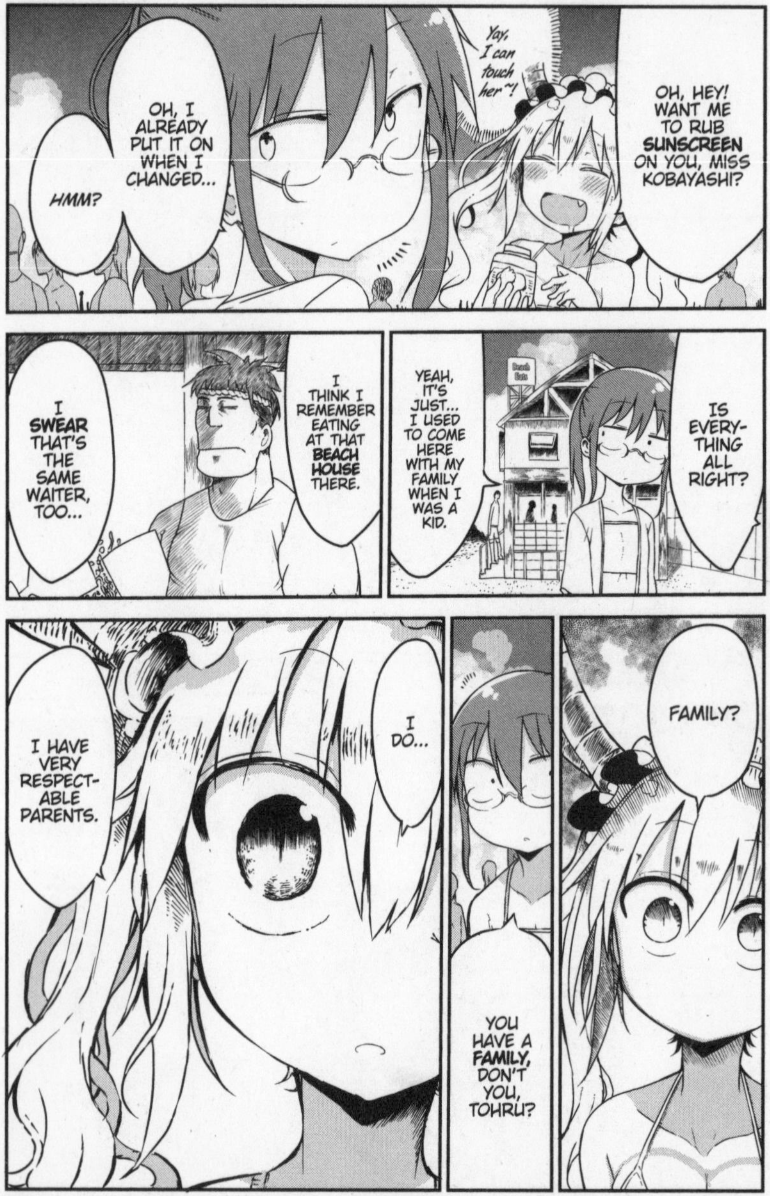
OH, HEY! WANT ME TO RUB SUNSCREEN ON YOU, MISS KOBAYASHI?
Yay, I can touch her~!
OH, I ALREADY PUT IT ON WHEN I CHANGED...
HMM?
IS EVERY-THING ALL RIGHT?
YEAH, IT'S JUST... I USED TO COME HERE WITH MY FAMILY WHEN I WAS A KID.
I THINK I REMEMBER EATING AT THAT BEACH HOUSE THERE.
I SWEAR THAT'S THE SAME WAITER, TOO...
FAMILY?
YOU HAVE A FAMILY, DON'T YOU, TOHRU?
I DO...
I HAVE VERY RESPECT-ABLE PARENTS.

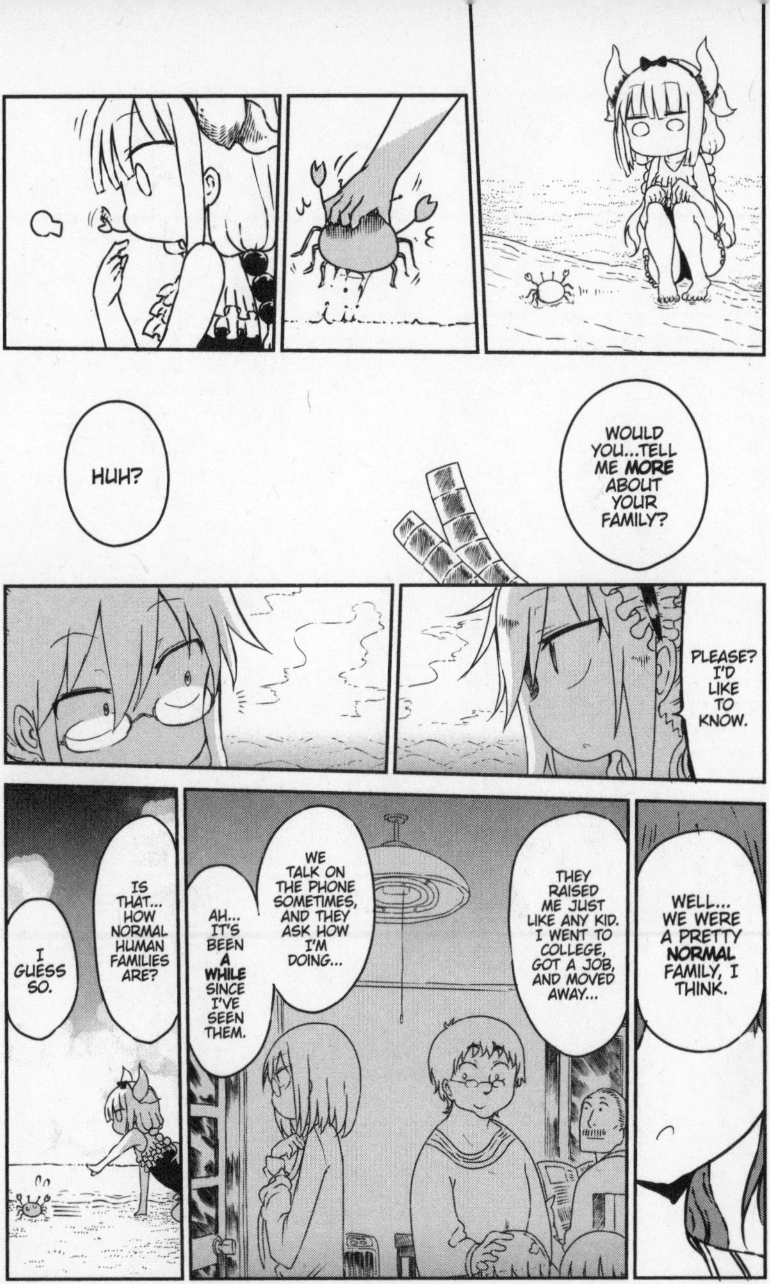
WOULD YOU...TELL ME MORE ABOUT YOUR FAMILY?
HUH?
PLEASE? I'D LIKE TO KNOW.
WELL... WE WERE A PRETTY NORMAL FAMILY, I THINK.
THEY RAISED ME JUST LIKE ANY KID. I WENT TO COLLEGE, GOT A JOB, AND MOVED AWAY...
WE TALK ON THE PHONE SOMETIMES, AND THEY ASK HOW I'M DOING...
AH... IT'S BEEN A WHILE SINCE I'VE SEEN THEM.
IS THAT... HOW NORMAL HUMAN FAMILIES ARE?
I GUESS SO.

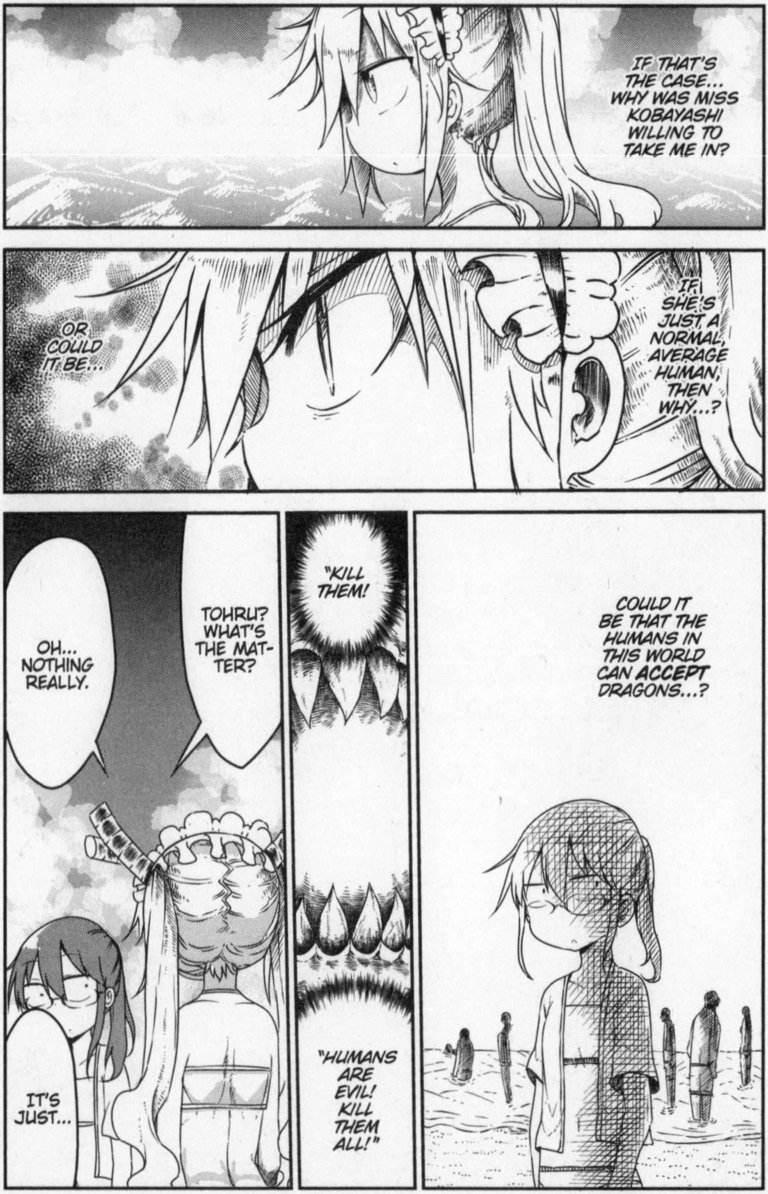
IF THAT'S THE CASE... WHY WAS MISS KOBAYASHI WILLING TO TAKE ME IN?
IF SHE'S JUST A NORMAL, AVERAGE HUMAN, THEN WHY...?
OR COULD IT BE...
COULD IT BE THAT THE HUMANS IN THIS WORLD CAN ACCEPT DRAGONS...?
"KILL THEM!
"HUMANS ARE EVIL! KILL THEM ALL!"
TOHRU? WHAT'S THE MAT-TER?
OH... NOTHING REALLY.
IT'S JUST...

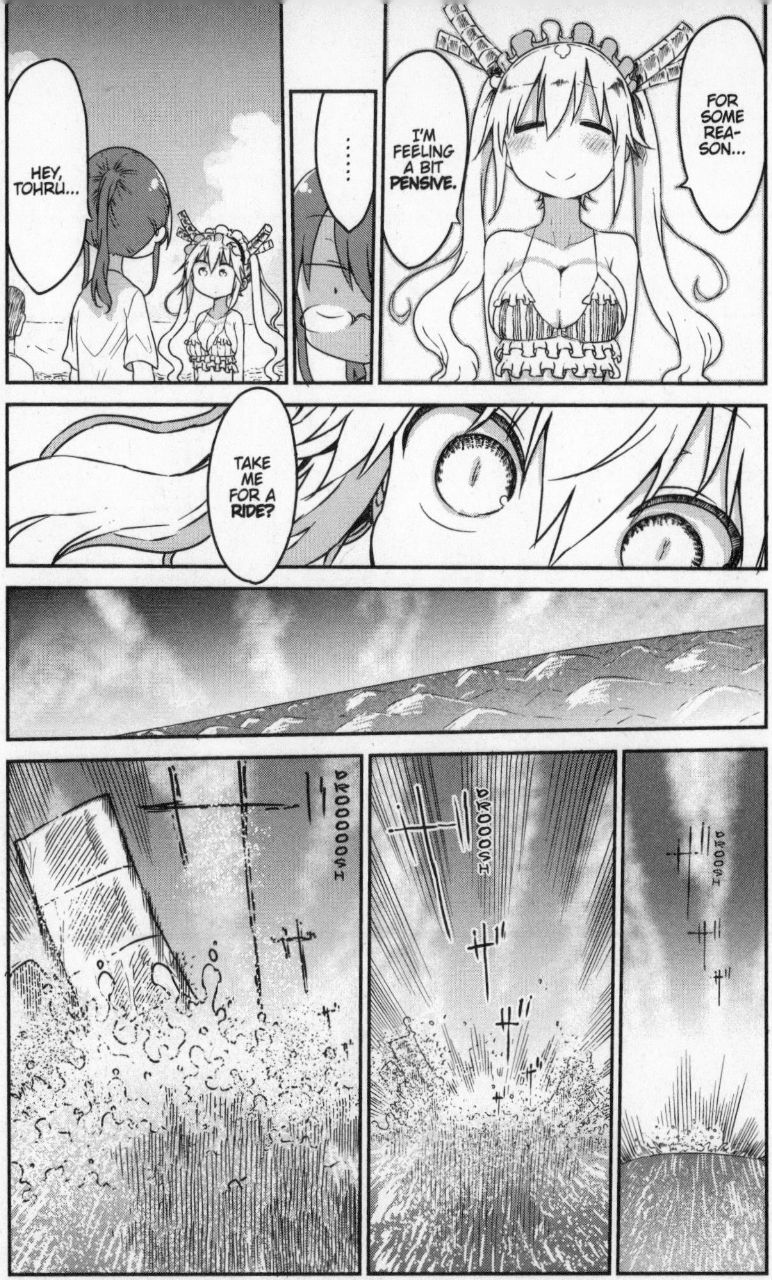
FOR SOME REA-SON...
I'M FEELING A BIT PENSIVE.
......
HEY, TOHRU...
TAKE ME FOR A RIDE?
DROOSH
DROOOSH
DROOOOOSH

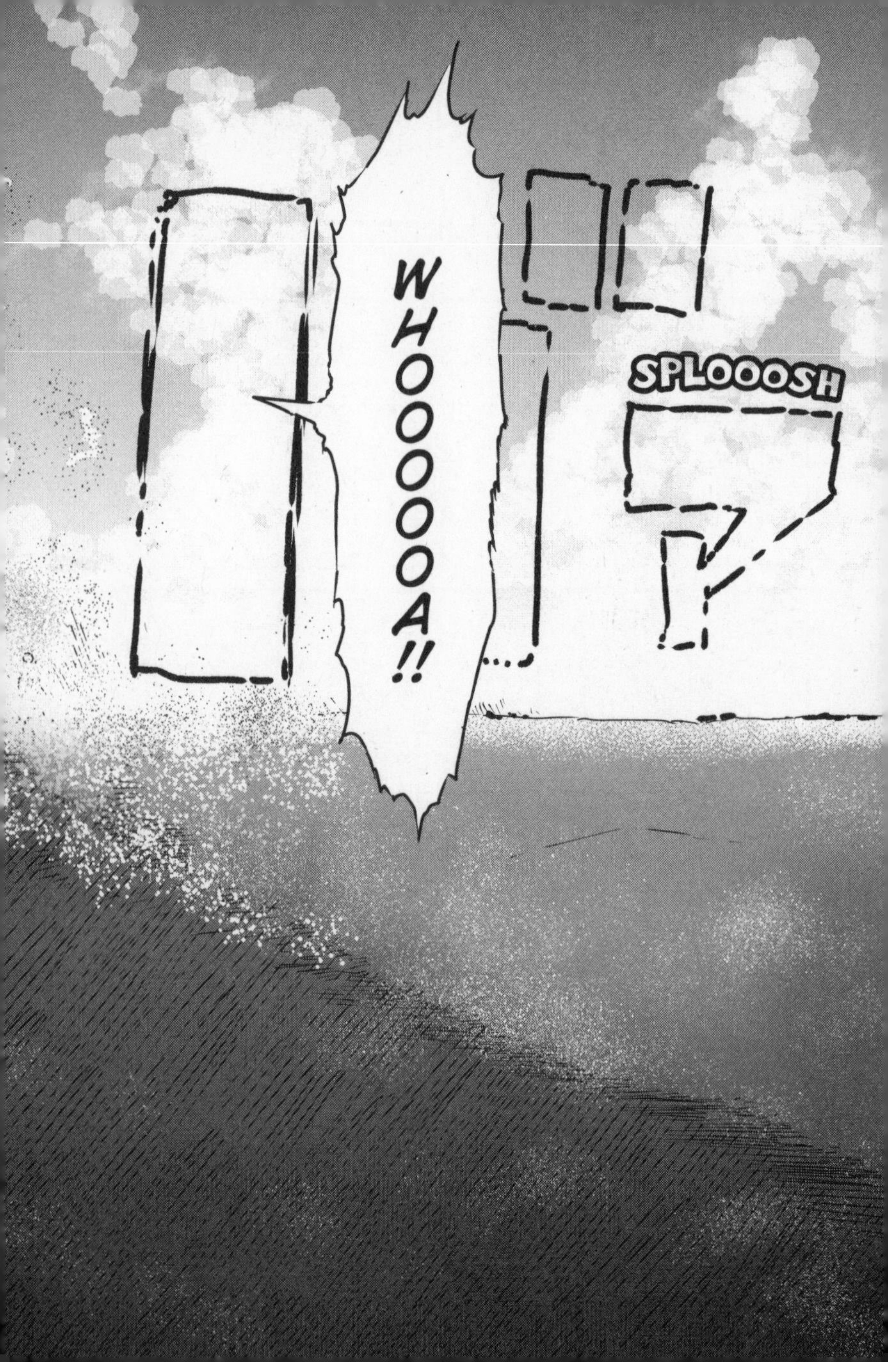
WHOOOOOOA!!
SPLOOOSH

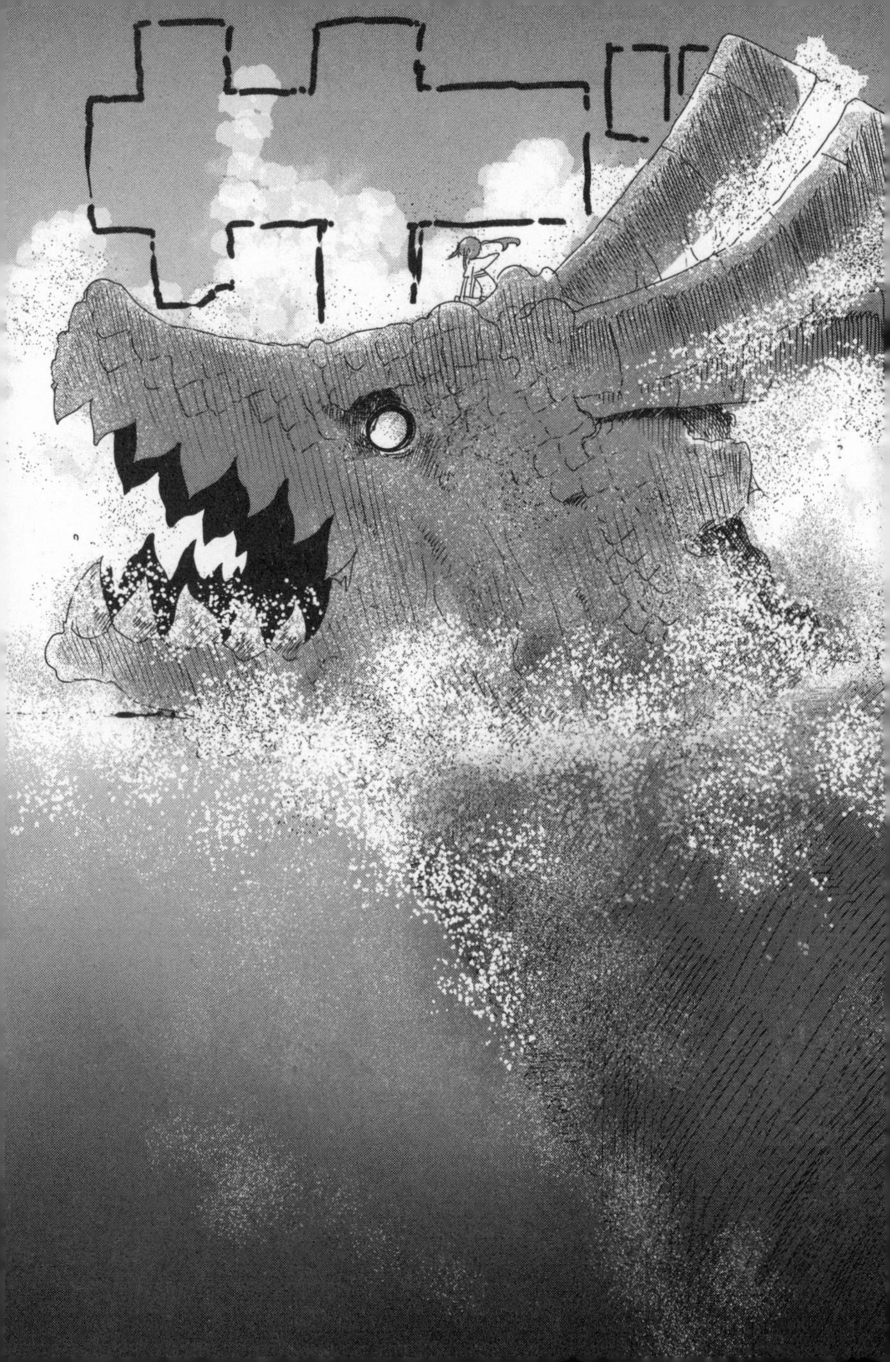

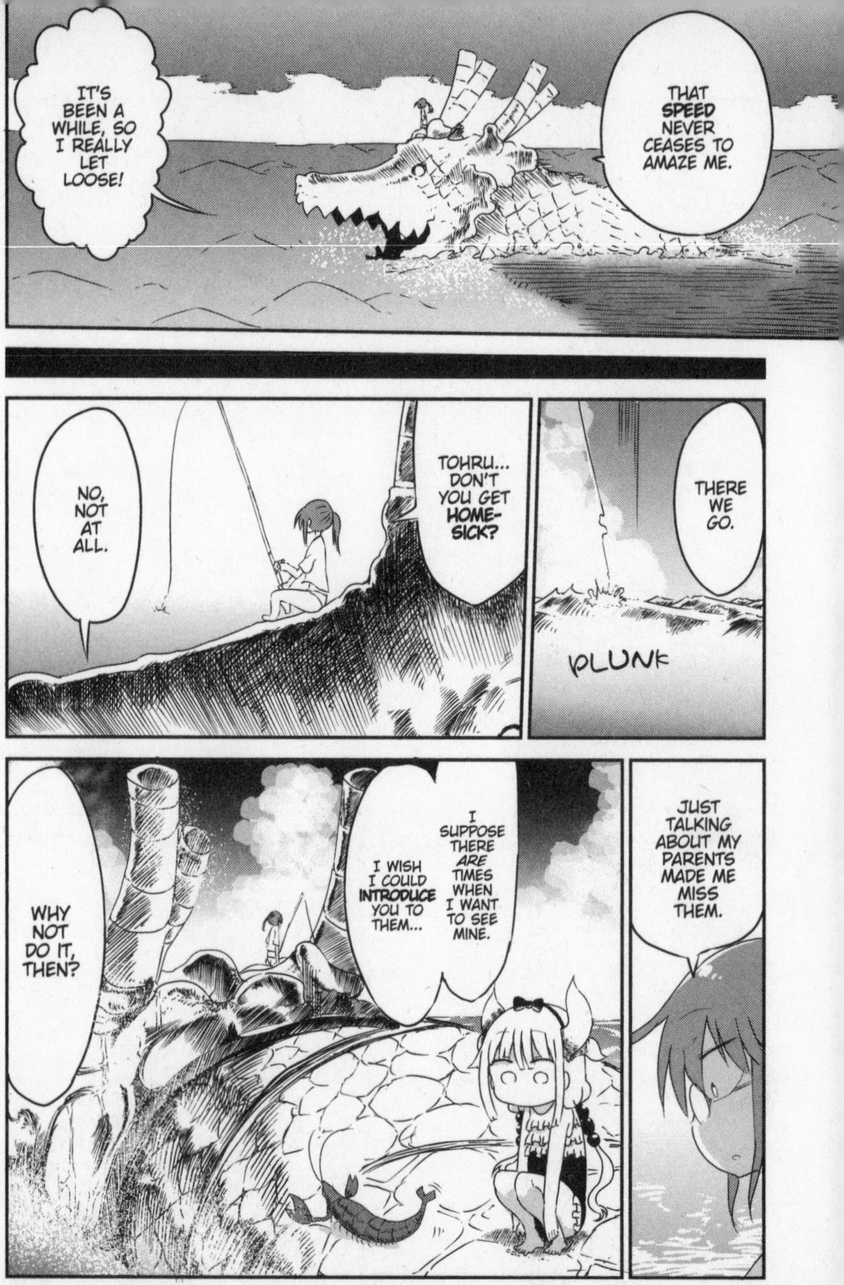
THAT SPEED NEVER CEASES TO AMAZE ME.
IT'S BEEN A WHILE, SO I REALLY LET LOOSE!
THERE WE GO.
PLUNK
TOHRU... DON'T YOU GET HOMESICK?
NO, NOT AT ALL.
JUST TALKING ABOUT MY PARENTS MADE ME MISS THEM.
I SUPPOSE THERE ARE TIMES WHEN I WANT TO SEE MINE.
I WISH I COULD INTRODUCE YOU TO THEM...
WHY NOT DO IT, THEN?

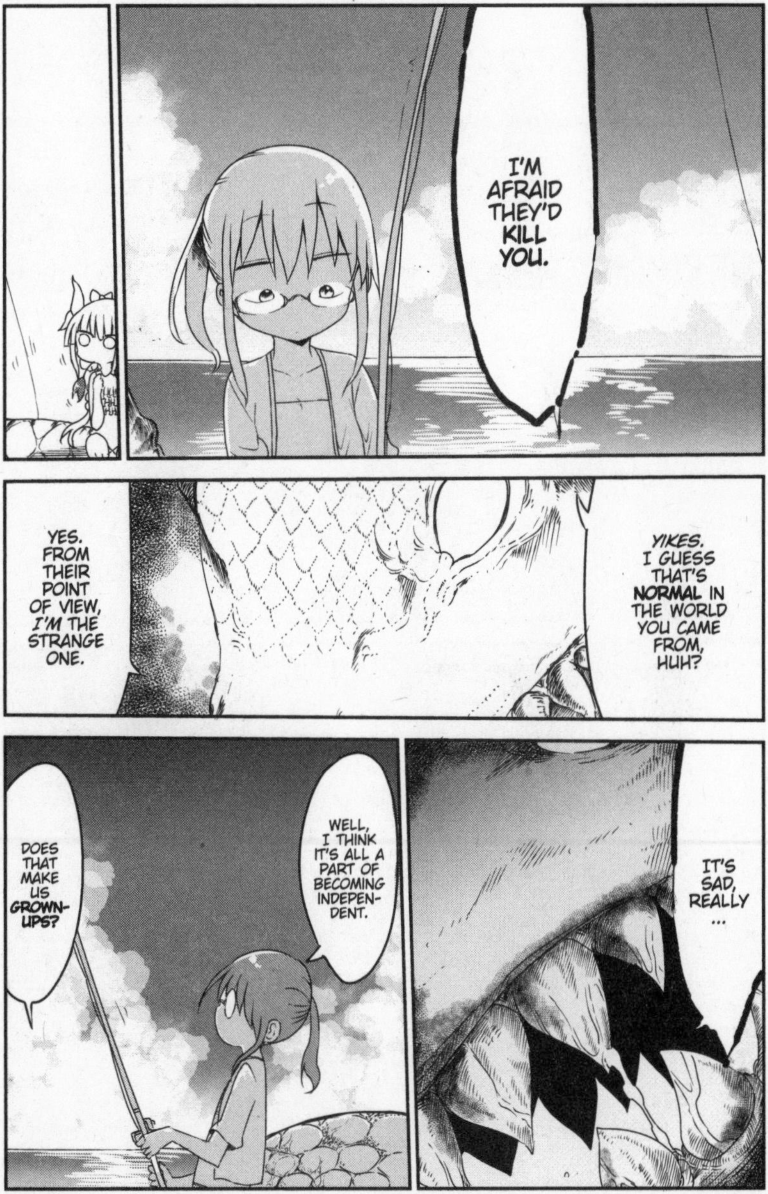
I'M AFRAID THEY'D KILL YOU.
YIKES. I GUESS THAT'S NORMAL IN THE WORLD YOU CAME FROM, HUH?
YES. FROM THEIR POINT OF VIEW, I'M THE STRANGE ONE.
IT'S SAD, REALLY...
WELL, I THINK IT'S ALL A PART OF BECOMING INDEPEN-DENT.
DOES THAT MAKE US GROWN-UPS?

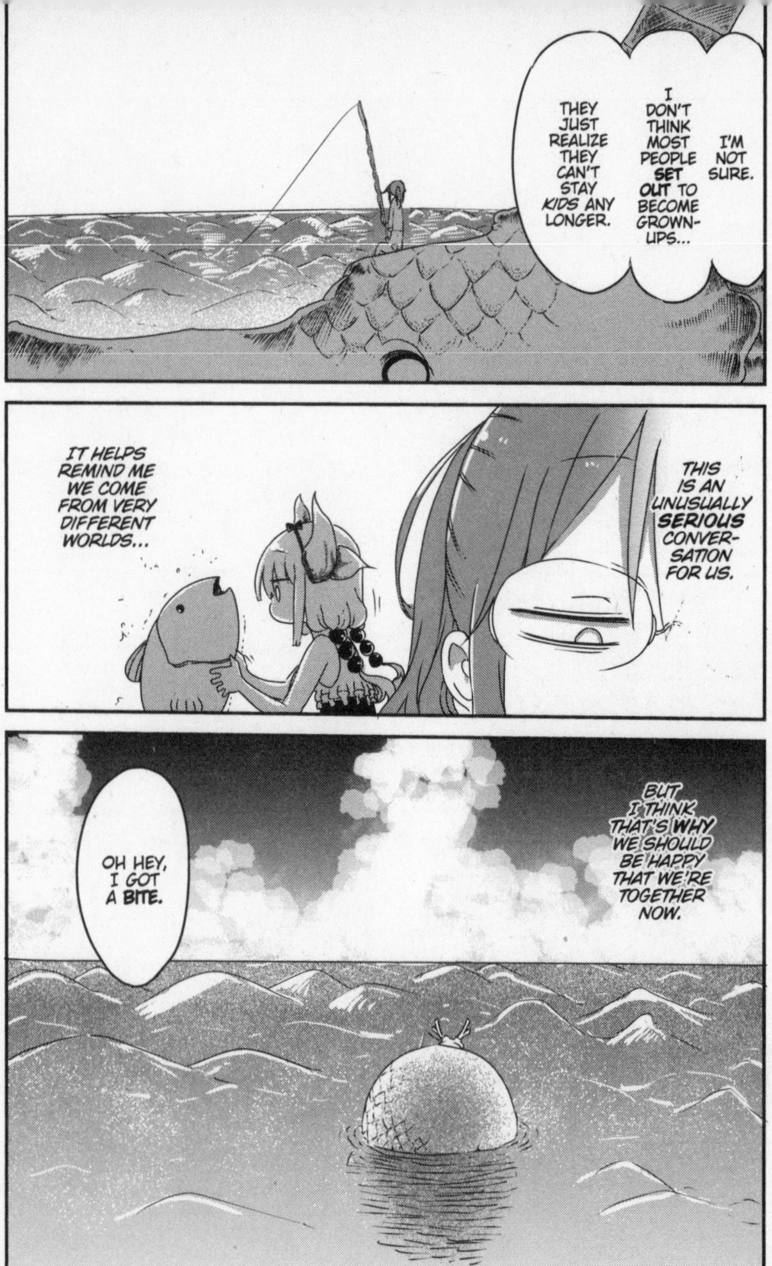
I'M NOT SURE.
I DON'T THINK MOST PEOPLE SET OUT TO BECOME GROWN-UPS...
THEY JUST REALIZE THEY CAN'T STAY KIDS ANY LONGER.
THIS IS AN UNUSUALLY SERIOUS CONVERSATION FOR US.
IT HELPS REMIND ME WE COME FROM VERY DIFFERENT WORLDS...
BUT I THINK THAT'S WHY WE SHOULD BE HAPPY THAT WE'RE TOGETHER NOW.
OH HEY, I GOT A BITE.

CHAPTER 16/END

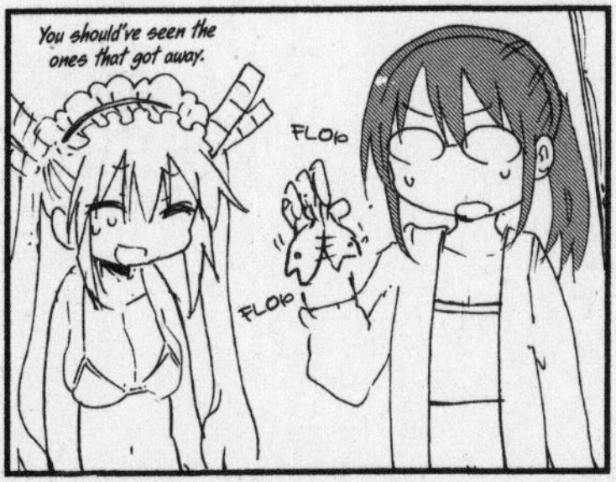
You should've seen the ones that got away.
FLOP
FLOP

Miss Kobayashi's Dragon Maid

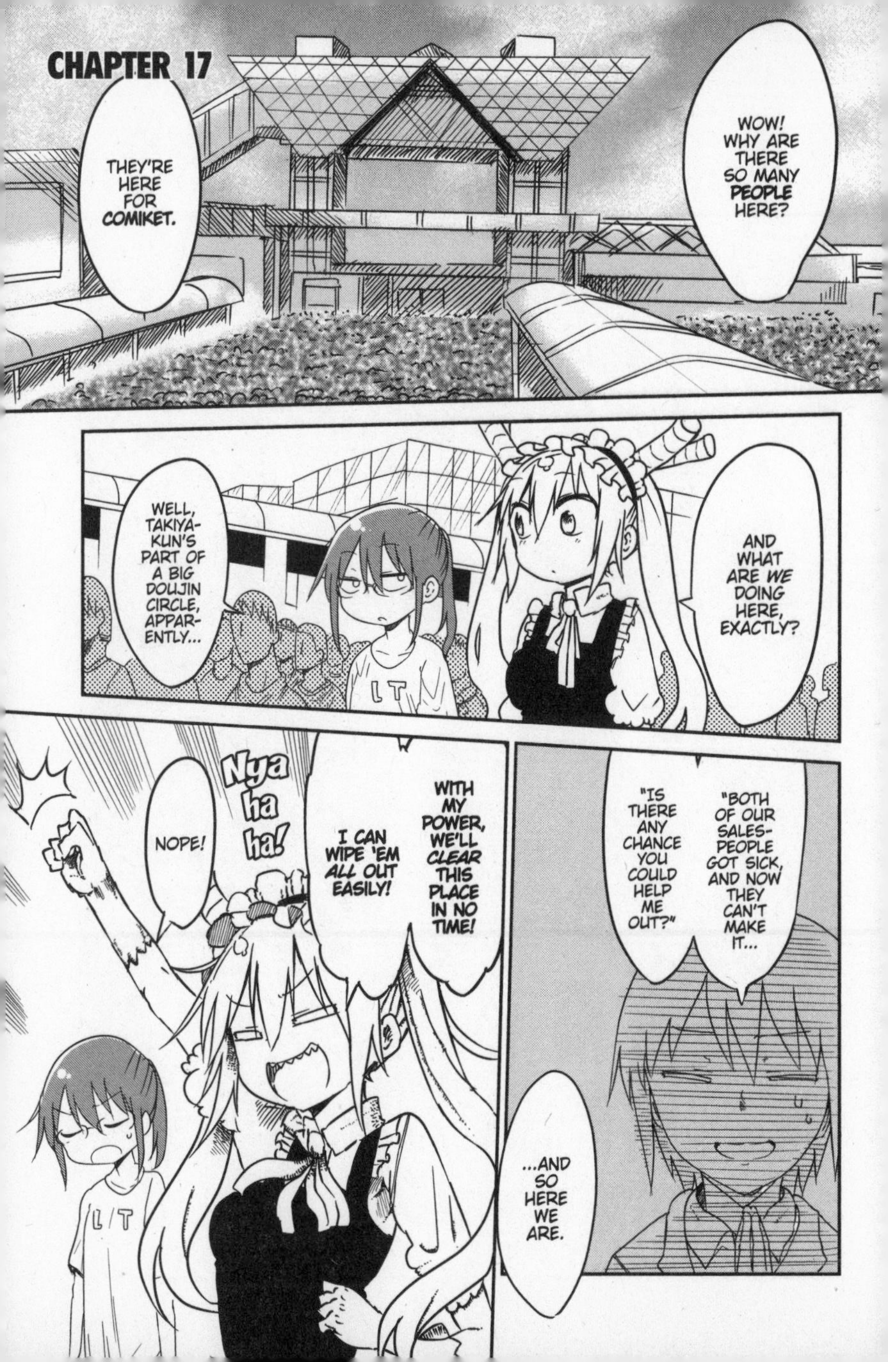
CHAPTER 17
WOW! WHY ARE THERE SO MANY PEOPLE HERE?
THEY'RE HERE FOR COMIKET.
AND WHAT ARE WE DOING HERE, EXACTLY?
WELL, TAKIYA-KUN'S PART OF A BIG DOUJIN CIRCLE, APPARENTLY...
"BOTH OF OUR SALES-PEOPLE GOT SICK, AND NOW THEY CAN'T MAKE IT...
"IS THERE ANY CHANCE YOU COULD HELP ME OUT?"
...AND SO HERE WE ARE.
WITH MY POWER, WE'LL CLEAR THIS PLACE IN NO TIME!
I CAN WIPE 'EM ALL OUT EASILY!
Nya ha ha!
NOPE!

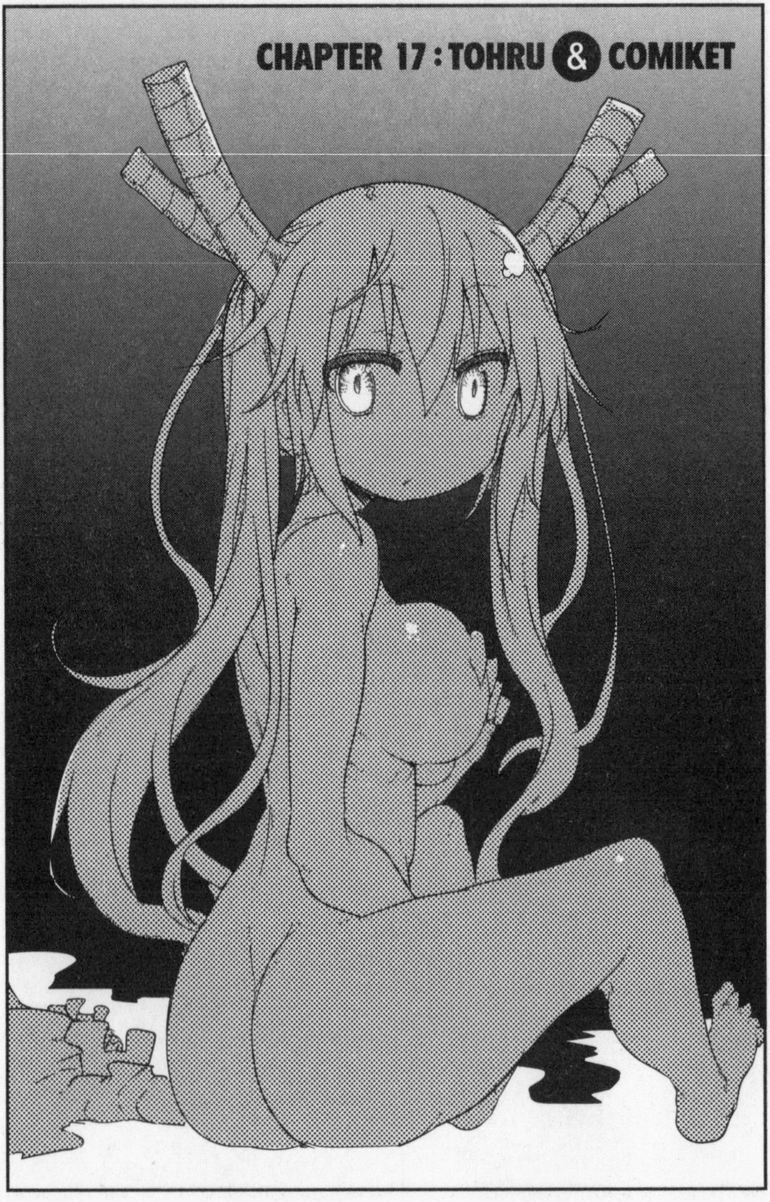
CHAPTER 17 : TOHRU & COMIKET

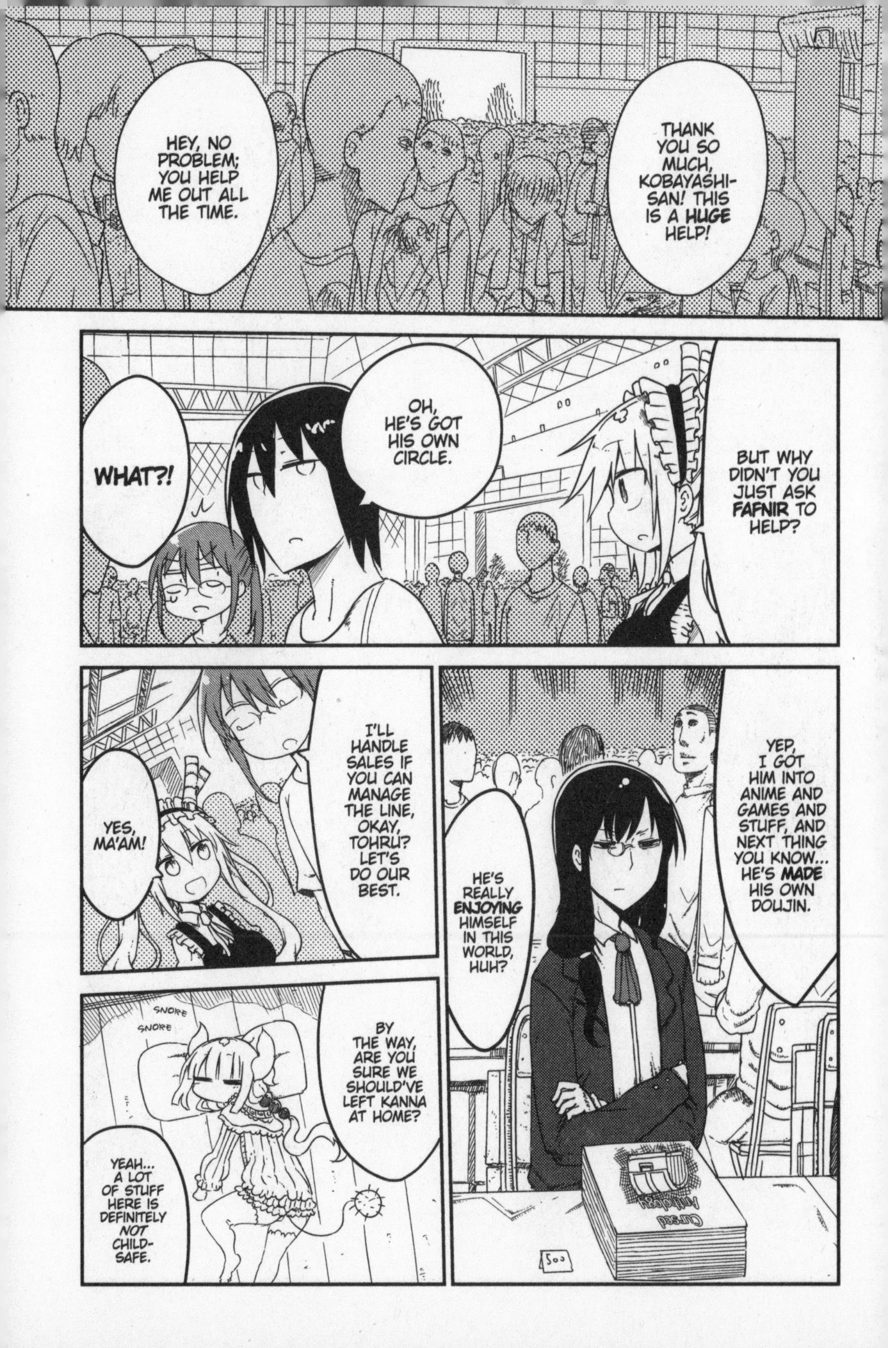
THANK YOU SO MUCH, KOBAYASHI-SAN! THIS IS A HUGE HELP!
HEY, NO PROBLEM; YOU HELP ME OUT ALL THE TIME.
BUT WHY DIDN'T YOU JUST ASK FAFNIR TO HELP?
OH, HE'S GOT HIS OWN CIRCLE.
WHAT?!
YEP, I GOT HIM INTO ANIME AND GAMES AND STUFF, AND NEXT THING YOU KNOW... HE'S MADE HIS OWN DOUJIN.
HE'S REALLY ENJOYING HIMSELF IN THIS WORLD, HUH?
Cursed Anthology
500
I'LL HANDLE SALES IF YOU CAN MANAGE THE LINE, OKAY, TOHRU? LET'S DO OUR BEST.
YES, MA'AM!
BY THE WAY, ARE YOU SURE WE SHOULD'VE LEFT KANNA AT HOME?
SNORE
SNORE
YEAH... A LOT OF STUFF HERE IS DEFINITELY NOT CHILD-SAFE.

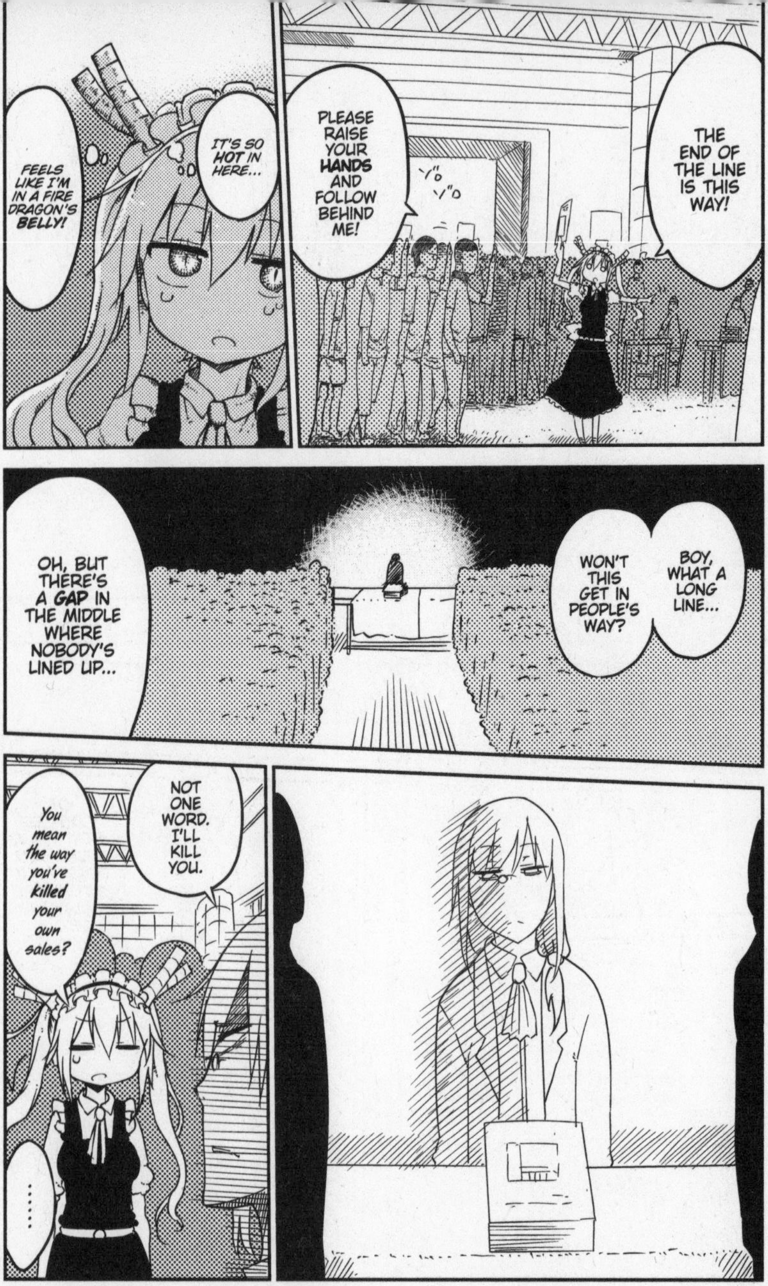

THE END OF THE LINE IS THIS WAY!
PLEASE RAISE YOUR HANDS AND FOLLOW BEHIND ME!
IT'S SO HOT IN HERE...
FEELS LIKE I'M IN A FIRE DRAGON'S BELLY!
BOY, WHAT A LONG LINE...
WON'T THIS GET IN PEOPLE'S WAY?
OH, BUT THERE'S A GAP IN THE MIDDLE WHERE NOBODY'S LINED UP...
NOT ONE WORD. I'LL KILL YOU.
You mean the way you've killed your own sales?
......

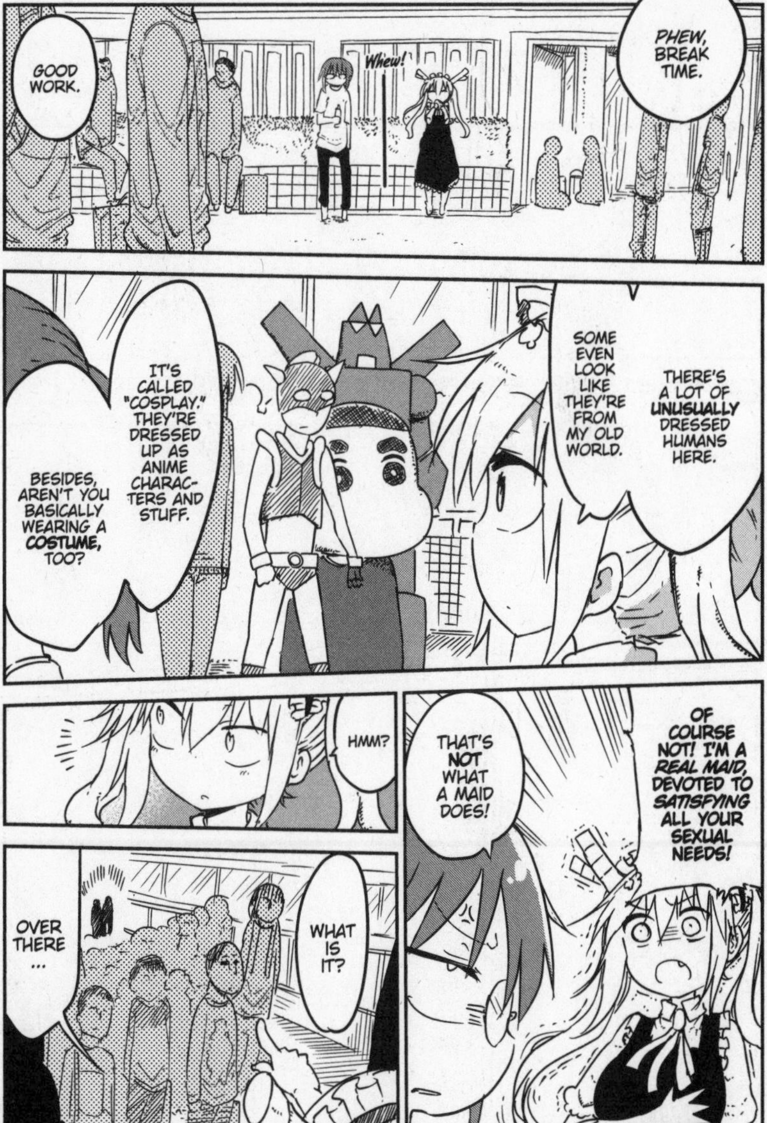
PHEW, BREAK TIME.
Whew!
GOOD WORK.
THERE'S A LOT OF UNUSUALLY DRESSED HUMANS HERE.
SOME EVEN LOOK LIKE THEY'RE FROM MY OLD WORLD.
IT'S CALLED "COSPLAY." THEY'RE DRESSED UP AS ANIME CHARACTERS AND STUFF.
BESIDES, AREN'T YOU BASICALLY WEARING A COSTUME, TOO?
OF COURSE NOT! I'M A REAL MAID, DEVOTED TO SATISFYING ALL YOUR SEXUAL NEEDS!
THAT'S NOT WHAT A MAID DOES!
Tch!
HMM?
WHAT IS IT?
OVER THERE ...

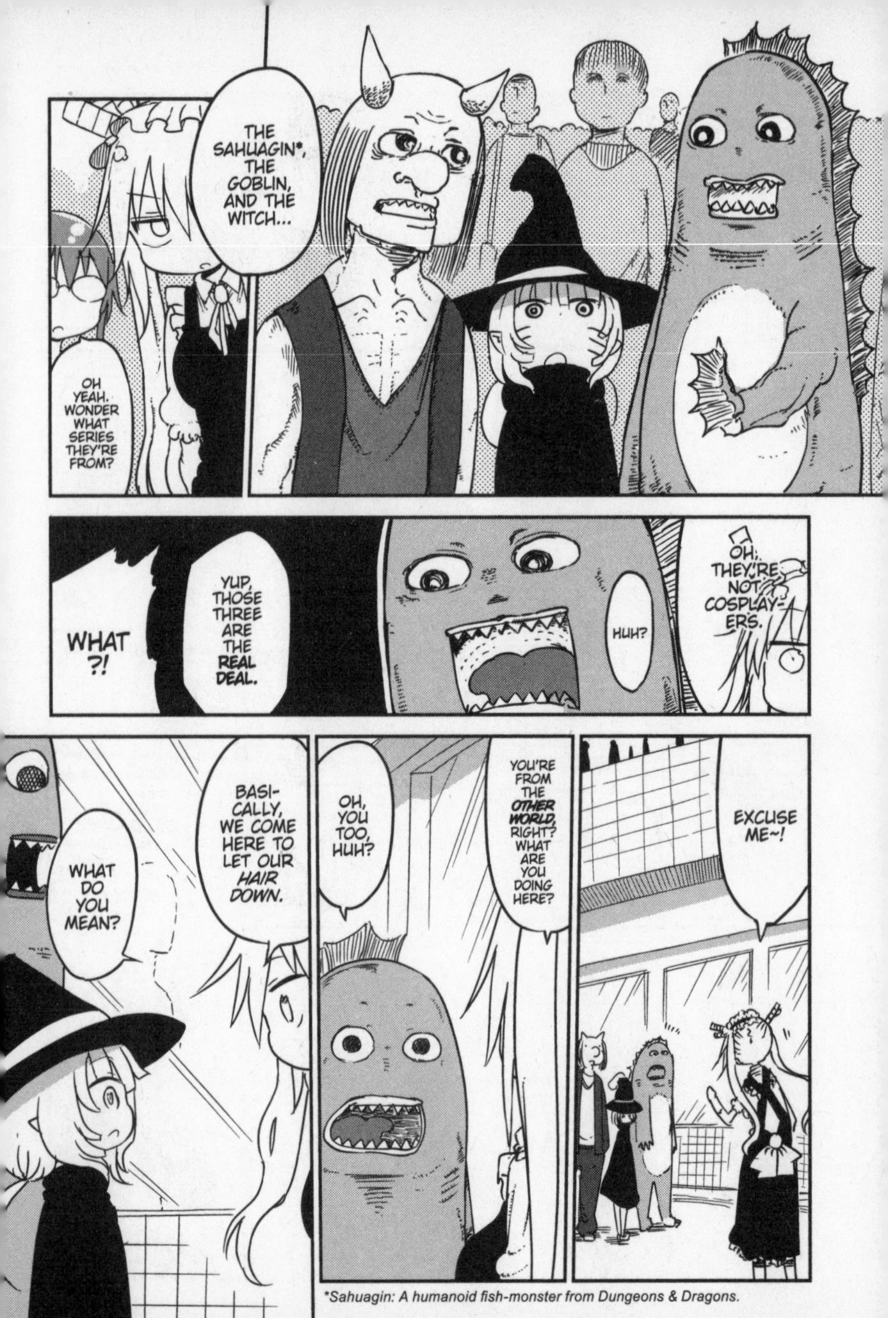
THE SAHUAGIN*, THE GOBLIN, AND THE WITCH...
OH YEAH. WONDER WHAT SERIES THEY'RE FROM?
OH, THEY'RE NOT COSPLAYERS.
HUH?
YUP, THOSE THREE ARE THE REAL DEAL.
WHAT?!
EXCUSE ME~!
YOU'RE FROM THE OTHER WORLD, RIGHT? WHAT ARE YOU DOING HERE?
OH, YOU TOO, HUH?
BASICALLY, WE COME HERE TO LET OUR HAIR DOWN.
WHAT DO YOU MEAN?

*Sahuagin: A humanoid fish-monster from Dungeons & Dragons.

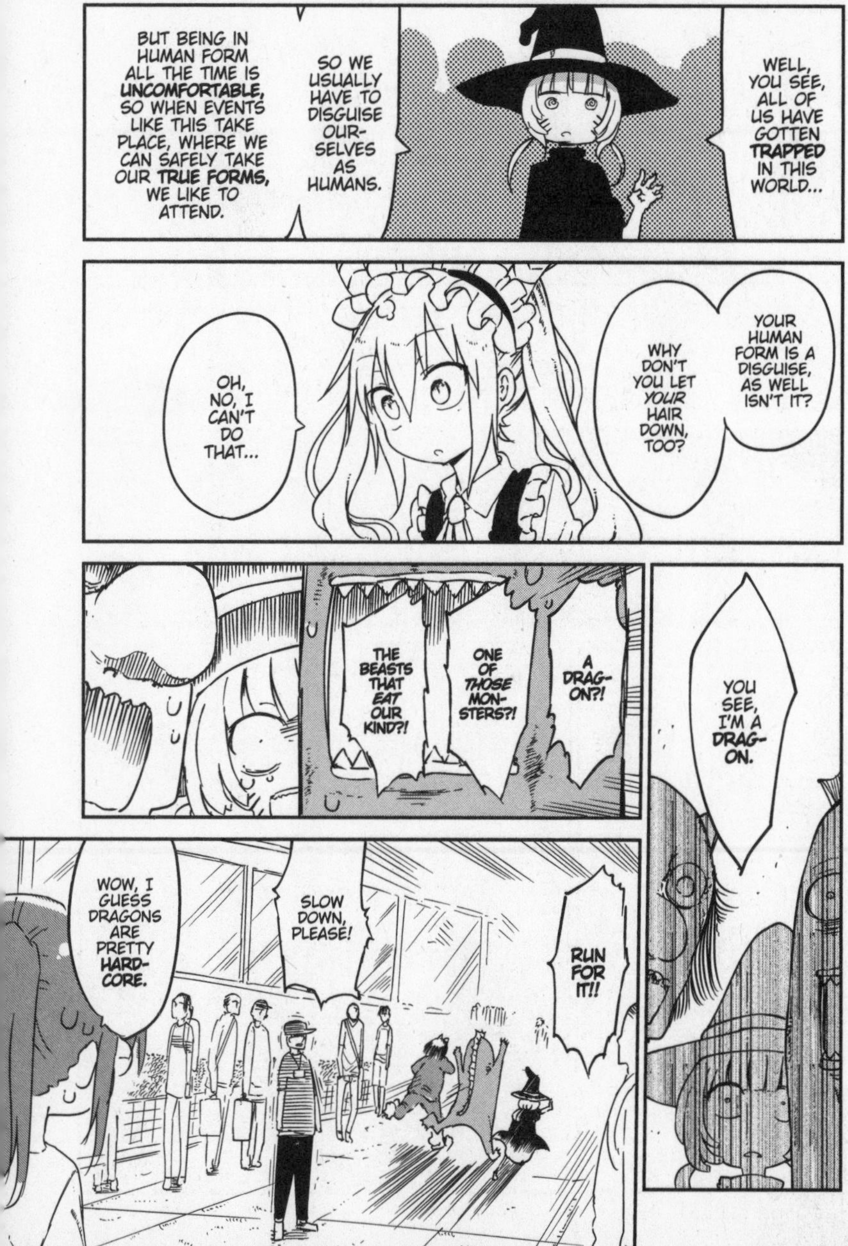
WELL, YOU SEE, ALL OF US HAVE GOTTEN **TRAPPED** IN THIS WORLD...
SO WE USUALLY HAVE TO DISGUISE OURSELVES AS HUMANS.
BUT BEING IN HUMAN FORM ALL THE TIME IS **UNCOMFORTABLE,** SO WHEN EVENTS LIKE THIS TAKE PLACE, WHERE WE CAN SAFELY TAKE OUR **TRUE FORMS,** WE LIKE TO ATTEND.
YOUR HUMAN FORM IS A DISGUISE, AS WELL ISN'T IT?
WHY DON'T YOU LET *YOUR* HAIR DOWN, TOO?
OH, NO, I CAN'T DO THAT...
YOU SEE, I'M A **DRAGON.**
A DRAGON?!
ONE OF *THOSE* MONSTERS?!
THE BEASTS THAT *EAT* OUR KIND?!
RUN FOR IT!!
SLOW DOWN, PLEASE!
WOW, I GUESS DRAGONS ARE PRETTY **HARDCORE.**

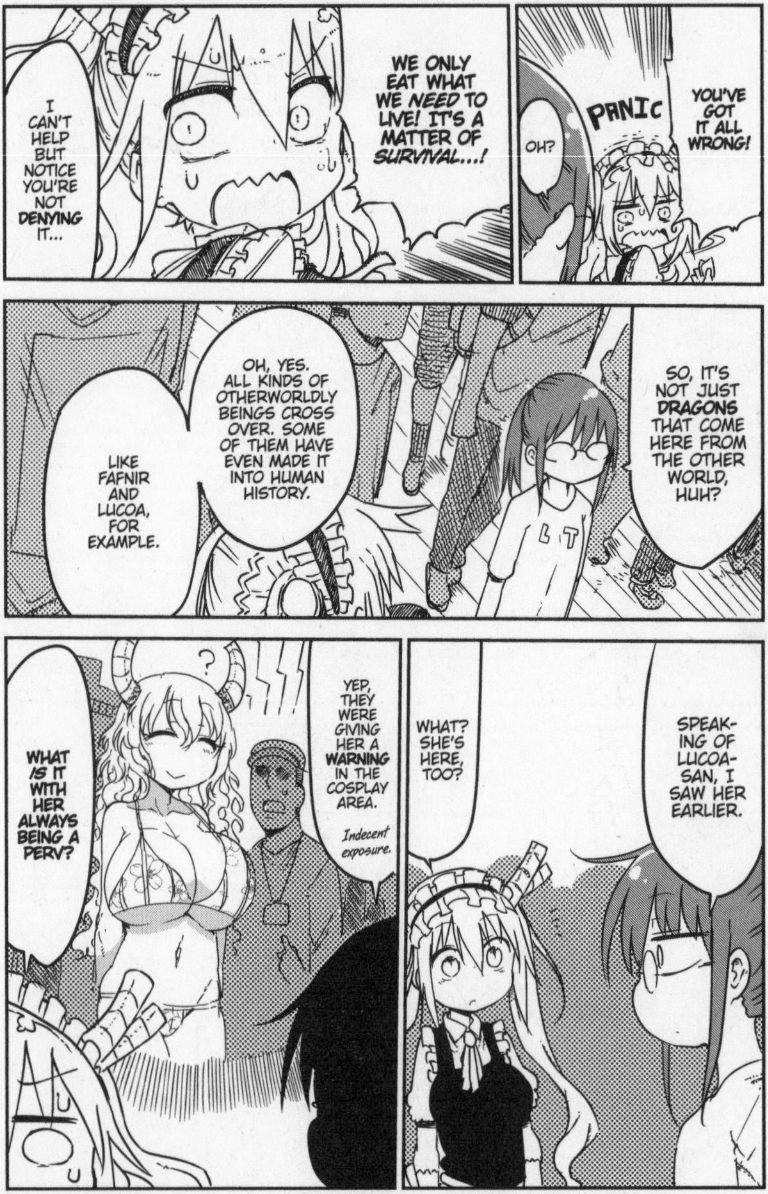
YOU'VE GOT IT ALL WRONG!
PANIC
OH?
WE ONLY EAT WHAT WE NEED TO LIVE! IT'S A MATTER OF SURVIVAL...!
I CAN'T HELP BUT NOTICE YOU'RE NOT DENYING IT...
SO, IT'S NOT JUST DRAGONS THAT COME HERE FROM THE OTHER WORLD, HUH?
OH, YES. ALL KINDS OF OTHERWORLDLY BEINGS CROSS OVER. SOME OF THEM HAVE EVEN MADE IT INTO HUMAN HISTORY.
LIKE FAFNIR AND LUCOA, FOR EXAMPLE.
SPEAK-ING OF LUCOA-SAN, I SAW HER EARLIER.
WHAT? SHE'S HERE, TOO?
YEP, THEY WERE GIVING HER A WARNING IN THE COSPLAY AREA.
Indecent exposure.
WHAT IS IT WITH HER ALWAYS BEING A PERV?

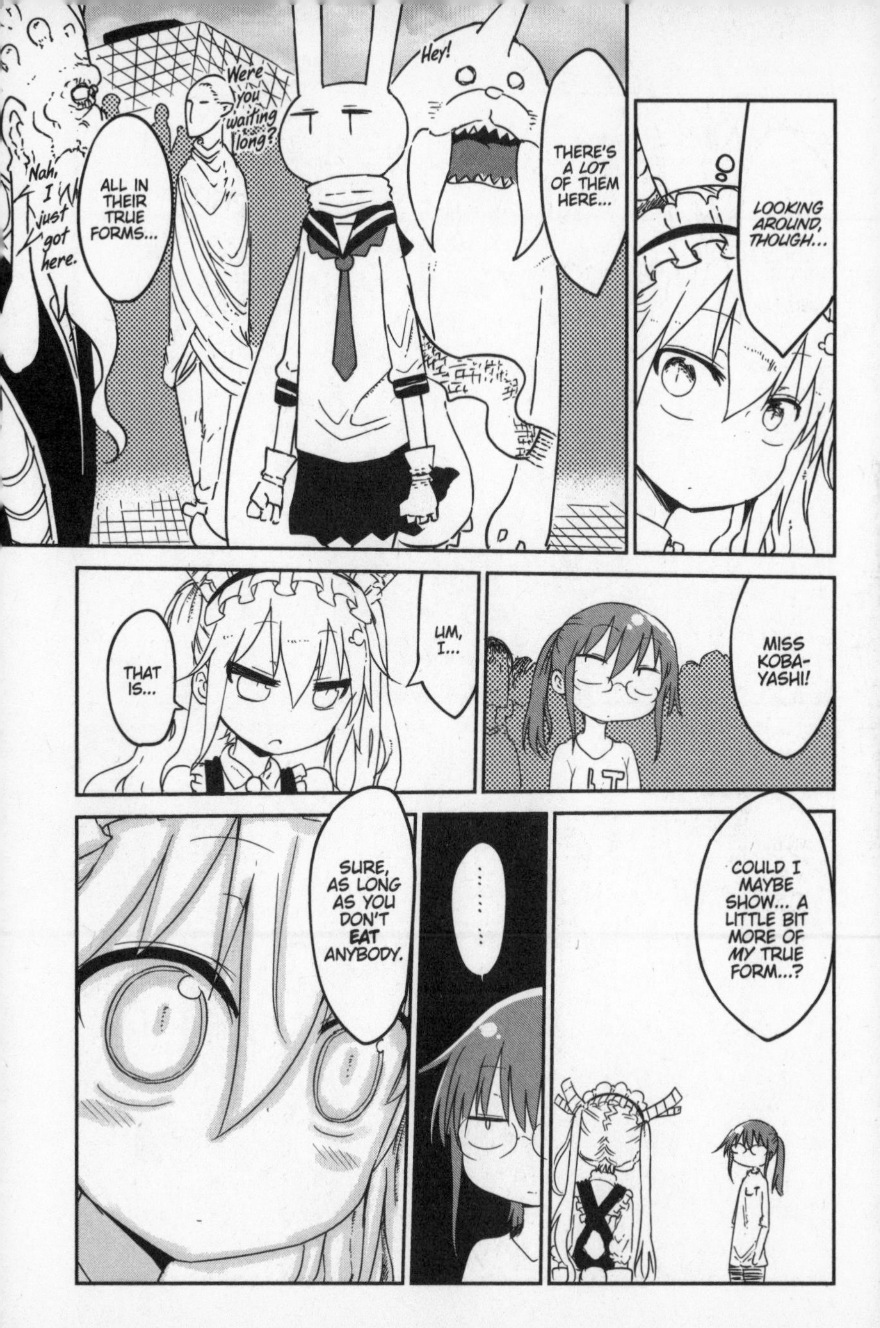
LOOKING AROUND, THOUGH...
THERE'S A *LOT* OF THEM HERE...
Hey!
Were you waiting long?
ALL IN THEIR TRUE FORMS...
Nah, I just got here.
MISS KOBA-YASHI!
UM, I...
THAT IS...
COULD I MAYBE SHOW... A LITTLE BIT MORE OF *MY* TRUE FORM...?
......
SURE, AS LONG AS YOU DON'T **EAT** ANYBODY.

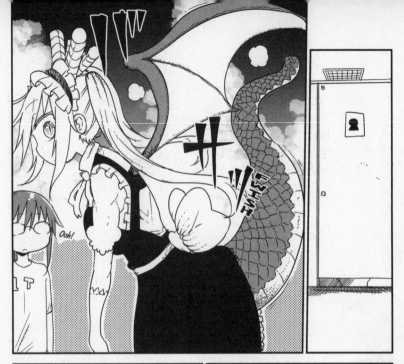

Ooh!

YES, MA'AM!

IS IT OKAY IF I TAKE A PICTURE?

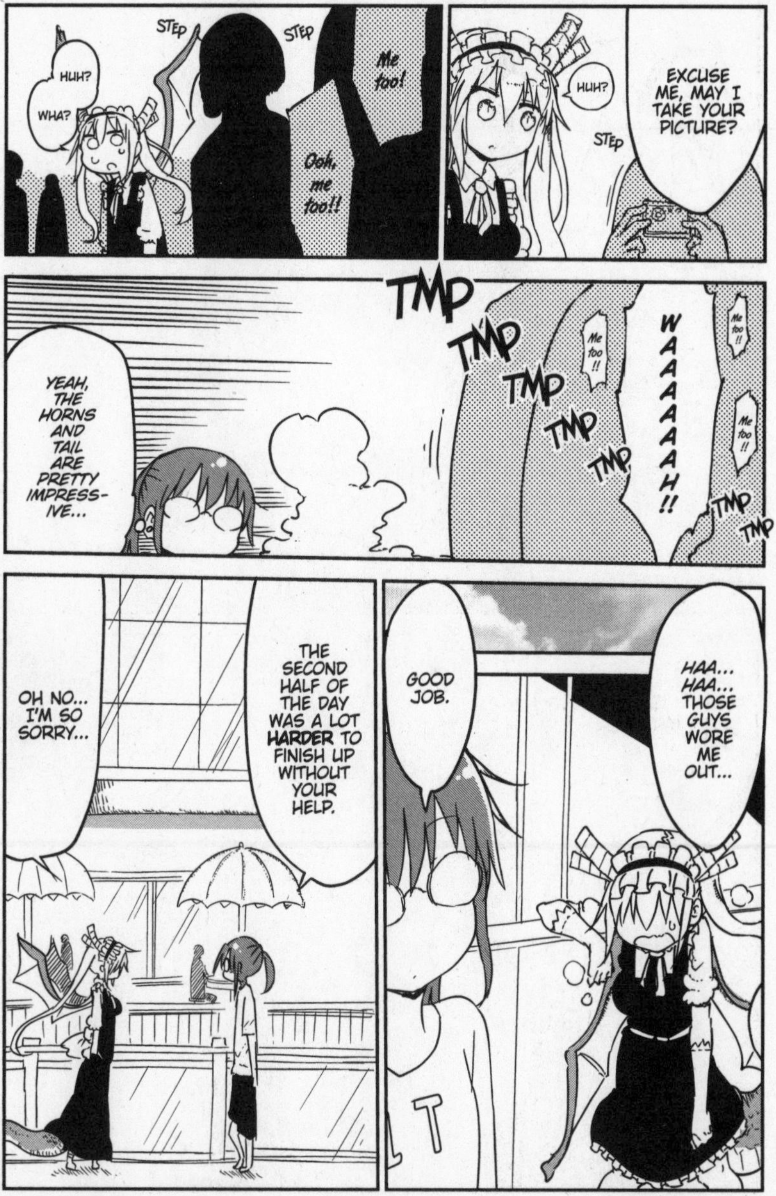
EXCUSE ME, MAY I TAKE YOUR PICTURE?
HUH?
STEP
STEP
Me too!
STEP
Ooh, me too!!
HUH?
WHA?
Me too!!
WAAAAAAAH!!
Me too!!
Me too!!
TMP
TMP
TMP
TMP
TMP
TMP
TMP
YEAH, THE HORNS AND TAIL ARE PRETTY IMPRESSIVE...
HAA... HAA... THOSE GUYS WORE ME OUT...
GOOD JOB.
THE SECOND HALF OF THE DAY WAS A LOT **HARDER** TO FINISH UP WITHOUT YOUR HELP.
OH NO... I'M SO SORRY...

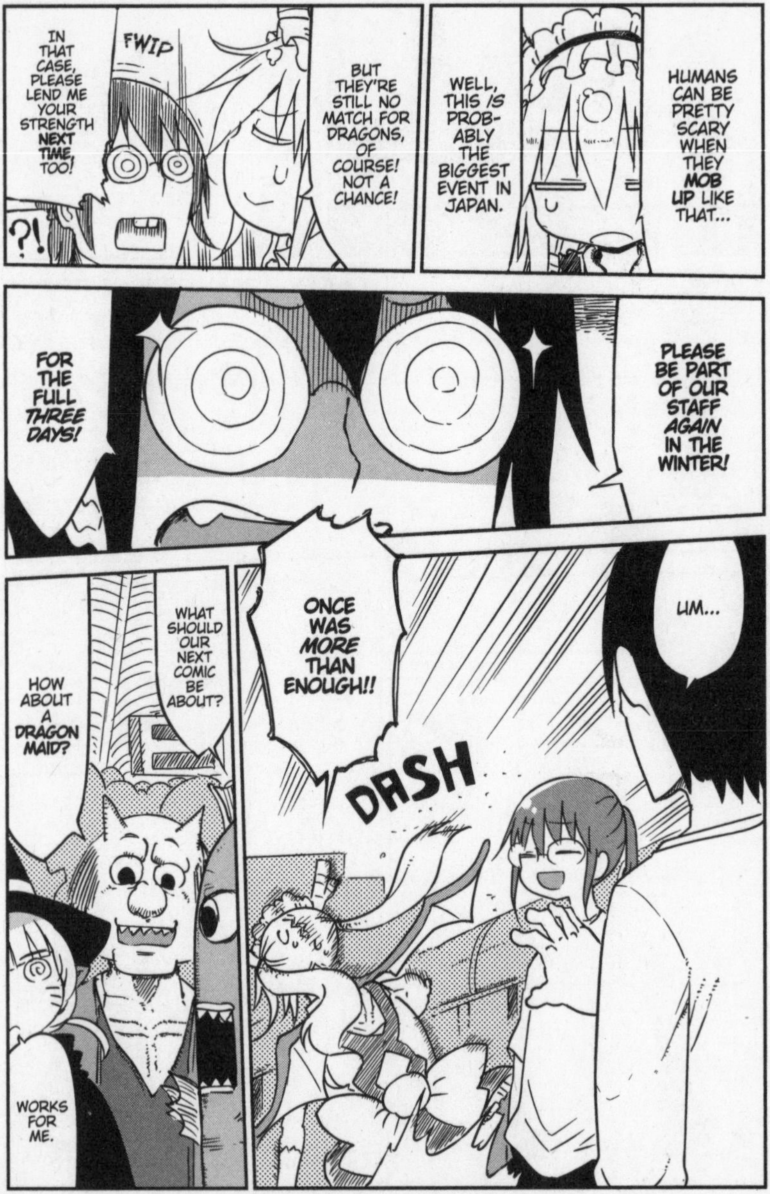
HUMANS CAN BE PRETTY SCARY WHEN THEY MOB UP LIKE THAT...
WELL, THIS IS PROBABLY THE BIGGEST EVENT IN JAPAN.
BUT THEY'RE STILL NO MATCH FOR DRAGONS, OF COURSE! NOT A CHANCE!
FWIP
IN THAT CASE, PLEASE LEND ME YOUR STRENGTH NEXT TIME, TOO!
?!
PLEASE BE PART OF OUR STAFF AGAIN IN THE WINTER!
FOR THE FULL THREE DAYS!
UM...
ONCE WAS MORE THAN ENOUGH!!
DASH
WHAT SHOULD OUR NEXT COMIC BE ABOUT?
HOW ABOUT A DRAGON MAID?
WORKS FOR ME.

CHAPTER 17/END

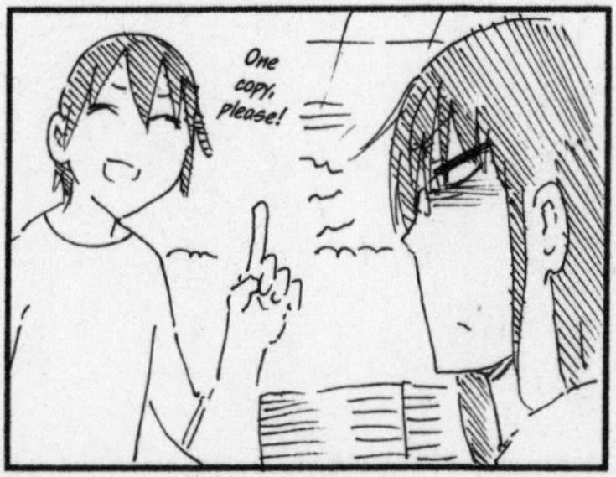
One copy, please!

Miss Kobayashi's
Dragon maid

CHAPTER 18

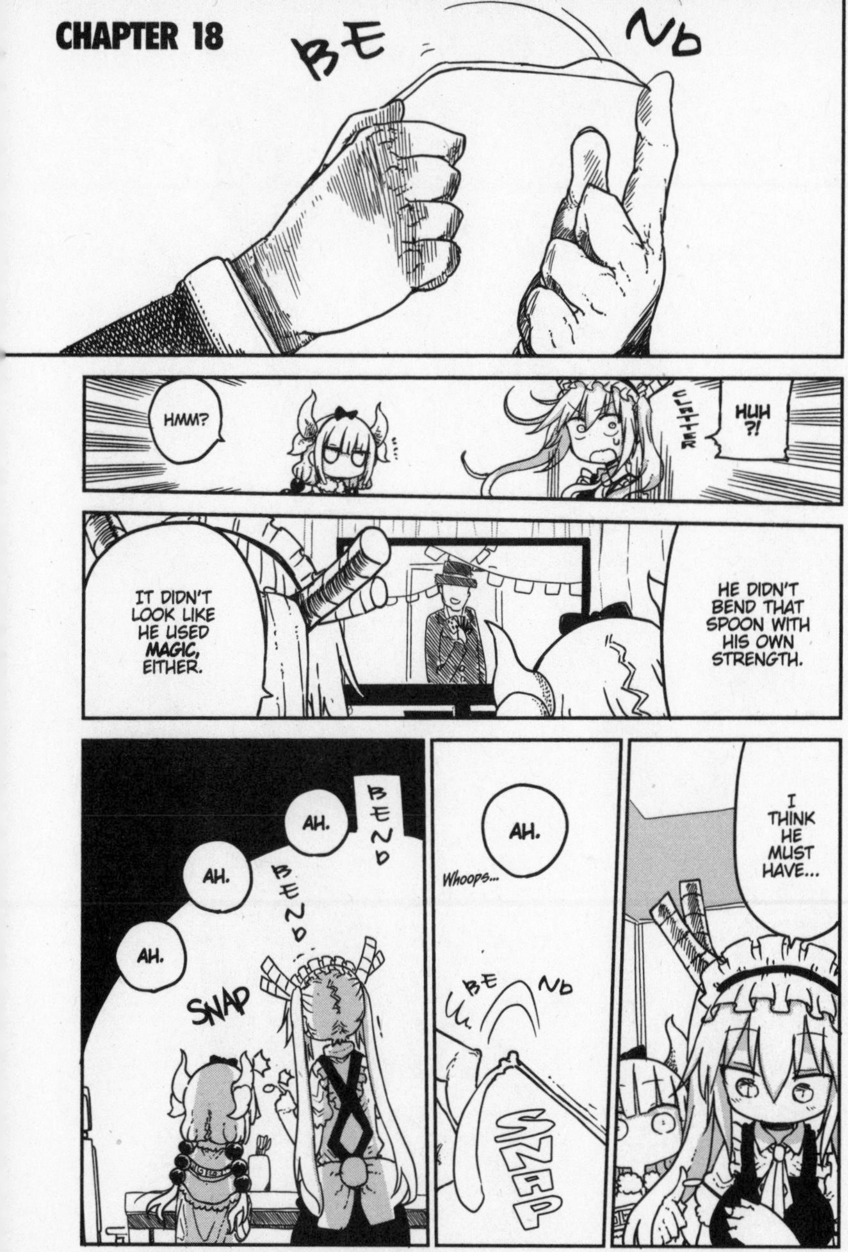

BEND
HUH?!
CLATTER
HMM?
HE DIDN'T BEND THAT SPOON WITH HIS OWN STRENGTH.
IT DIDN'T LOOK LIKE HE USED **MAGIC**, EITHER.
I THINK HE MUST HAVE...
AH.
Whoops...
BEND
SNAP
BEND
AH.
AH.
BEND
AH.
SNAP

CHAPTER 18: TOHRU & ESP

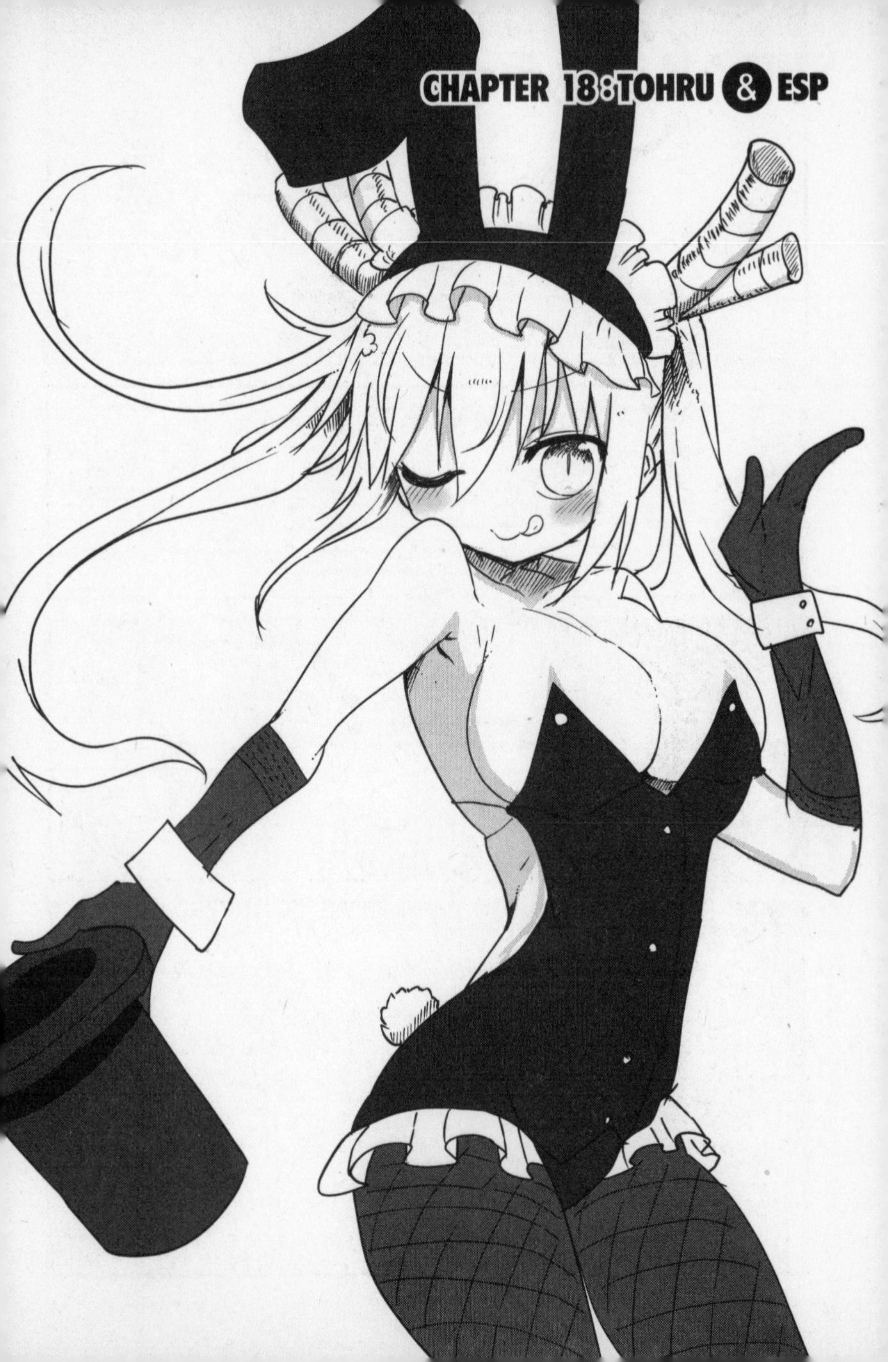

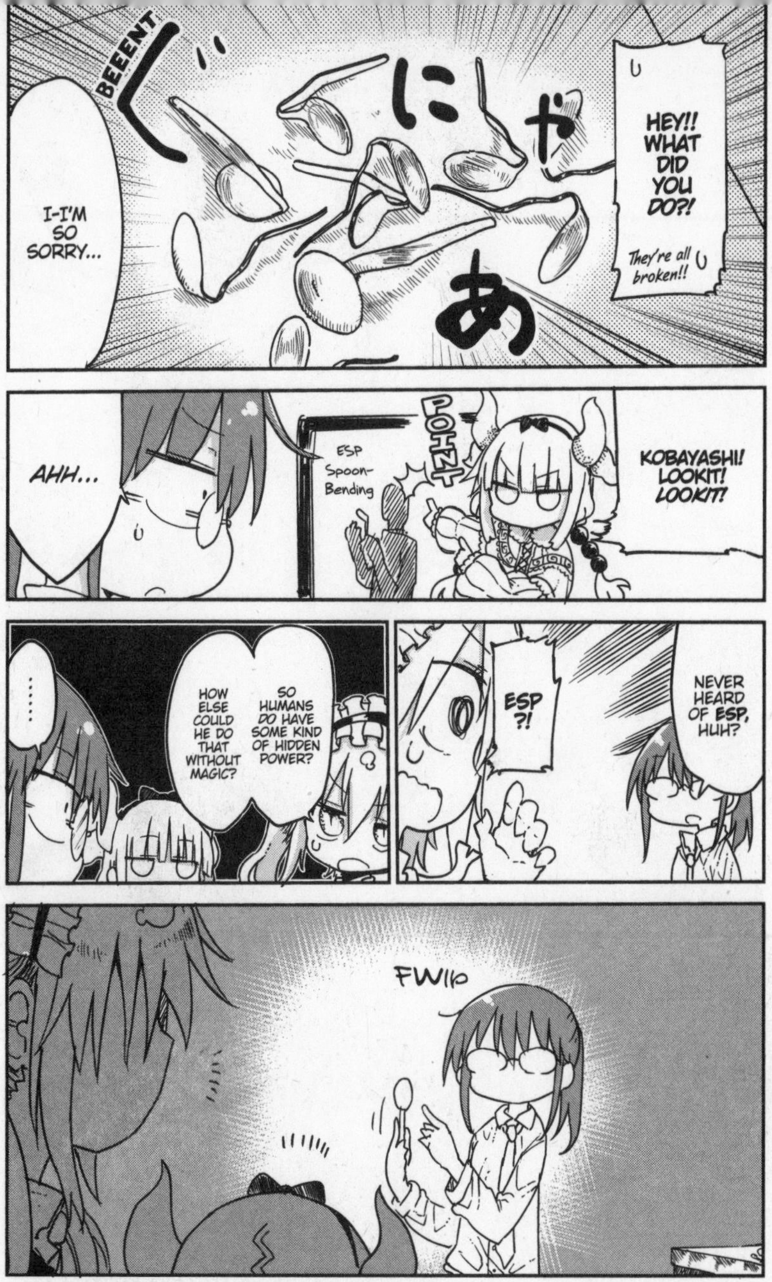
HEY!! WHAT DID YOU DO?!
They're all broken!!
ぐにゃあ
BEEENT
I-I'M SO SORRY...
KOBAYASHI! LOOKIT! LOOKIT!
POINT
ESP Spoon-Bending
AHH...
NEVER HEARD OF ESP, HUH?
ESP?!
SO HUMANS DO HAVE SOME KIND OF HIDDEN POWER?
HOW ELSE COULD HE DO THAT WITHOUT MAGIC?
......
FWIP

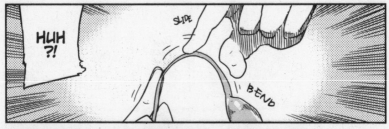

SLIDE
BEND
HUH ?!
I KNEW YOU WERE NO ORDINARY HUMAN, MISS KOBAYASHI!!
SHE'S A GOD! ALL HAIL LORD KOBAYASHI!!
UH, GUYS...
IT'S JUST SLEIGHT OF HAND! ANYONE CAN LEARN IT!
ANY... ONE...?
I'VE HEARD ABOUT THIS... HUMANS ONLY USE 10% OF THEIR BRAINS. SO, IF THEY FELT LIKE IT, ANY HUMAN COULD MASTER THESE ABILITIES... IT'S JUST THAT MOST OF THEM LACK THE MOTIVATION. A CUNNING YET CARELESS SPECIES... I CAN'T ALLOW THIS! I WON'T!!
YOU'RE THINKING SOME-THING WEIRD AGAIN, AREN'T YOU?

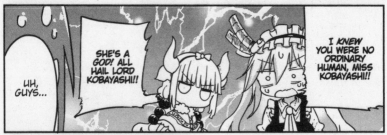

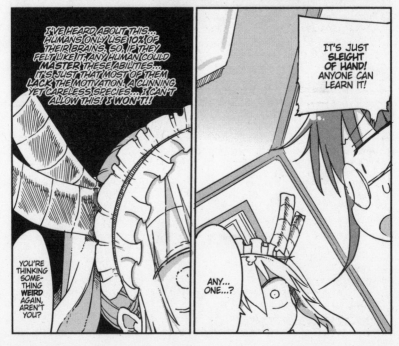

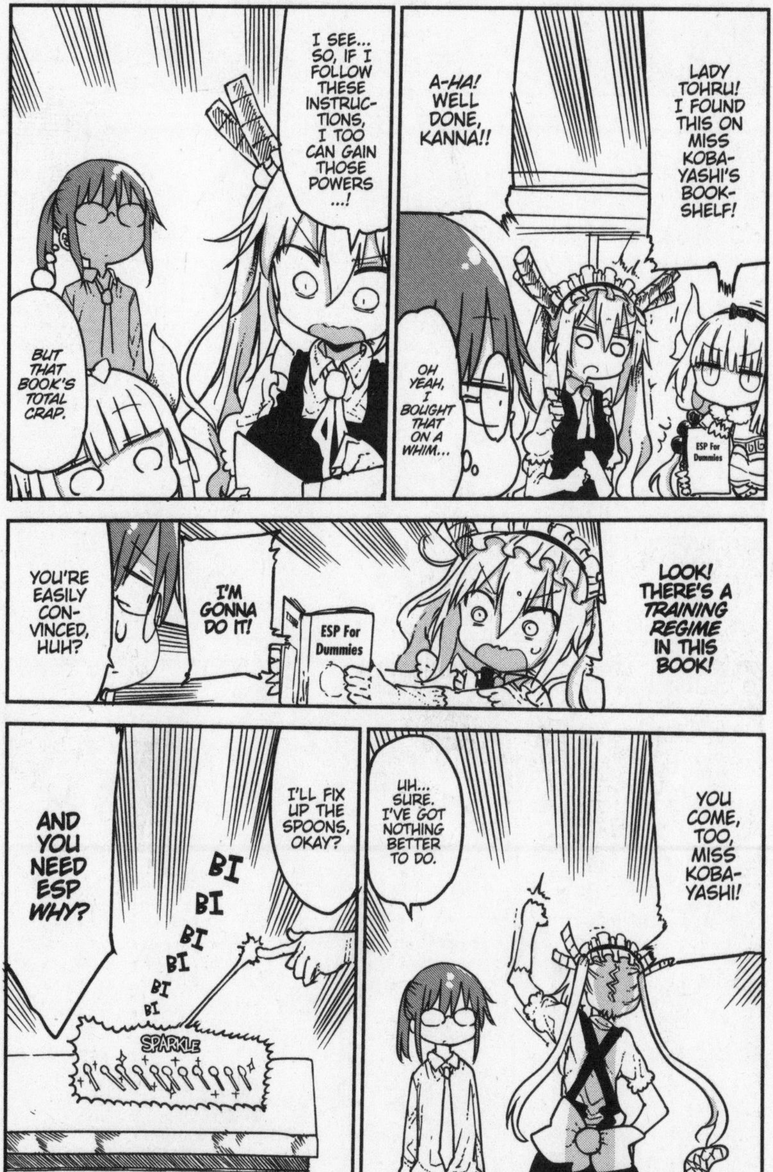
LADY TOHRU! I FOUND THIS ON MISS KOBA-YASHI'S BOOK-SHELF!
A-HA! WELL DONE, KANNA!!
ESP For Dummies
OH YEAH, I BOUGHT THAT ON A WHIM...
I SEE... SO, IF I FOLLOW THESE INSTRUC-TIONS, I TOO CAN GAIN THOSE POWERS ...!
BUT THAT BOOK'S TOTAL CRAP.
LOOK! THERE'S A TRAINING REGIME IN THIS BOOK!
ESP For Dummies
I'M GONNA DO IT!
YOU'RE EASILY CON-VINCED, HUH?
YOU COME, TOO, MISS KOBA-YASHI!
UH... SURE. I'VE GOT NOTHING BETTER TO DO.
I'LL FIX UP THE SPOONS, OKAY?
BI BI BI BI BI BI
SPARKLE
AND YOU NEED ESP WHY?

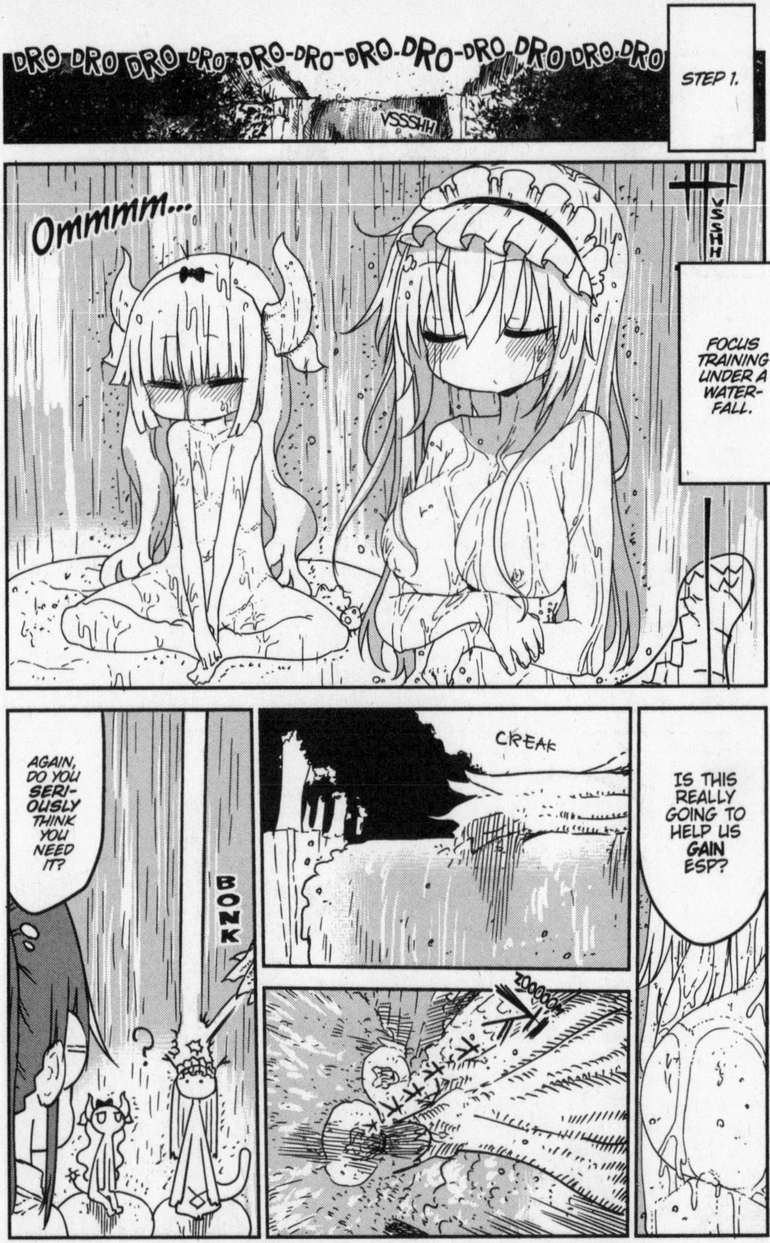
STEP 1.
DRO DRO DRO DRO DRO-DRO-DRO-DRO-DRO DRO DRO-DRO
VSSSHH
VSSHH
FOCUS TRAINING UNDER A WATER-FALL.
Ommmm...
IS THIS REALLY GOING TO HELP US GAIN ESP?
CREAK
ZOOOOOM
BONK
AGAIN, DO YOU SERI-OUSLY THINK YOU NEED IT?

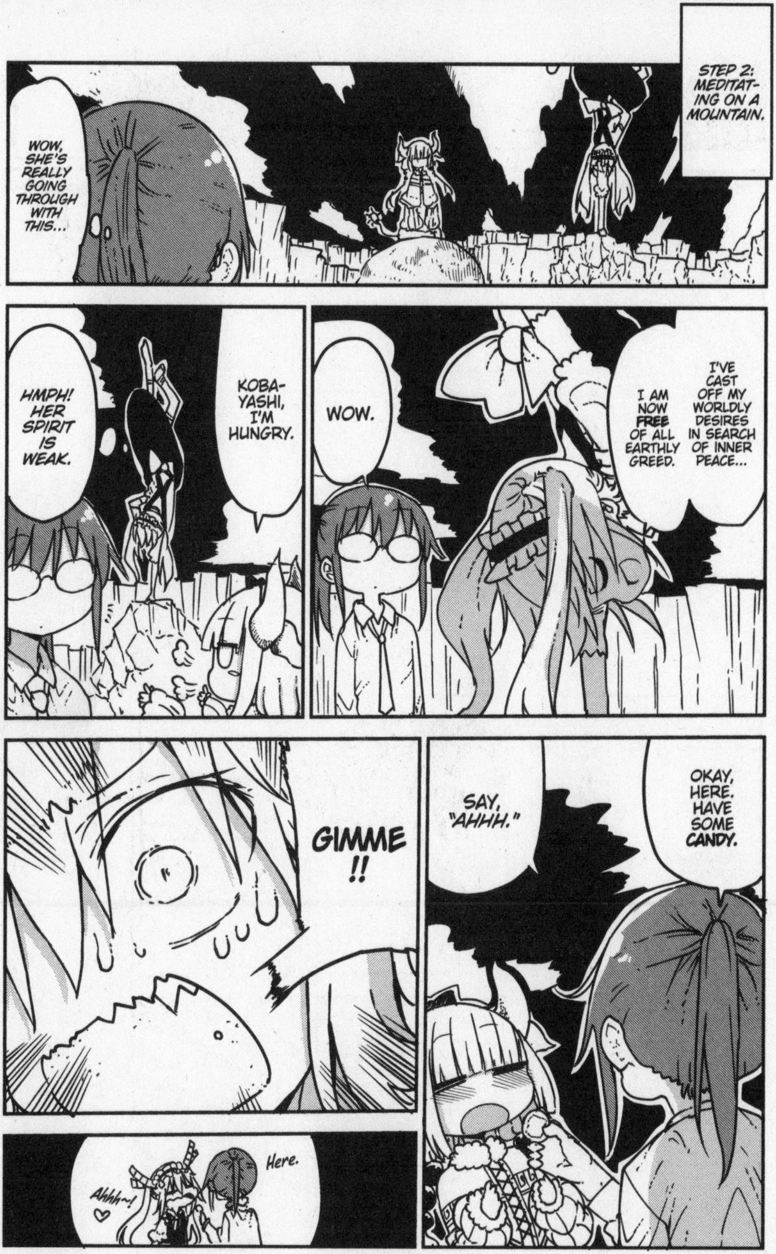
STEP 2: MEDITATING ON A MOUNTAIN.
WOW, SHE'S REALLY GOING THROUGH WITH THIS...
I'VE CAST OFF MY WORLDLY DESIRES IN SEARCH OF INNER PEACE...
I AM NOW **FREE** OF ALL EARTHLY GREED.
WOW.
KOBAYASHI, I'M HUNGRY.
HMPH! HER SPIRIT IS WEAK.
OKAY, HERE. HAVE SOME **CANDY**.
SAY, "AHHH."
GIMME!!
Here.
Ahhh~!

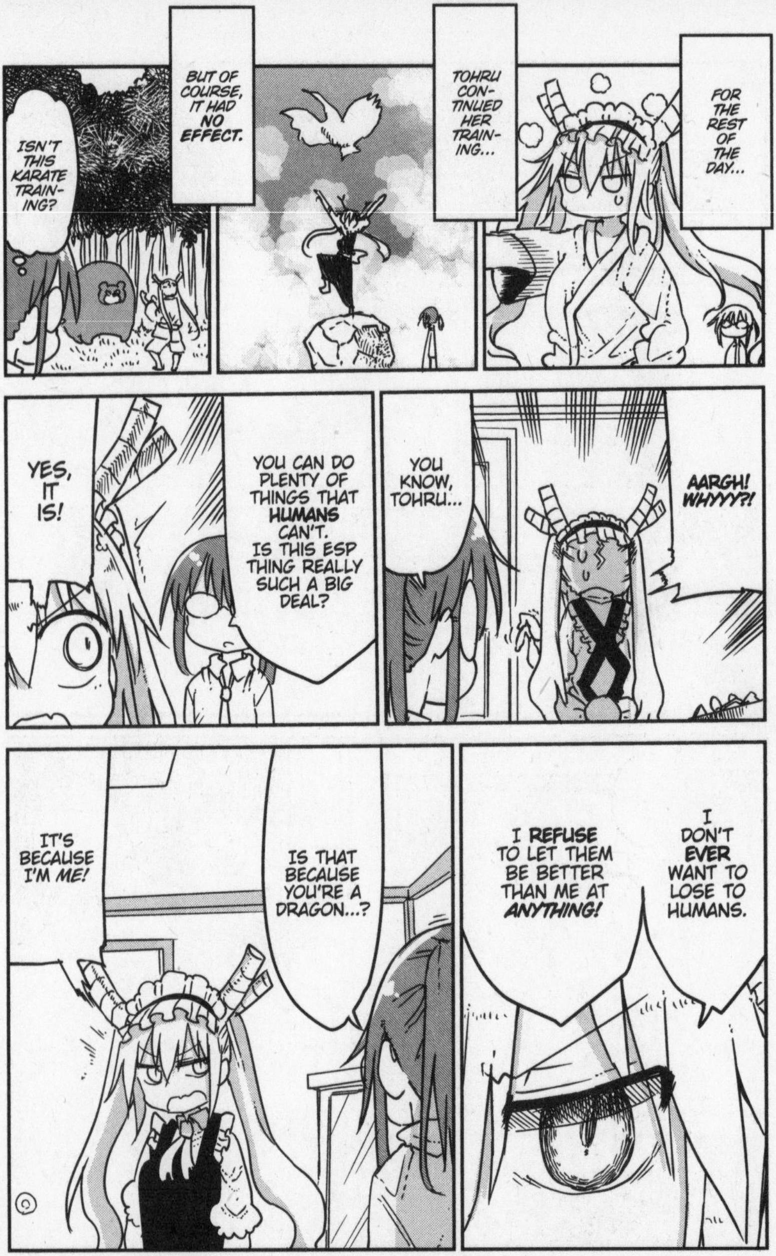
FOR THE REST OF THE DAY...
TOHRU CONTINUED HER TRAINING...
BUT OF COURSE, IT HAD NO EFFECT.
ISN'T THIS KARATE TRAINING?
AARGH! WHYYY?!
YOU KNOW, TOHRU...
YOU CAN DO PLENTY OF THINGS THAT HUMANS CAN'T. IS THIS ESP THING REALLY SUCH A BIG DEAL?
YES, IT IS!
I DON'T EVER WANT TO LOSE TO HUMANS.
I REFUSE TO LET THEM BE BETTER THAN ME AT ANYTHING!
IS THAT BECAUSE YOU'RE A DRAGON...?
IT'S BECAUSE I'M ME!

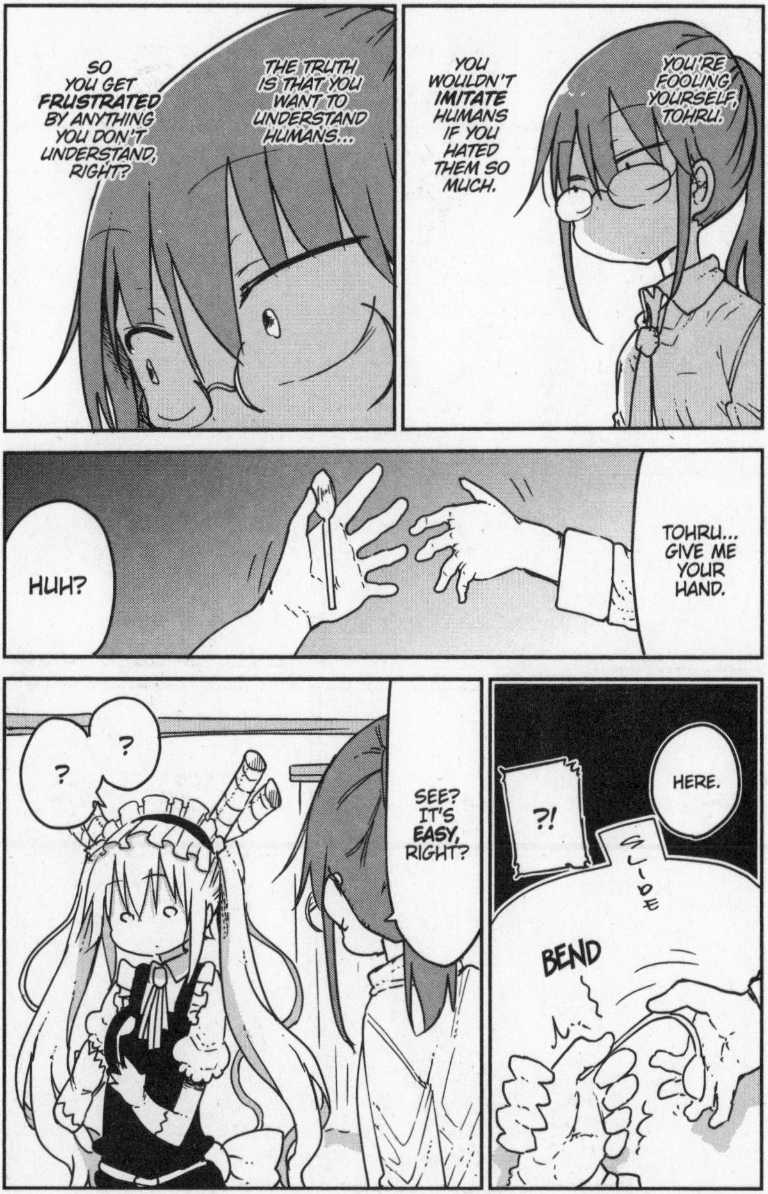
YOU'RE FOOLING YOURSELF, TOHRU.
YOU WOULDN'T IMITATE HUMANS IF YOU HATED THEM SO MUCH.
THE TRUTH IS THAT YOU WANT TO UNDERSTAND HUMANS...
SO YOU GET FRUSTRATED BY ANYTHING YOU DON'T UNDERSTAND, RIGHT?
TOHRU... GIVE ME YOUR HAND.
HUH?
HERE.
?!
SLIDE
BEND
SEE? IT'S EASY, RIGHT?
? ?

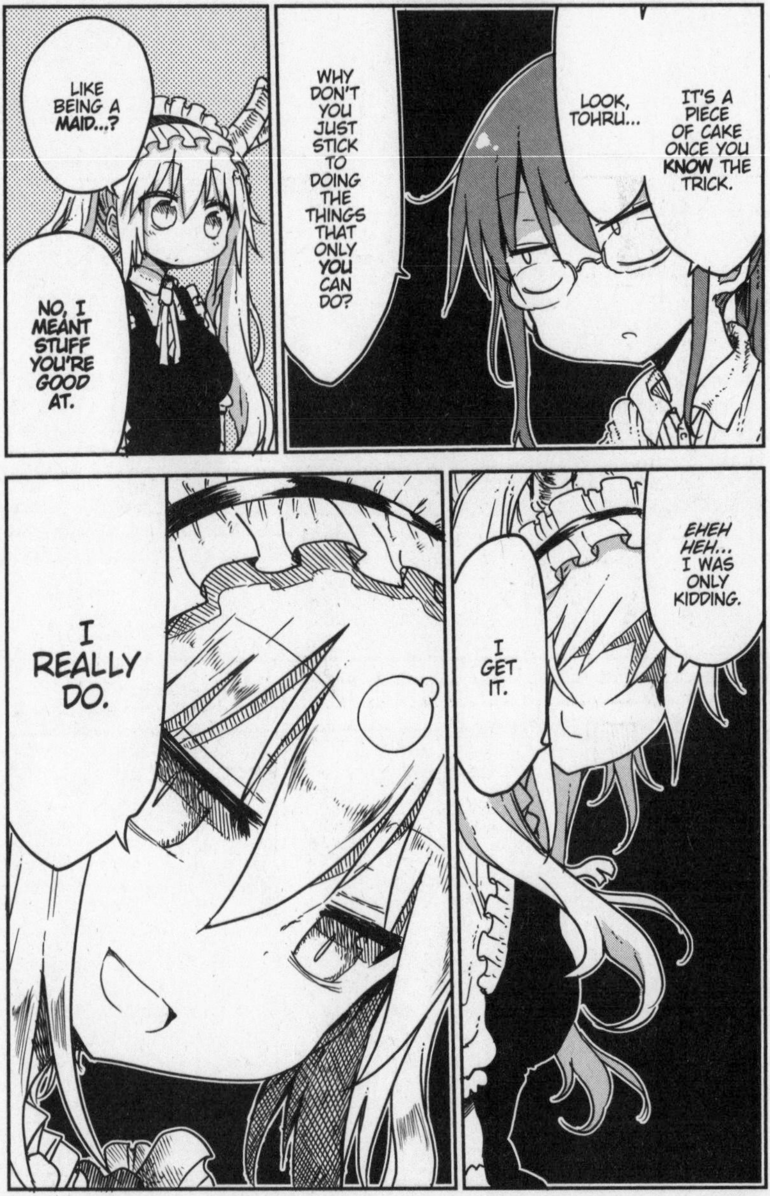
IT'S A PIECE OF CAKE ONCE YOU KNOW THE TRICK.
LOOK, TOHRU...
WHY DON'T YOU JUST STICK TO DOING THE THINGS THAT ONLY YOU CAN DO?
LIKE BEING A MAID...?
NO, I MEANT STUFF YOU'RE GOOD AT.
EHEH HEH... I WAS ONLY KIDDING.
I GET IT.
I REALLY DO.

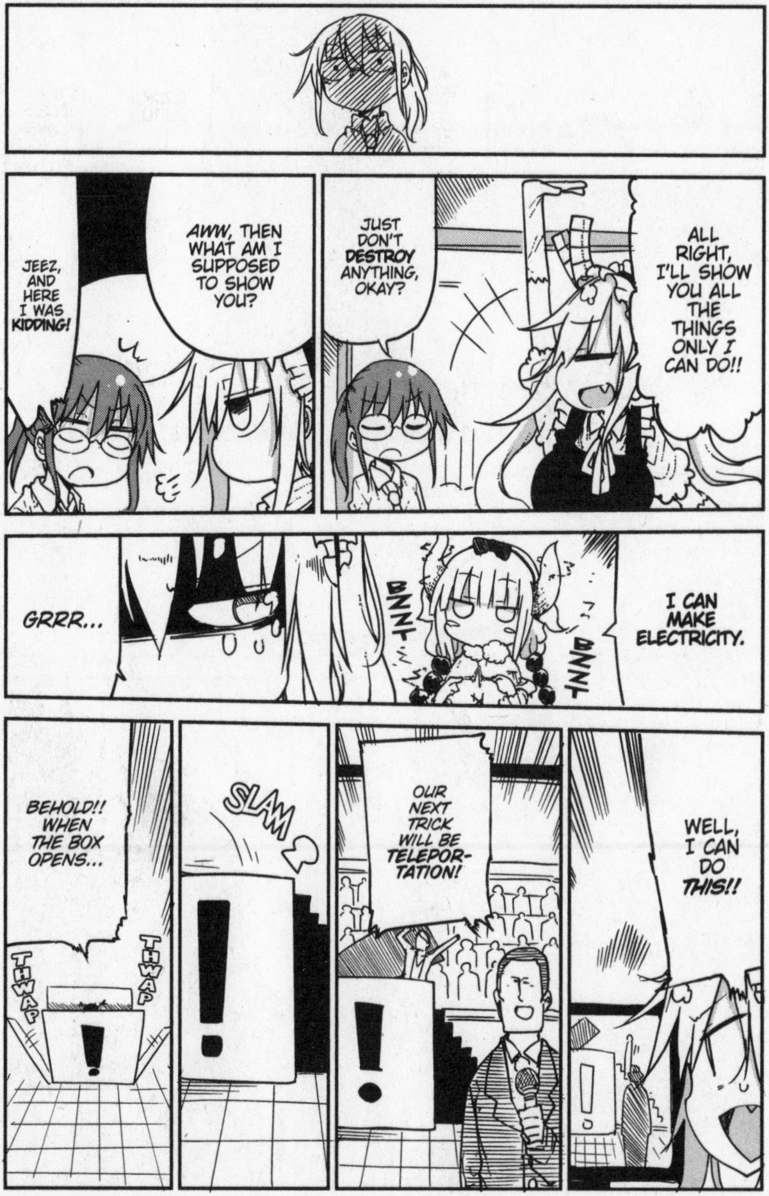
ALL RIGHT, I'LL SHOW YOU ALL THE THINGS ONLY *I* CAN DO!!
JUST DON'T **DESTROY** ANYTHING, OKAY?
AWW, THEN WHAT AM I SUPPOSED TO SHOW YOU?
JEEZ, AND HERE I WAS **KIDDING!**
I CAN MAKE ELECTRICITY.
BZZT
BZZT
GRRR...
WELL, I CAN DO *THIS!!*
OUR NEXT TRICK WILL BE TELEPORTATION!
SLAM
BEHOLD!! WHEN THE BOX OPENS...
THWAP
THWAP

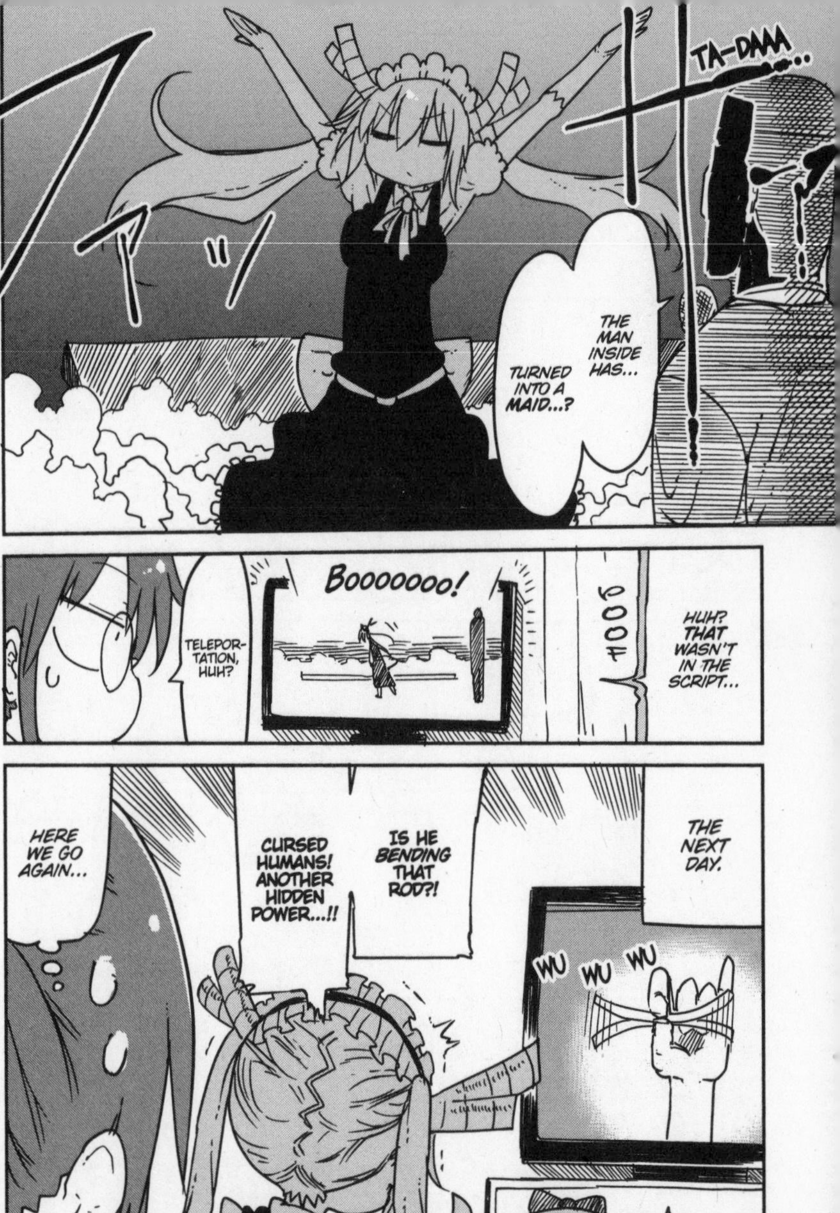
TA-DAAA...
THE MAN INSIDE HAS...
TURNED INTO A MAID...?
HUH? THAT WASN'T IN THE SCRIPT...
Booooooo!
TELEPORTATION, HUH?
THE NEXT DAY.
IS HE BENDING THAT ROD?!
CURSED HUMANS! ANOTHER HIDDEN POWER...!!
WU WU WU
HERE WE GO AGAIN...

CHAPTER 18/END

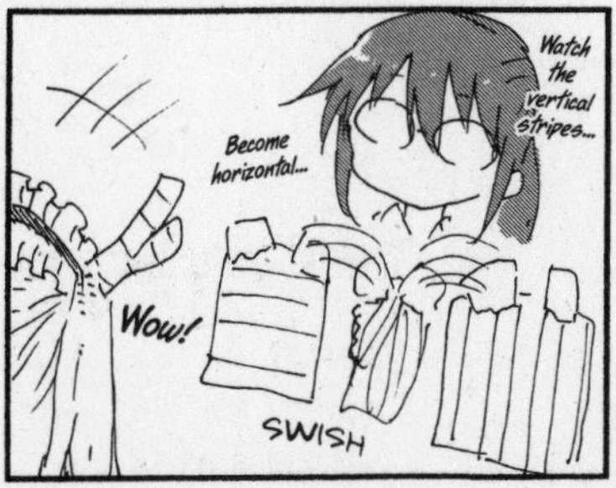
Watch the vertical stripes...
Become horizontal...
Wow!
SWISH

Miss Kobayashi's
Dragon Maid

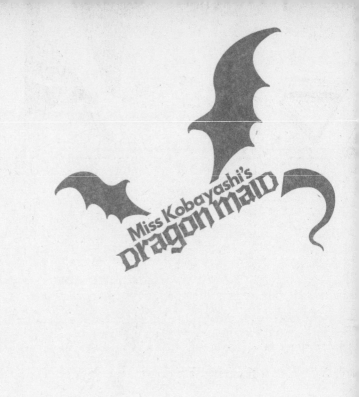

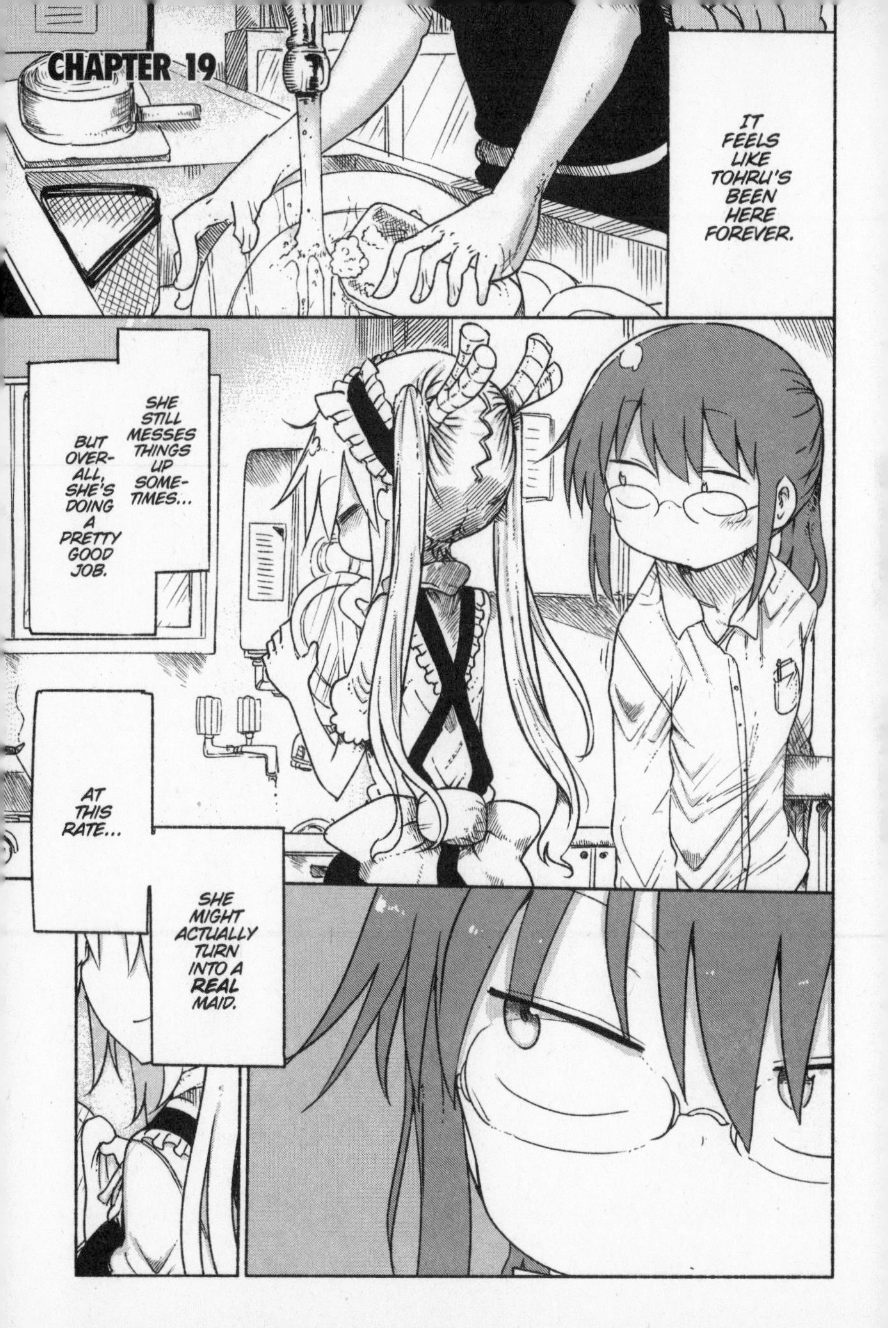
CHAPTER 19
IT FEELS LIKE TOHRU'S BEEN HERE FOREVER.
SHE STILL MESSES THINGS UP SOMETIMES...
BUT OVER-ALL, SHE'S DOING A PRETTY GOOD JOB.
AT THIS RATE...
SHE MIGHT ACTUALLY TURN INTO A REAL MAID.

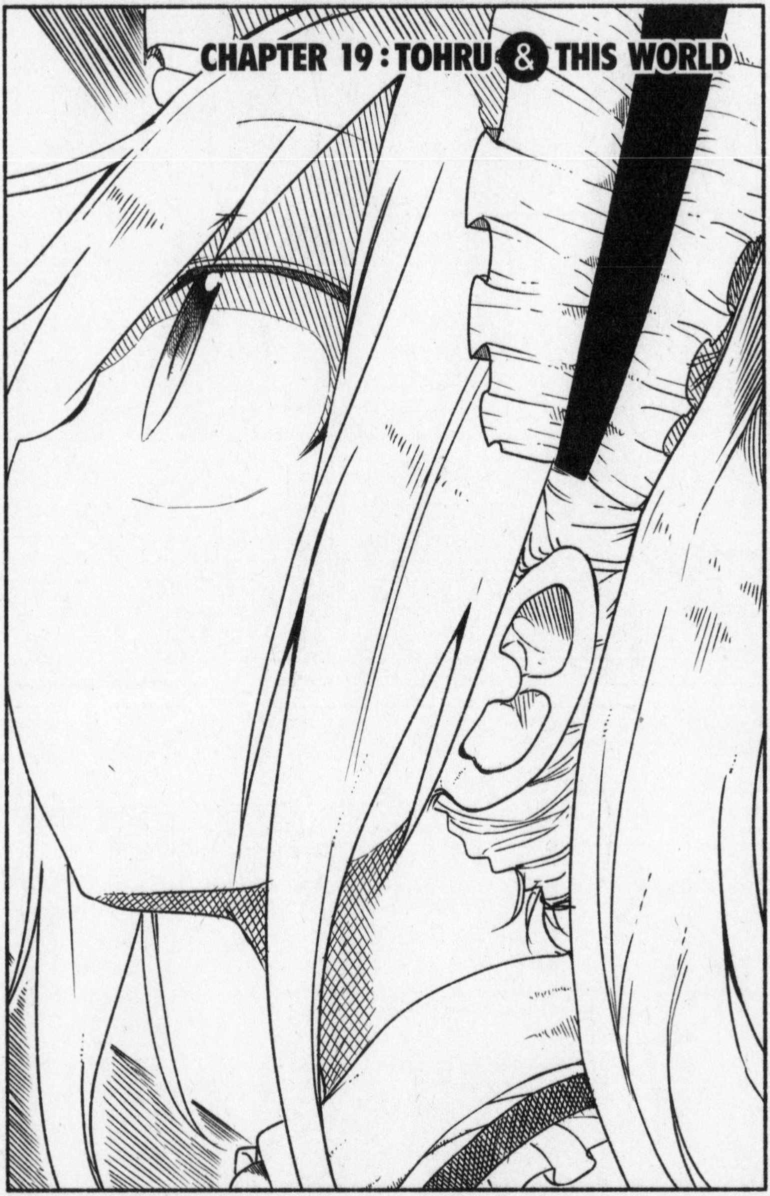
CHAPTER 19 : TOHRU & THIS WORLD

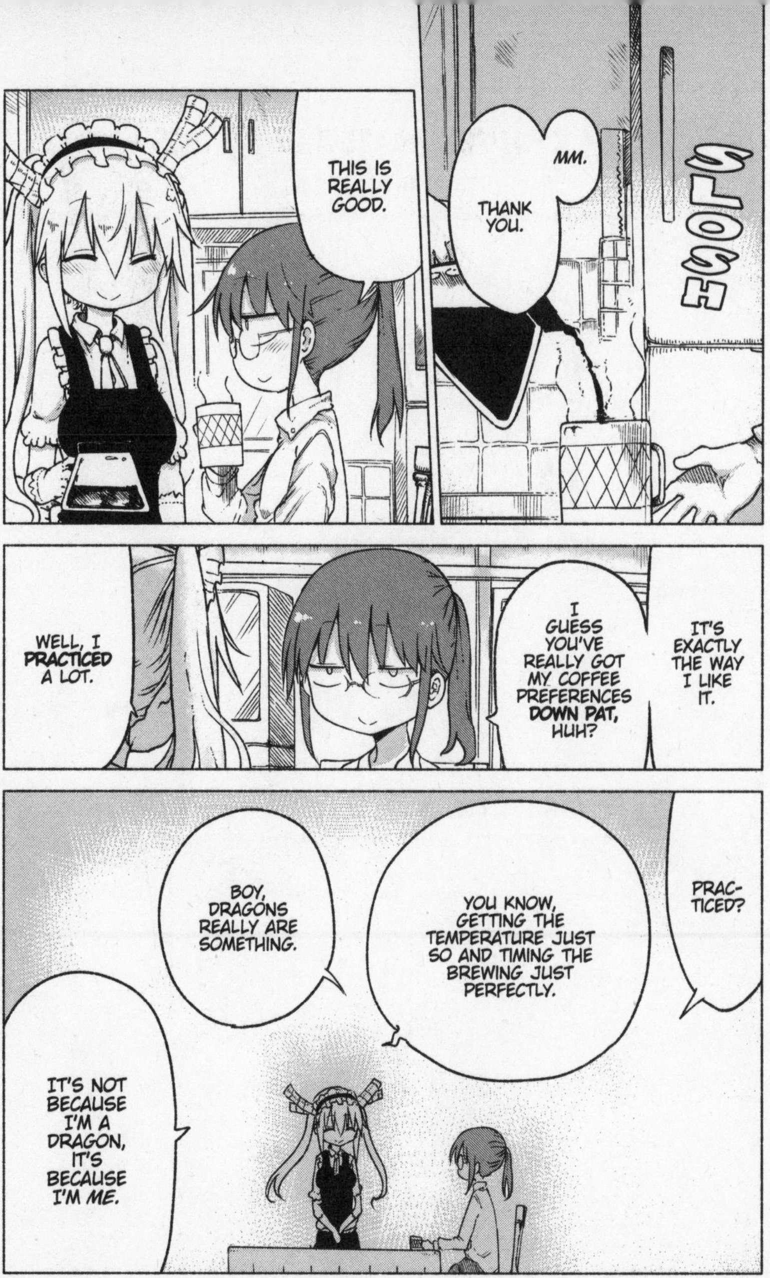
SLOSH
MM. THANK YOU.
THIS IS REALLY GOOD.
IT'S EXACTLY THE WAY I LIKE IT.
I GUESS YOU'VE REALLY GOT MY COFFEE PREFERENCES **DOWN PAT**, HUH?
WELL, I **PRACTICED** A LOT.
PRAC-TICED?
YOU KNOW, GETTING THE TEMPERATURE JUST SO AND TIMING THE BREWING JUST PERFECTLY.
BOY, DRAGONS REALLY ARE SOMETHING.
IT'S NOT BECAUSE I'M A DRAGON, IT'S BECAUSE I'M *ME*.

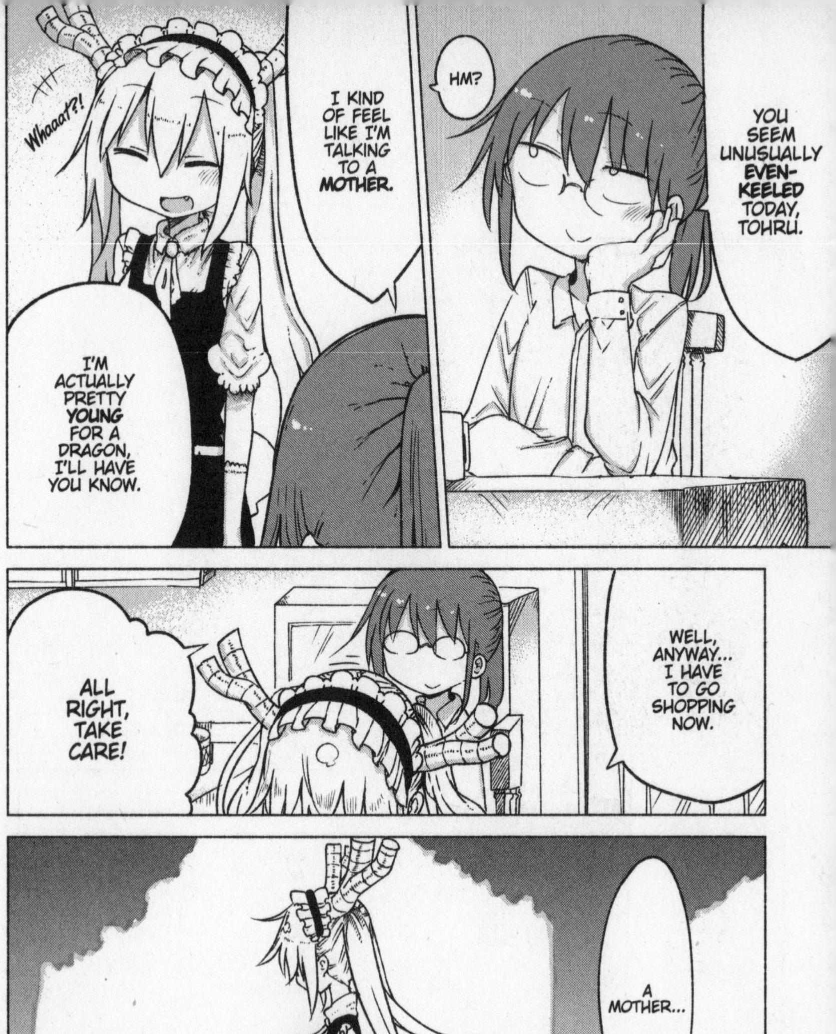
YOU SEEM UNUSUALLY EVEN-KEELED TODAY, TOHRU.
HM?
I KIND OF FEEL LIKE I'M TALKING TO A MOTHER.
Whaaat?!
I'M ACTUALLY PRETTY YOUNG FOR A DRAGON, I'LL HAVE YOU KNOW.
WELL, ANYWAY... I HAVE TO GO SHOPPING NOW.
ALL RIGHT, TAKE CARE!
A MOTHER...
HUNH.

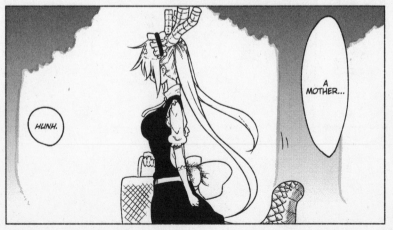

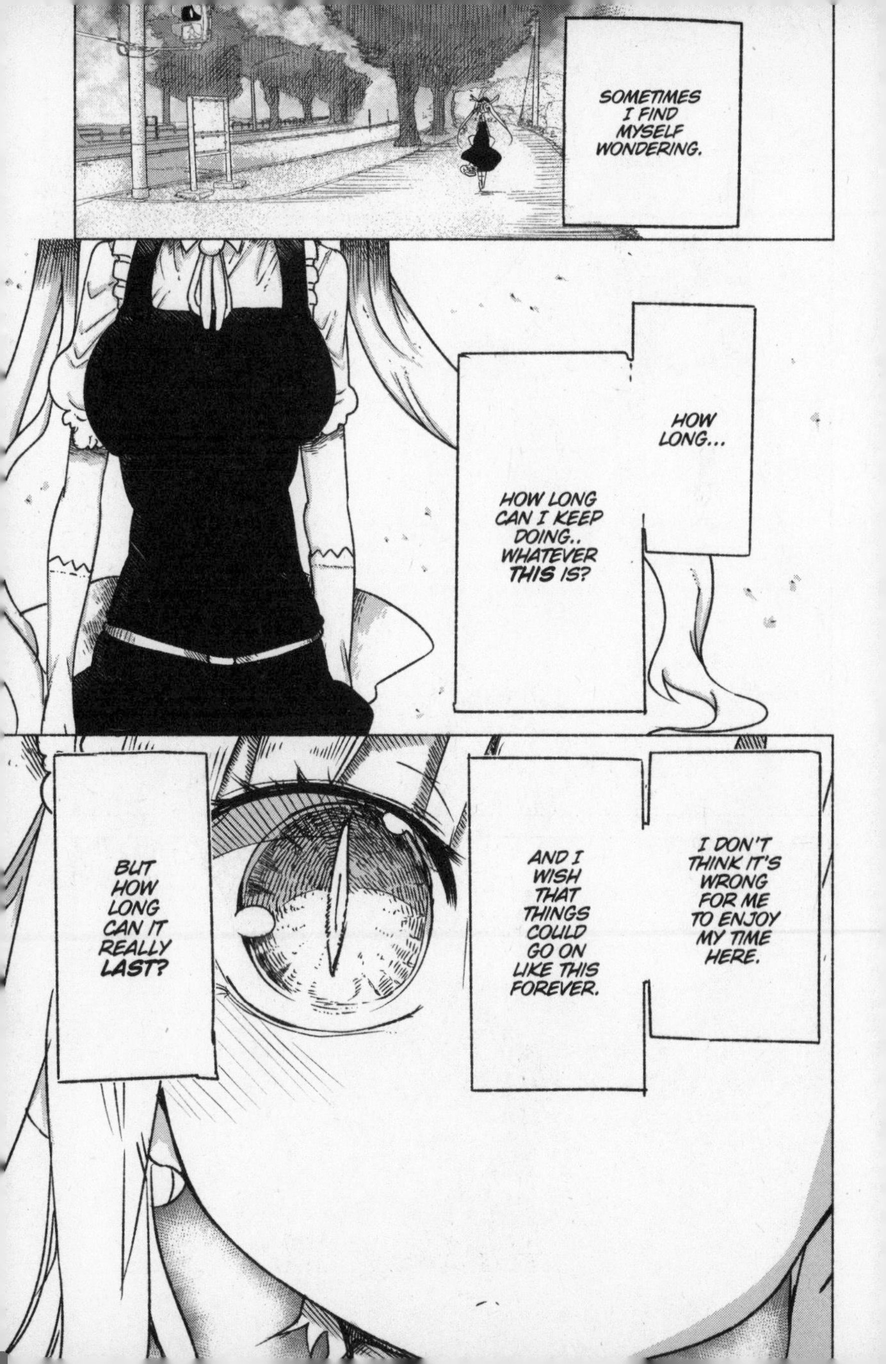
SOMETIMES I FIND MYSELF WONDERING.
HOW LONG...
HOW LONG CAN I KEEP DOING.. WHATEVER THIS IS?
I DON'T THINK IT'S WRONG FOR ME TO ENJOY MY TIME HERE.
AND I WISH THAT THINGS COULD GO ON LIKE THIS FOREVER.
BUT HOW LONG CAN IT REALLY LAST?

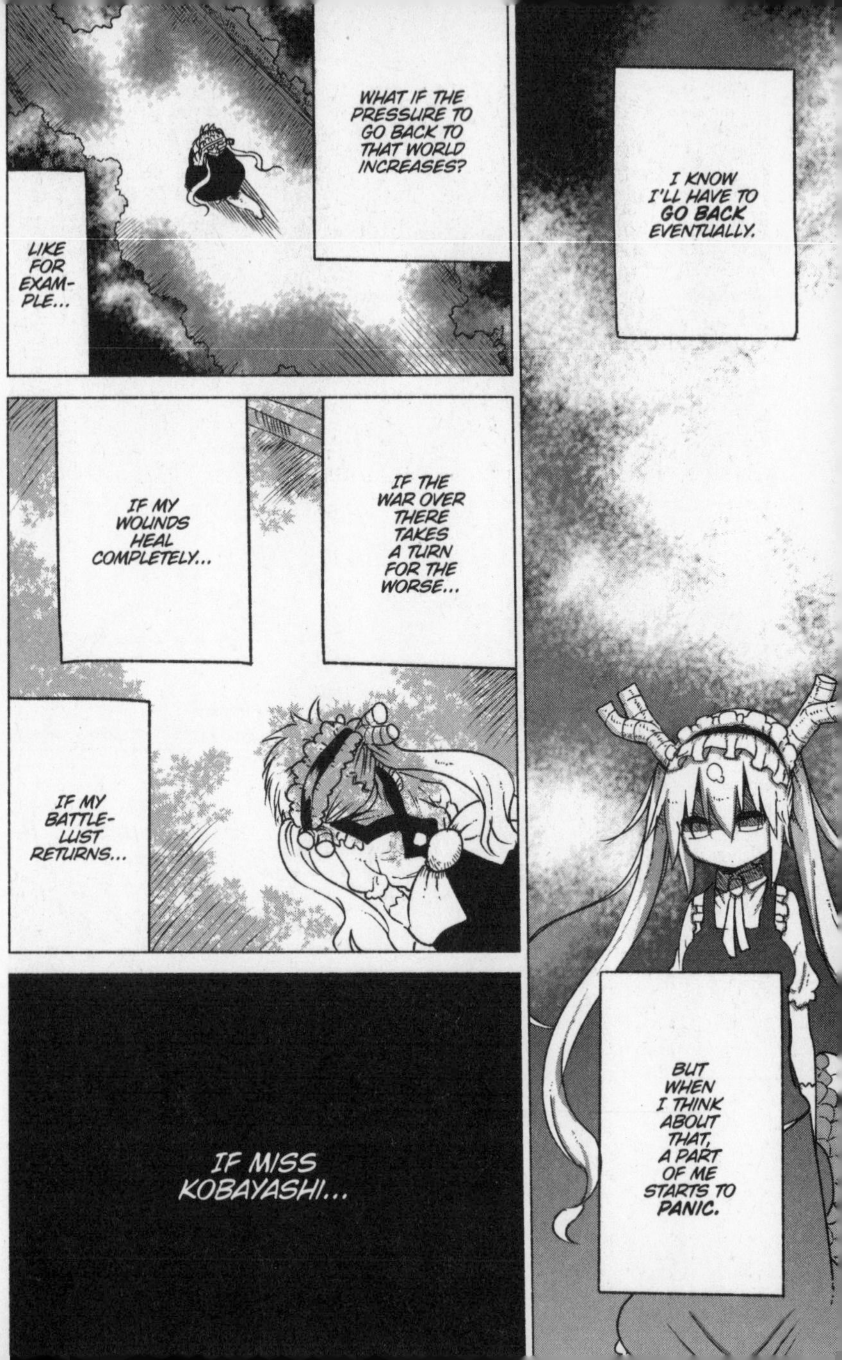

I KNOW I'LL HAVE TO GO BACK EVENTUALLY.
BUT WHEN I THINK ABOUT THAT, A PART OF ME STARTS TO PANIC.
WHAT IF THE PRESSURE TO GO BACK TO THAT WORLD INCREASES?
LIKE FOR EXAMPLE...
IF THE WAR OVER THERE TAKES A TURN FOR THE WORSE...
IF MY WOUNDS HEAL COMPLETELY...
IF MY BATTLE-LUST RETURNS...
IF MISS KOBAYASHI...

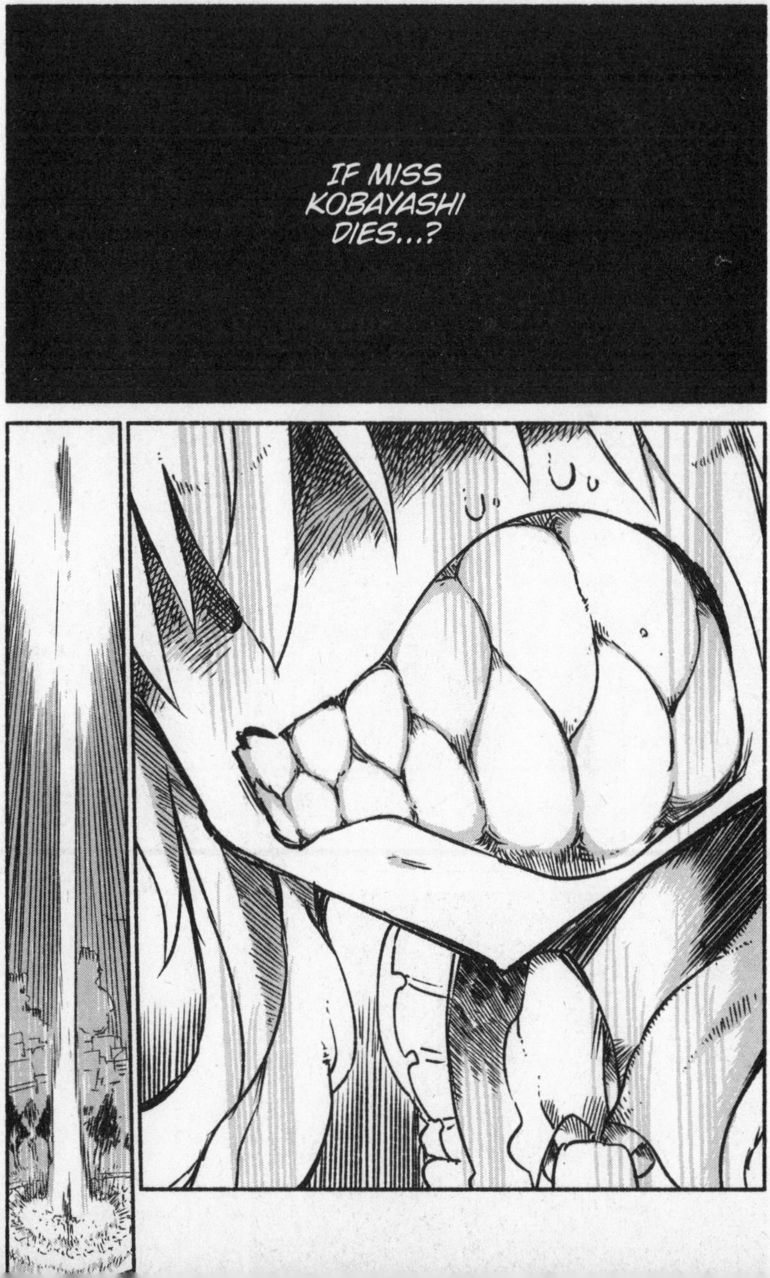
IF MISS KOBAYASHI DIES...?

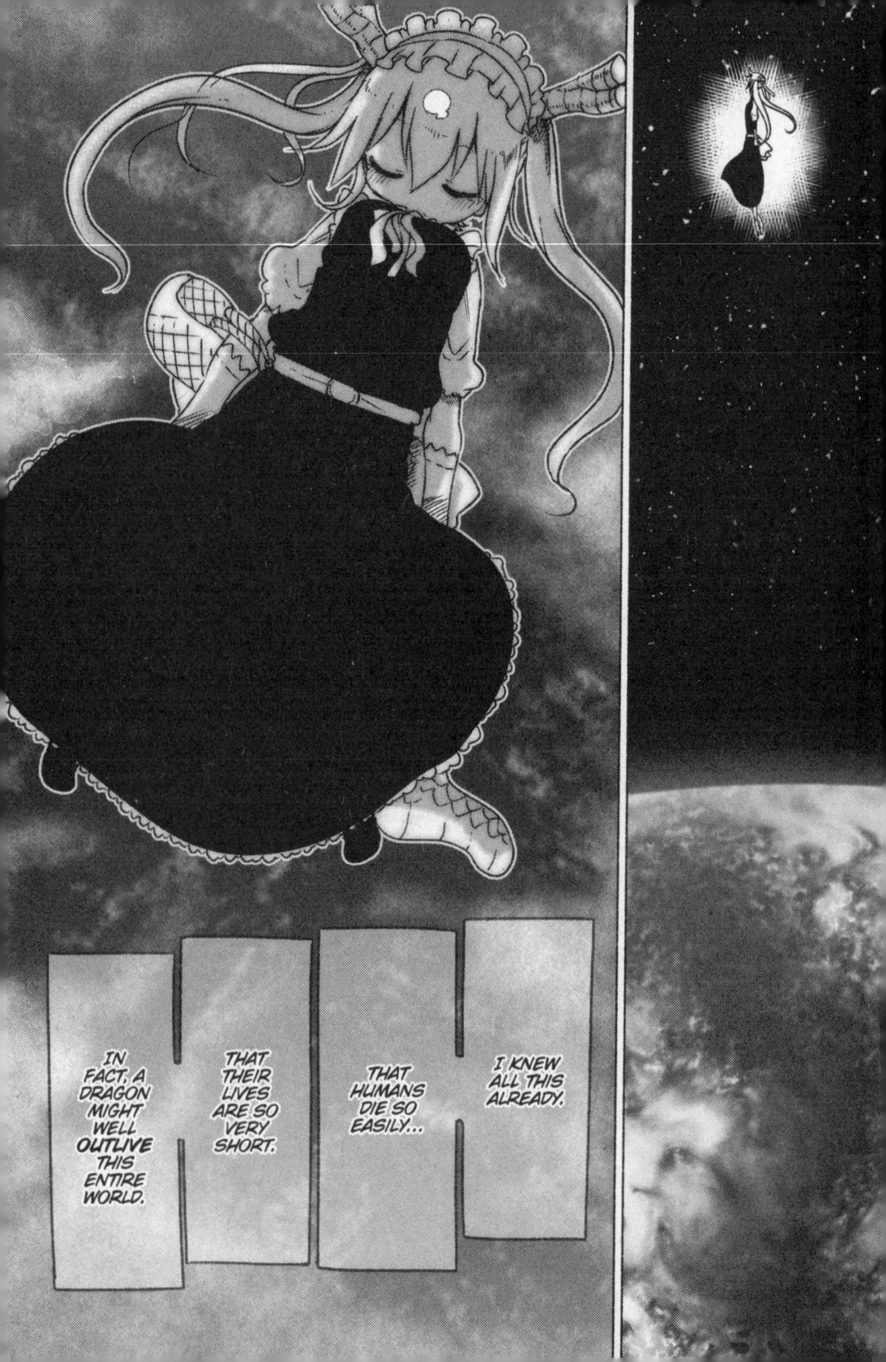
I KNEW ALL THIS ALREADY.
THAT HUMANS DIE SO EASILY...
THAT THEIR LIVES ARE SO VERY SHORT.
IN FACT, A DRAGON MIGHT WELL OUTLIVE THIS ENTIRE WORLD.

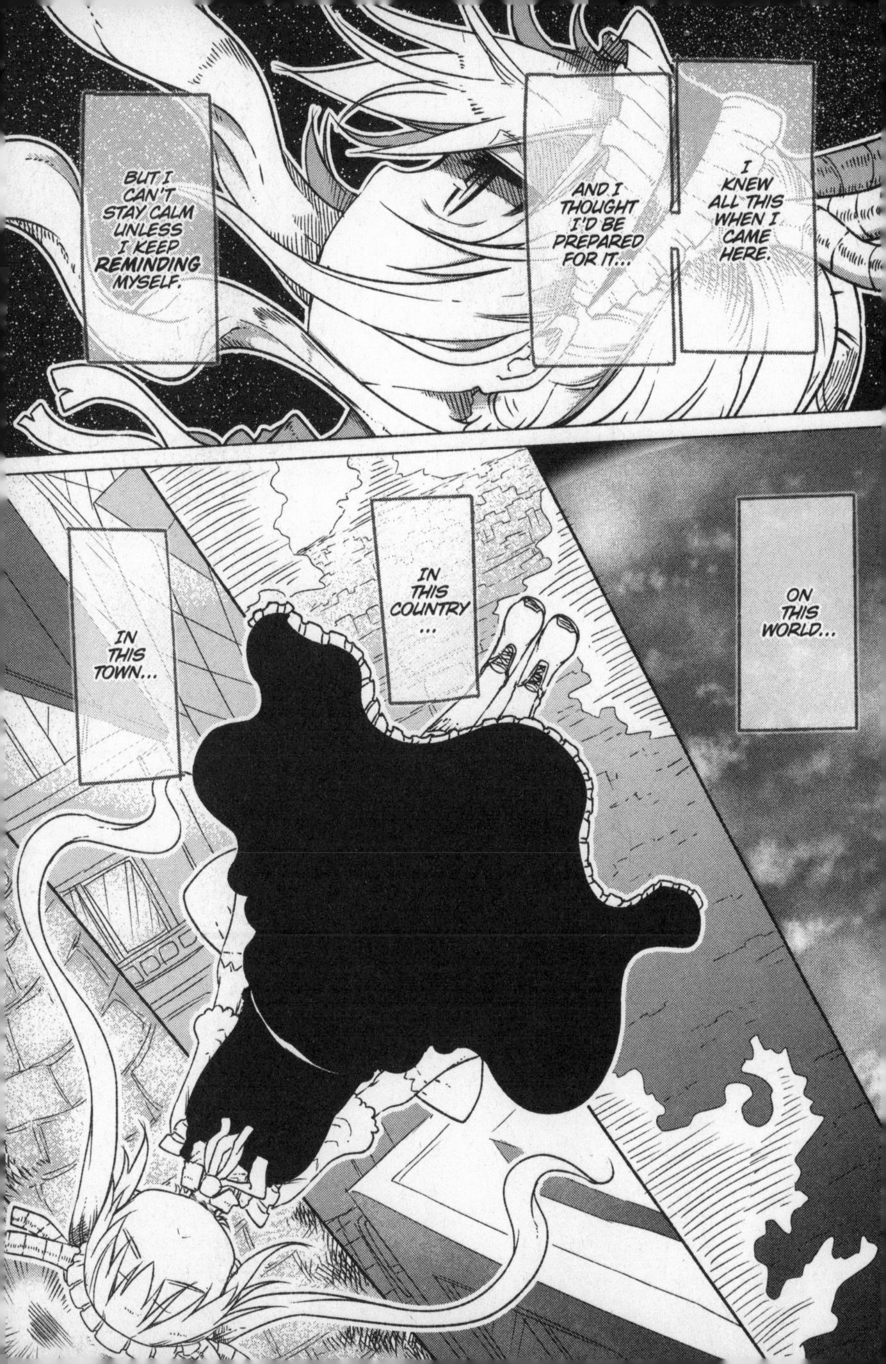
I KNEW ALL THIS WHEN I CAME HERE.
AND I THOUGHT I'D BE PREPARED FOR IT...
BUT I CAN'T STAY CALM UNLESS I KEEP REMINDING MYSELF.
ON THIS WORLD...
IN THIS COUNTRY...
IN THIS TOWN...

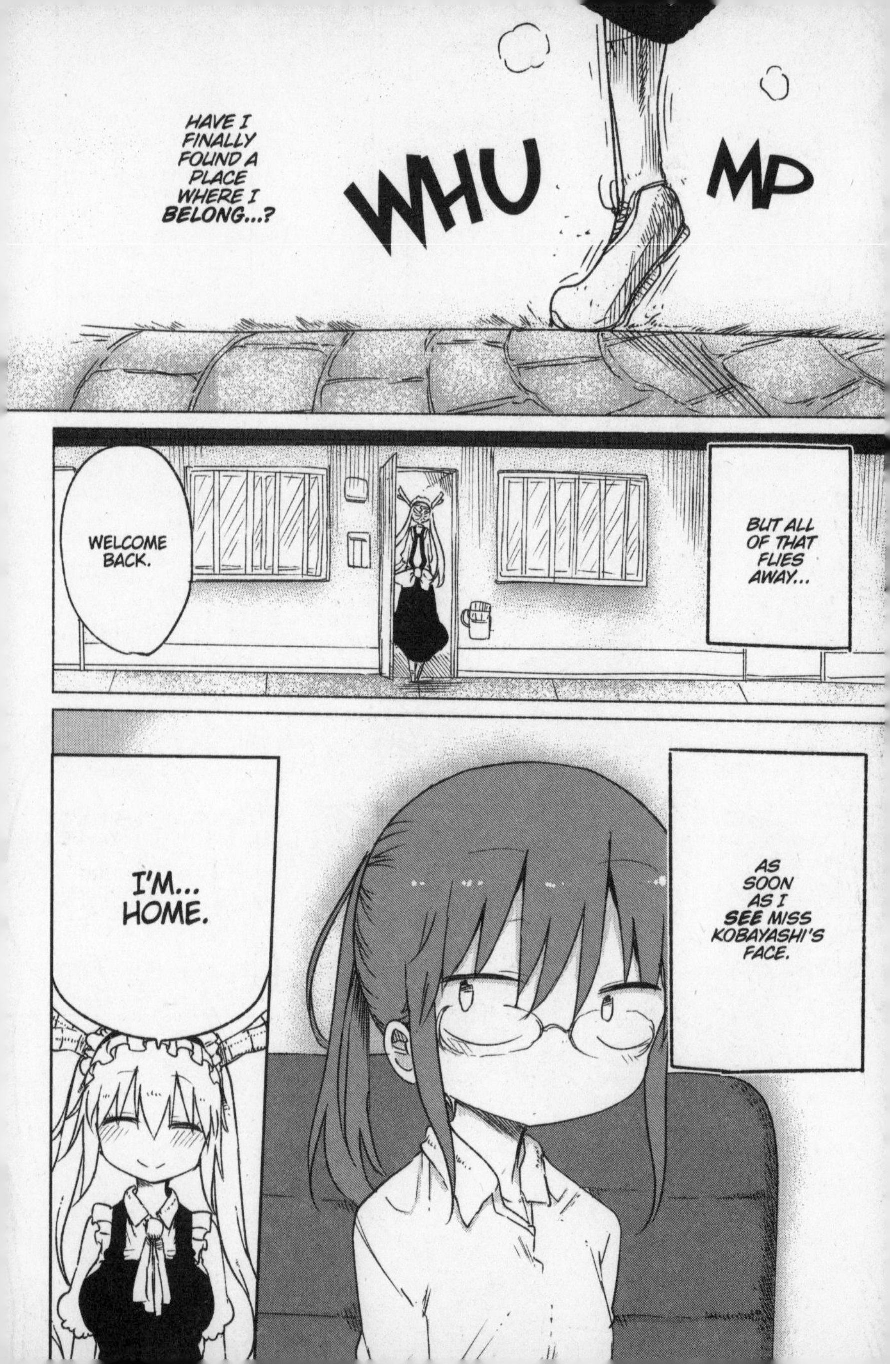
HAVE I FINALLY FOUND A PLACE WHERE I BELONG...?
WHUMP
BUT ALL OF THAT FLIES AWAY...
WELCOME BACK.
AS SOON AS I SEE MISS KOBAYASHI'S FACE.
I'M... HOME.

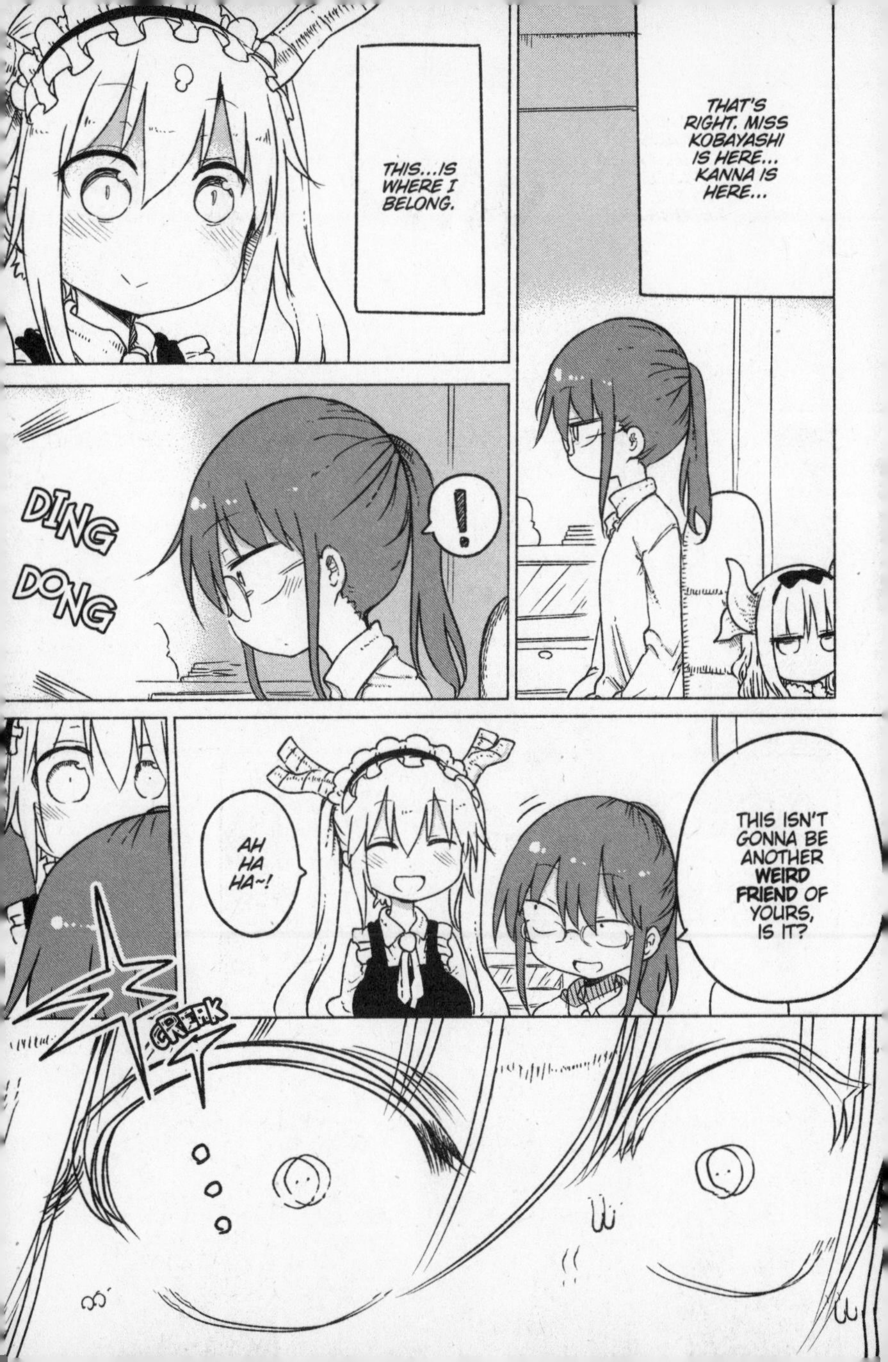
THAT'S RIGHT. MISS KOBAYASHI IS HERE... KANNA IS HERE...
THIS...IS WHERE I BELONG.
!
DING DONG
THIS ISN'T GONNA BE ANOTHER **WEIRD FRIEND** OF YOURS, IS IT?
AH HA HA~!
CREAK

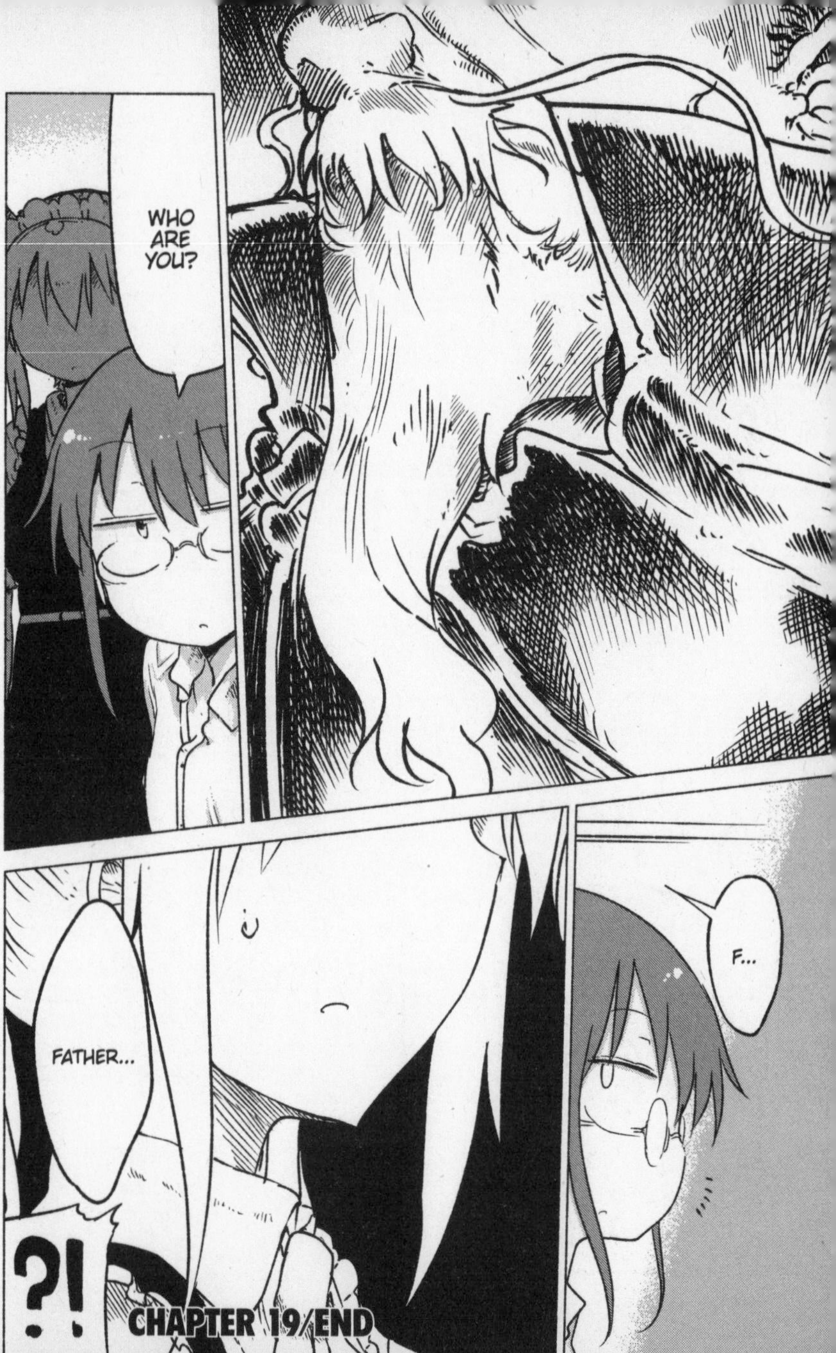
WHO ARE YOU?
F...
FATHER...
?!
CHAPTER 19/END

Coffee tastes better while I'm looking at Tohru...

Miss Kobayashi's Dragon Maid

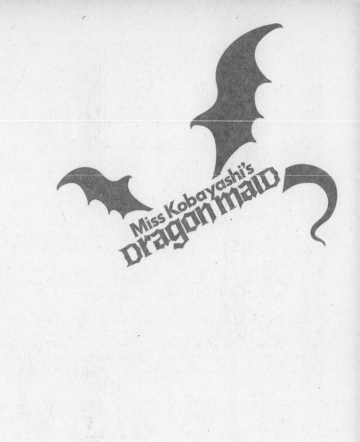

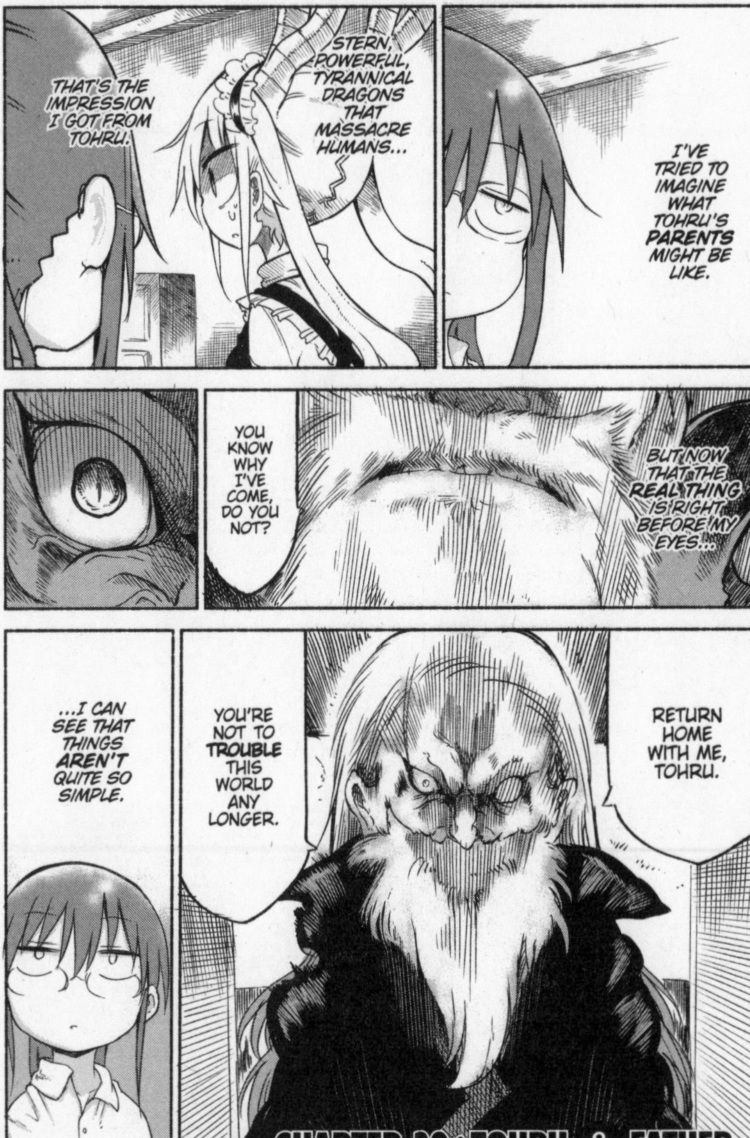
I'VE TRIED TO IMAGINE WHAT TOHRU'S PARENTS MIGHT BE LIKE.
STERN, POWERFUL, TYRANNICAL DRAGONS THAT MASSACRE HUMANS...
THAT'S THE IMPRESSION I GOT FROM TOHRU.
BUT NOW THAT THE REAL THING IS RIGHT BEFORE MY EYES...
YOU KNOW WHY I'VE COME, DO YOU NOT?
RETURN HOME WITH ME, TOHRU.
YOU'RE NOT TO TROUBLE THIS WORLD ANY LONGER.
CHAPTER 20: TOHRU & FATHER
...I CAN SEE THAT THINGS AREN'T QUITE SO SIMPLE.

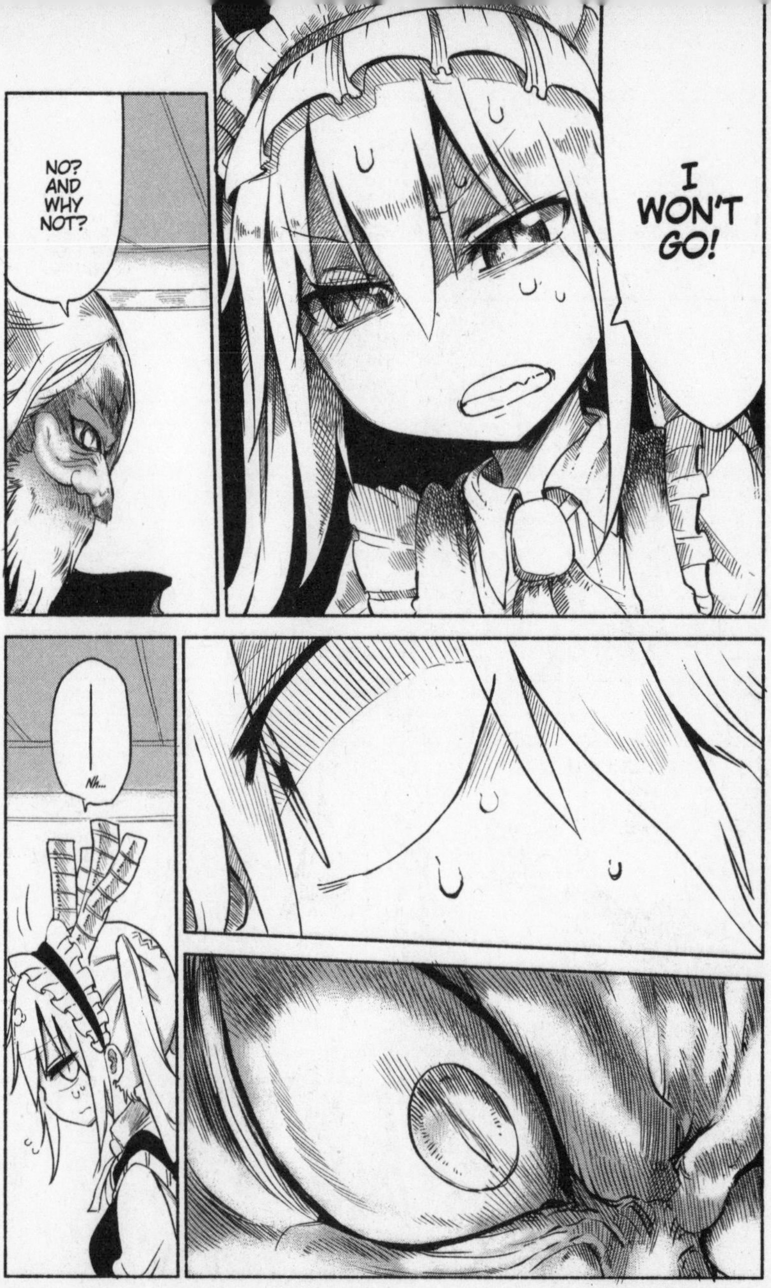
I WON'T GO!
NO? AND WHY NOT?
—
Nh...

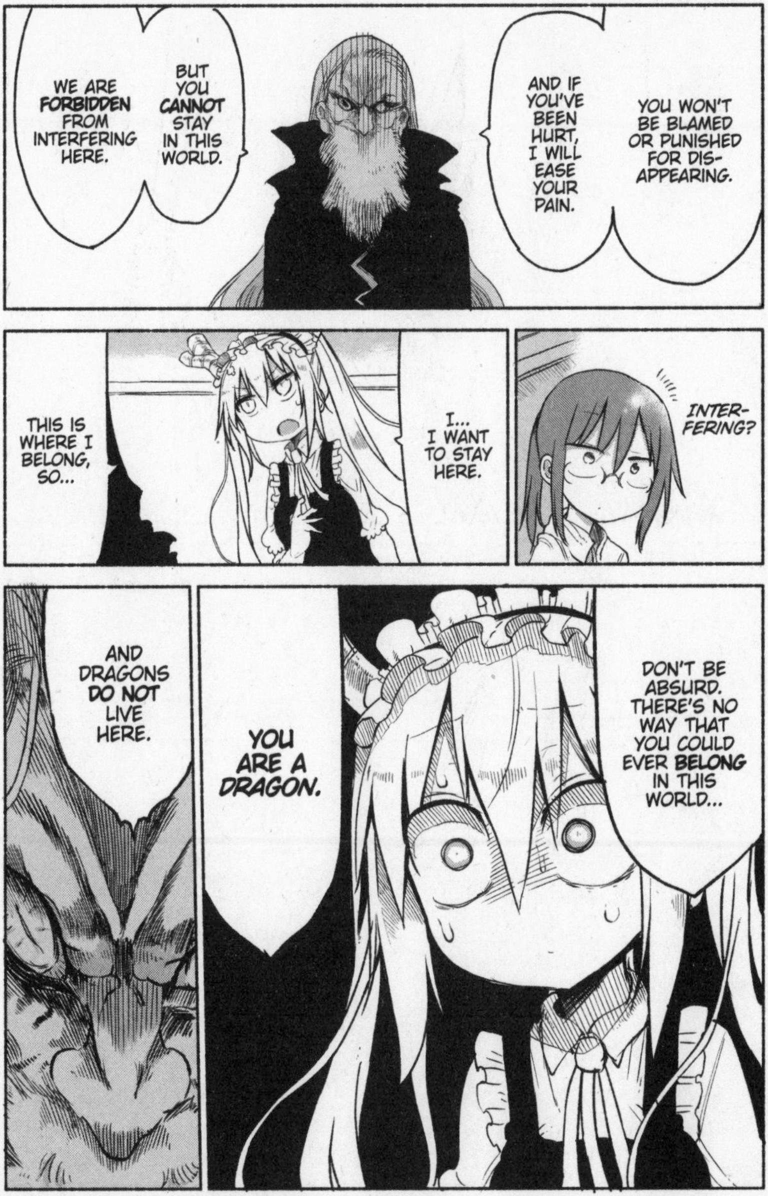
YOU WON'T BE BLAMED OR PUNISHED FOR DIS-APPEARING.
AND IF YOU'VE BEEN HURT, I WILL EASE YOUR PAIN.
BUT YOU **CANNOT** STAY IN THIS WORLD.
WE ARE **FORBIDDEN** FROM INTERFERING HERE.
INTER-FERING?
I... I WANT TO STAY HERE.
THIS IS WHERE I BELONG, SO...
DON'T BE ABSURD. THERE'S NO WAY THAT YOU COULD EVER **BELONG** IN THIS WORLD...
YOU ARE A DRAGON.
AND DRAGONS **DO NOT** LIVE HERE.

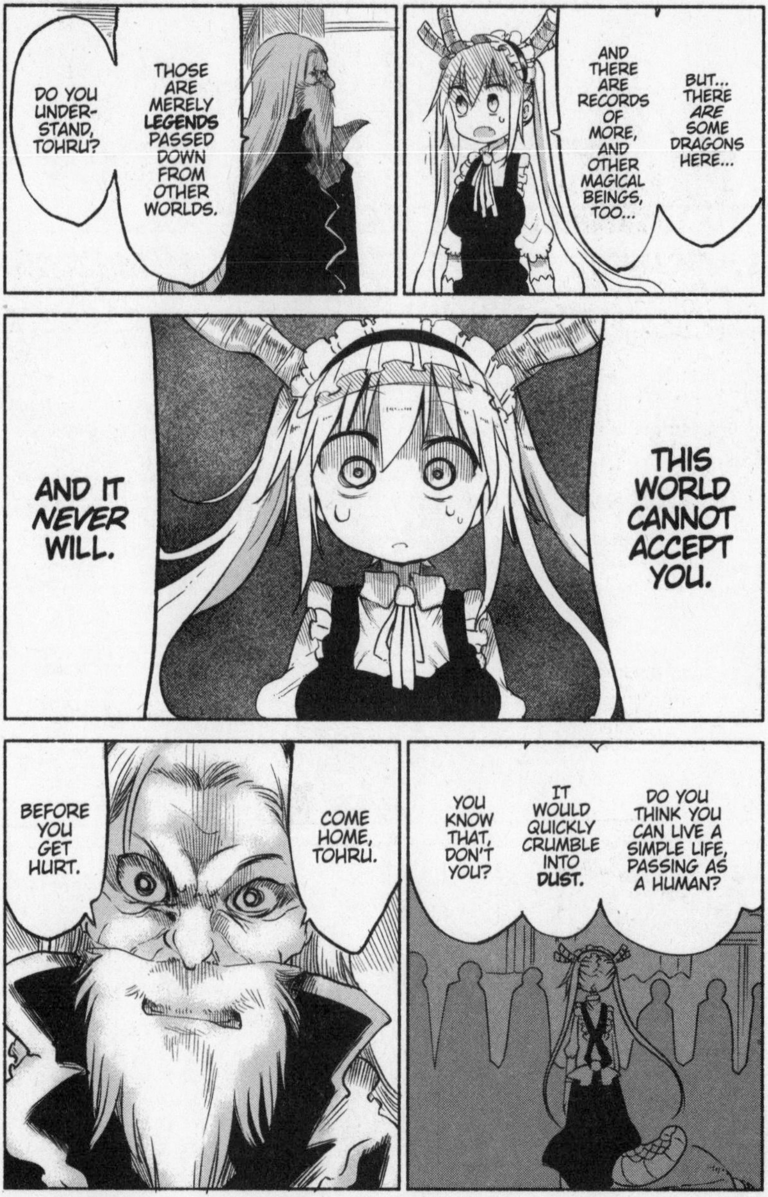
BUT... THERE ARE SOME DRAGONS HERE...
AND THERE ARE RECORDS OF MORE, AND OTHER MAGICAL BEINGS, TOO...
THOSE ARE MERELY LEGENDS PASSED DOWN FROM OTHER WORLDS.
DO YOU UNDER-STAND, TOHRU?
THIS WORLD CANNOT ACCEPT YOU.
AND IT NEVER WILL.
DO YOU THINK YOU CAN LIVE A SIMPLE LIFE, PASSING AS A HUMAN?
IT WOULD QUICKLY CRUMBLE INTO DUST.
YOU KNOW THAT, DON'T YOU?
COME HOME, TOHRU.
BEFORE YOU GET HURT.

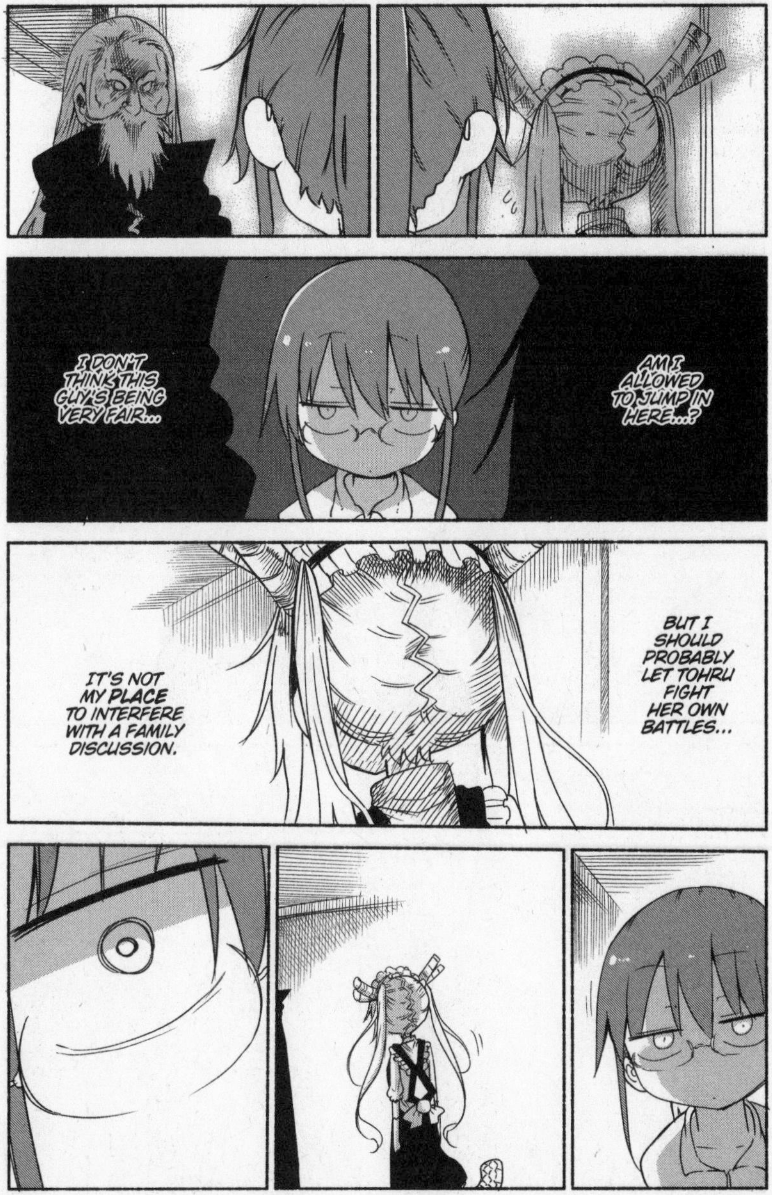
AM I ALLOWED TO JUMP IN HERE...?
I DON'T THINK THIS GUY'S BEING VERY FAIR...
BUT I SHOULD PROBABLY LET TOHRU FIGHT HER OWN BATTLES...
IT'S NOT MY PLACE TO INTERFERE WITH A FAMILY DISCUSSION.

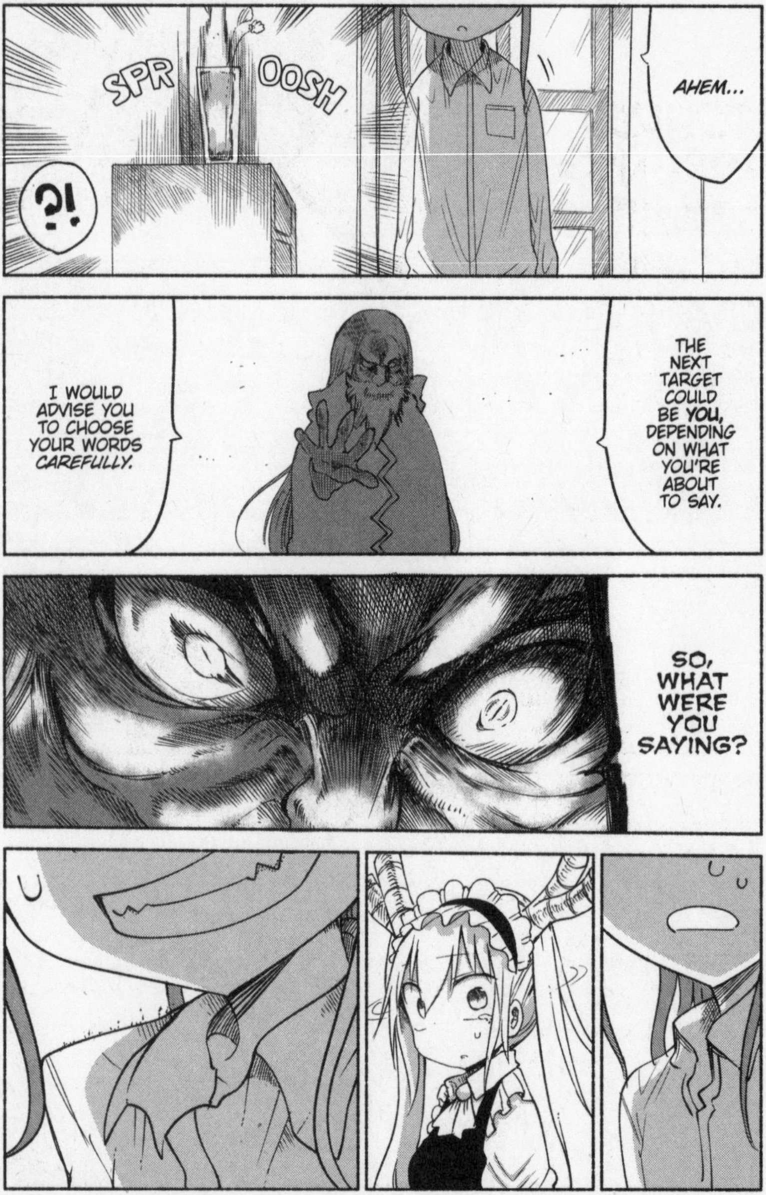
AHEM...
SPR OOSH
?!
THE NEXT TARGET COULD BE YOU, DEPENDING ON WHAT YOU'RE ABOUT TO SAY.
I WOULD ADVISE YOU TO CHOOSE YOUR WORDS CAREFULLY.
SO, WHAT WERE YOU SAYING?

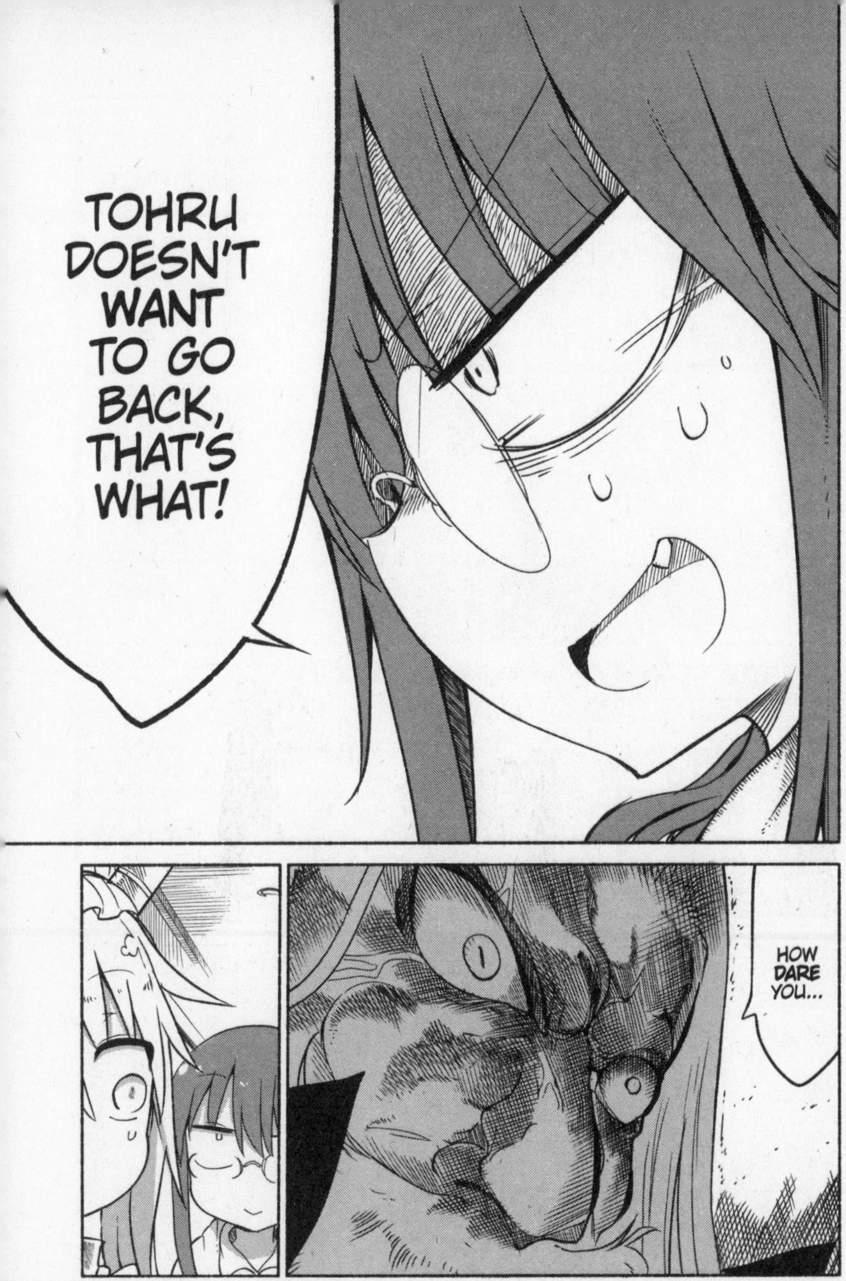
TOHRU DOESN'T WANT TO GO BACK, THAT'S WHAT!
HOW DARE YOU...

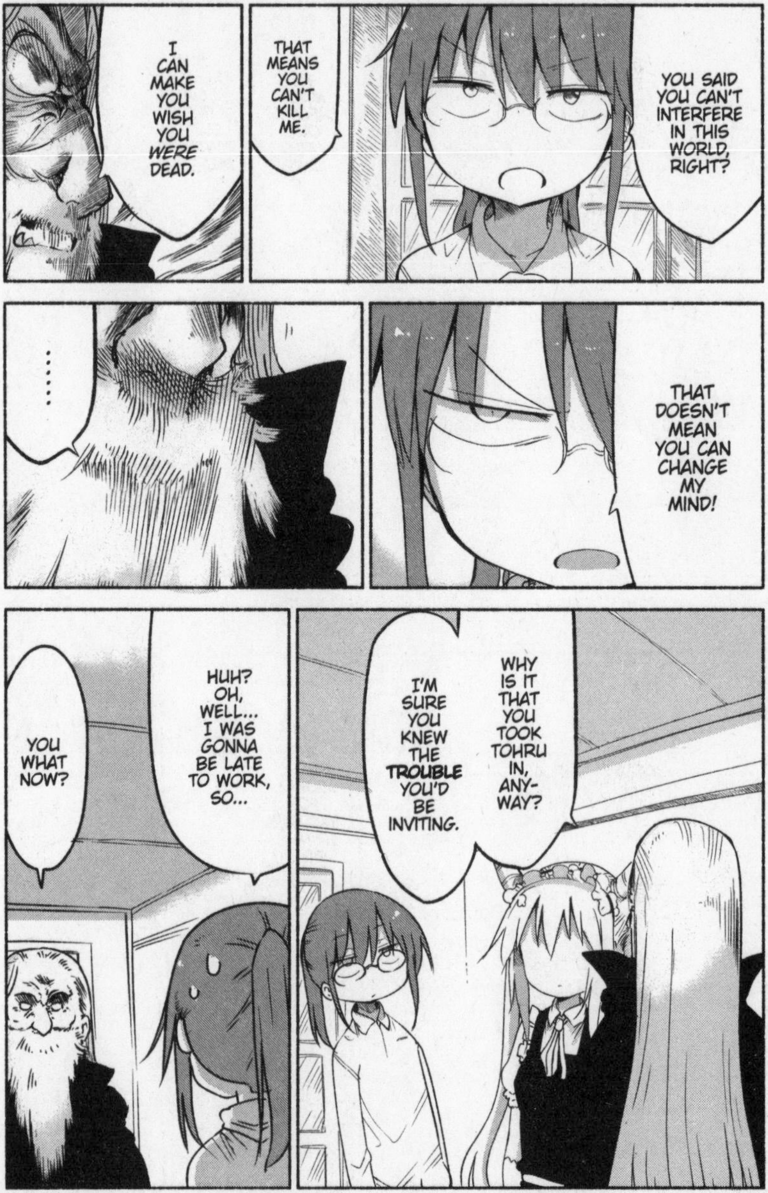
YOU SAID YOU CAN'T INTERFERE IN THIS WORLD, RIGHT?
THAT MEANS YOU CAN'T KILL ME.
I CAN MAKE YOU WISH YOU *WERE* DEAD.
THAT DOESN'T MEAN YOU CAN CHANGE MY MIND!
......
WHY IS IT THAT YOU TOOK TOHRU IN, ANYWAY?
I'M SURE YOU KNEW THE **TROUBLE** YOU'D BE INVITING.
HUH? OH, WELL... I WAS GONNA BE LATE TO WORK, SO...
YOU WHAT NOW?

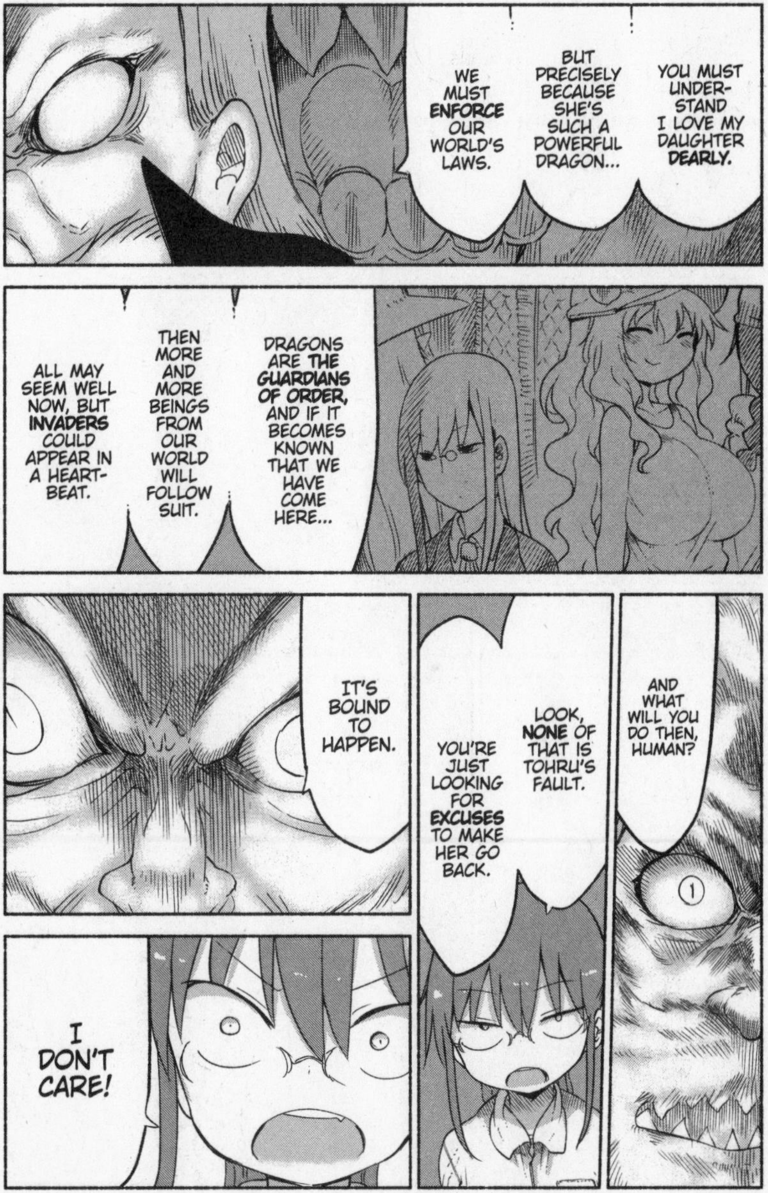
YOU MUST UNDERSTAND I LOVE MY DAUGHTER DEARLY.
BUT PRECISELY BECAUSE SHE'S SUCH A POWERFUL DRAGON...
WE MUST ENFORCE OUR WORLD'S LAWS.
DRAGONS ARE THE GUARDIANS OF ORDER, AND IF IT BECOMES KNOWN THAT WE HAVE COME HERE...
THEN MORE AND MORE BEINGS FROM OUR WORLD WILL FOLLOW SUIT.
ALL MAY SEEM WELL NOW, BUT INVADERS COULD APPEAR IN A HEART-BEAT.
AND WHAT WILL YOU DO THEN, HUMAN?
LOOK, NONE OF THAT IS TOHRU'S FAULT.
YOU'RE JUST LOOKING FOR EXCUSES TO MAKE HER GO BACK.
IT'S BOUND TO HAPPEN.
I DON'T CARE!

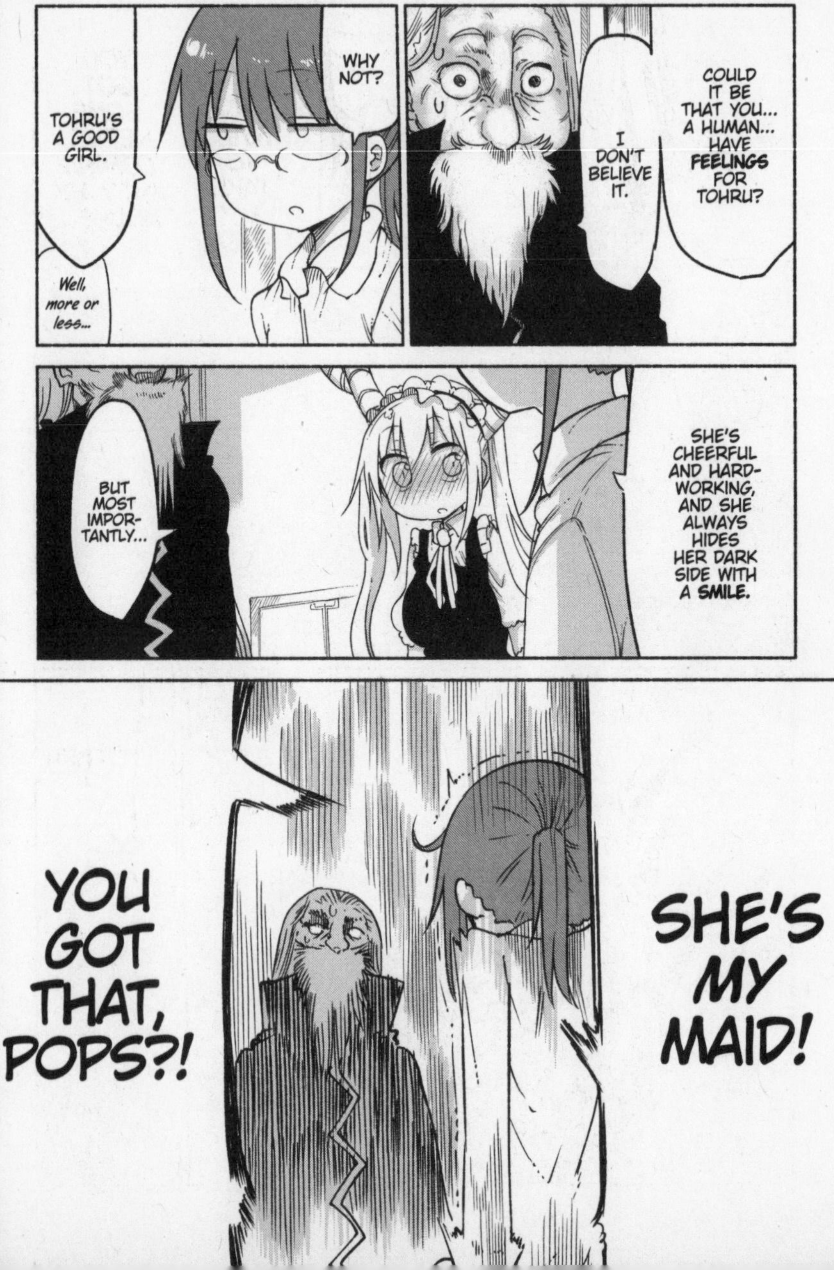

COULD IT BE THAT YOU... A HUMAN... HAVE **FEELINGS** FOR TOHRU?
I DON'T BELIEVE IT.
WHY NOT?
TOHRU'S A GOOD GIRL.
Well, more or less...
SHE'S CHEERFUL AND HARD-WORKING, AND SHE ALWAYS HIDES HER DARK SIDE WITH A **SMILE**.
BUT MOST IMPORTANTLY...
SHE'S *MY* MAID!
YOU GOT THAT, POPS?!

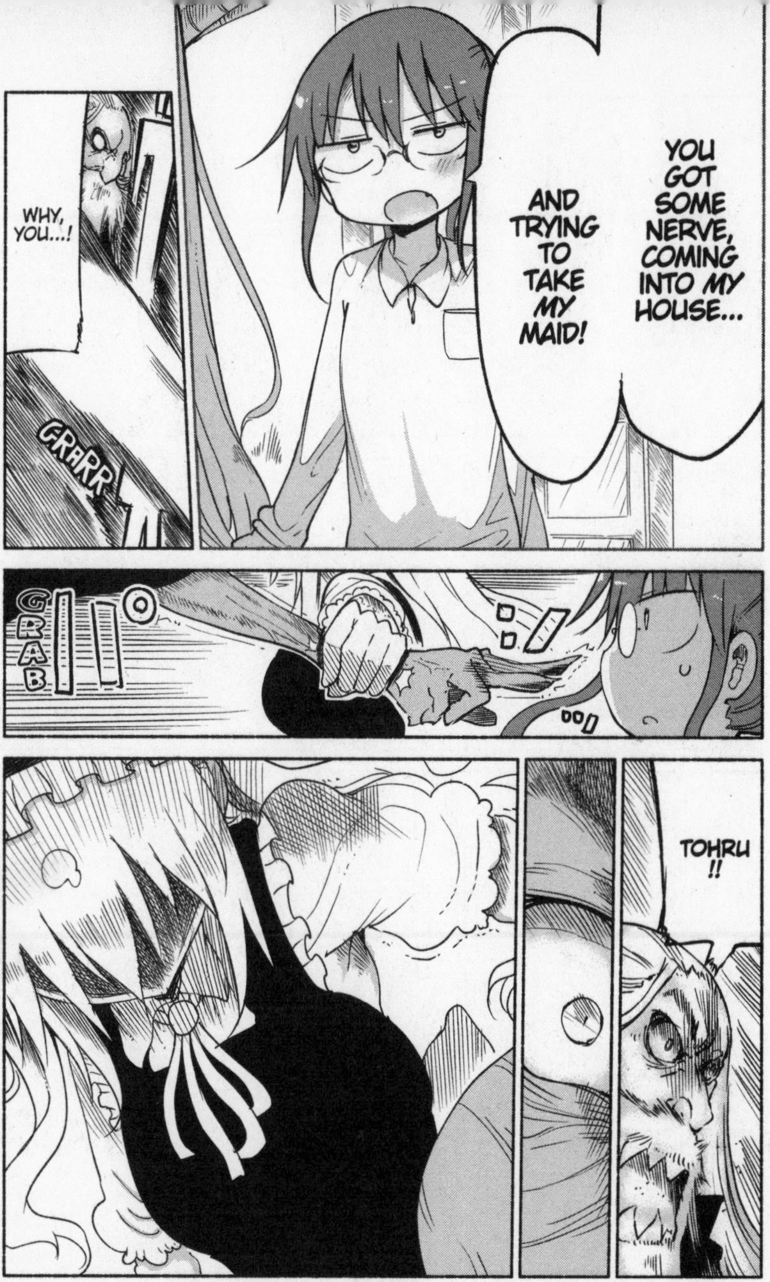
YOU GOT SOME NERVE, COMING INTO MY HOUSE...
AND TRYING TO TAKE MY MAID!
WHY, YOU...!
GRARRR
GRAB
TOHRU !!

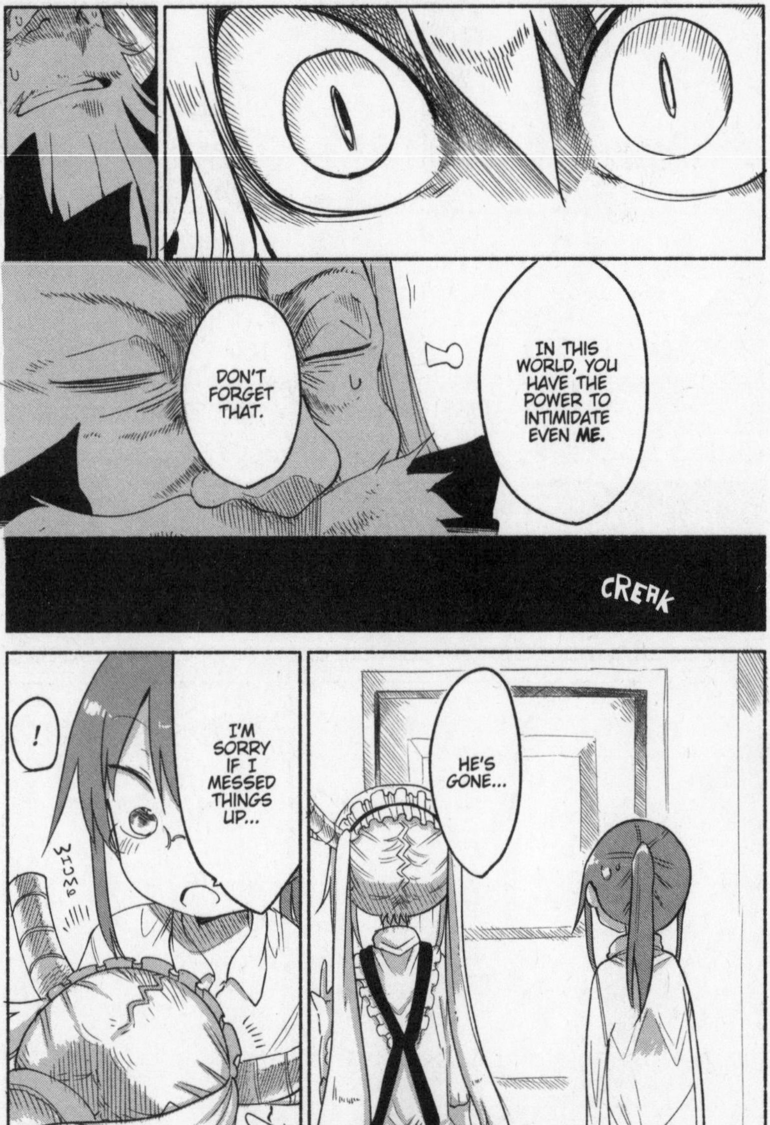
IN THIS WORLD, YOU HAVE THE POWER TO INTIMIDATE EVEN ME.
DON'T FORGET THAT.
CREAK
HE'S GONE...
I'M SORRY IF I MESSED THINGS UP...
!

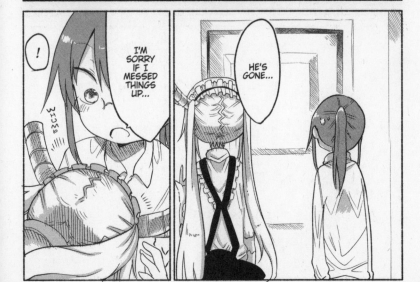

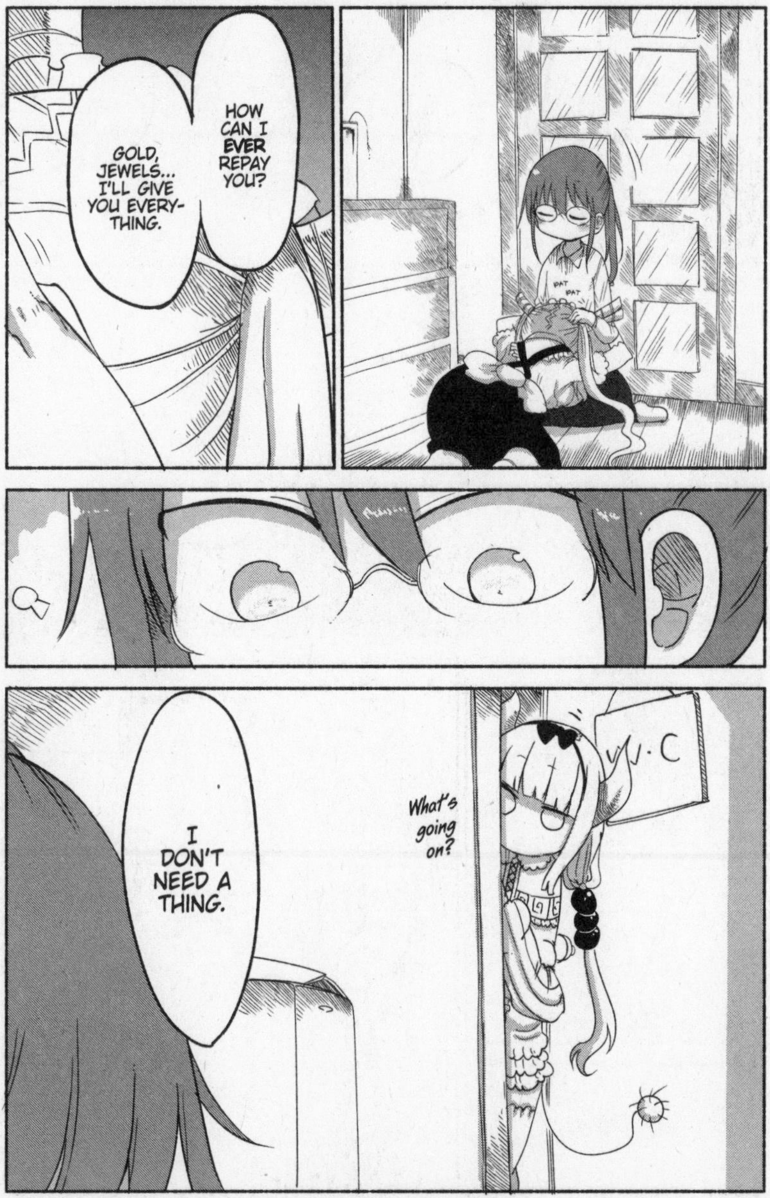
PAT PAT
HOW CAN I EVER REPAY YOU?
GOLD, JEWELS... I'LL GIVE YOU EVERY-THING.
What's going on?
I DON'T NEED A THING.

CHAPTER 20/END

AFTERWORD

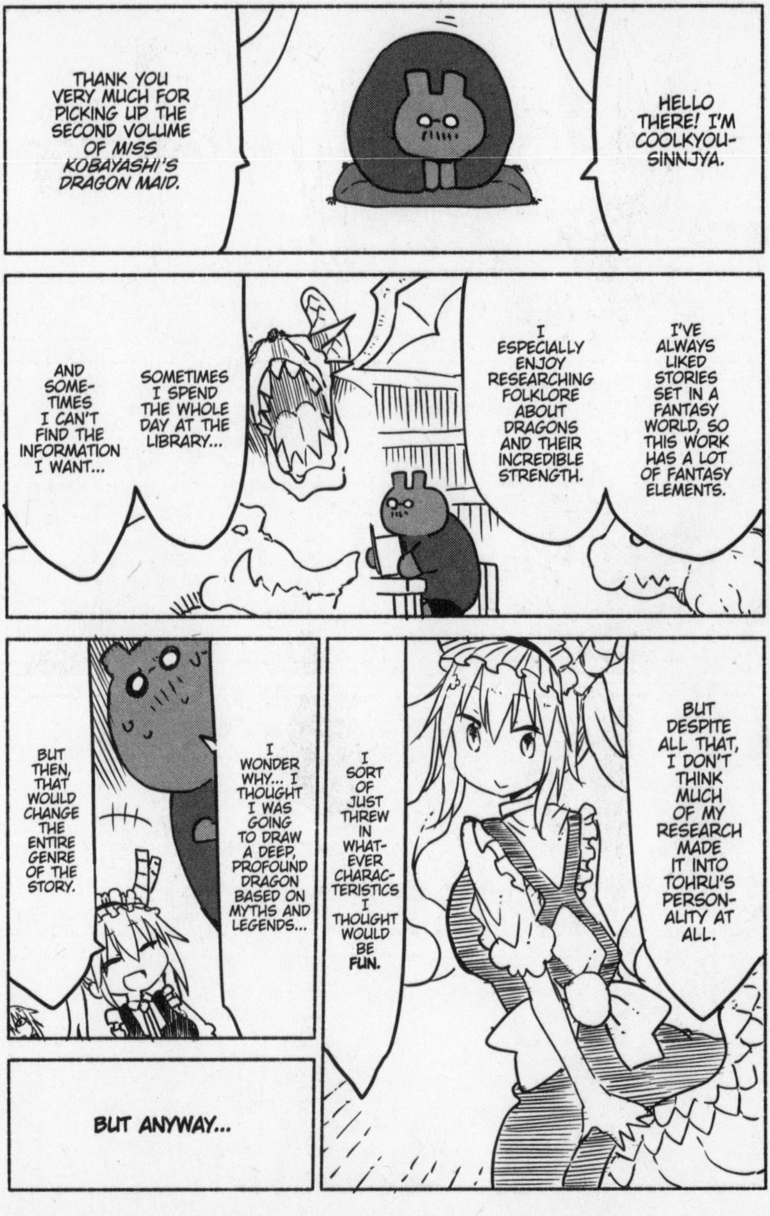

HELLO THERE! I'M COOLKYOU-SINNJYA.
THANK YOU VERY MUCH FOR PICKING UP THE SECOND VOLUME OF *MISS KOBAYASHI'S DRAGON MAID.*
I'VE ALWAYS LIKED STORIES SET IN A FANTASY WORLD, SO THIS WORK HAS A LOT OF FANTASY ELEMENTS.
I ESPECIALLY ENJOY RESEARCHING FOLKLORE ABOUT DRAGONS AND THEIR INCREDIBLE STRENGTH.
SOMETIMES I SPEND THE WHOLE DAY AT THE LIBRARY...
AND SOMETIMES I CAN'T FIND THE INFORMATION I WANT...
BUT DESPITE ALL THAT, I DON'T THINK MUCH OF MY RESEARCH MADE IT INTO TOHRU'S PERSONALITY AT ALL.
I SORT OF JUST THREW IN WHATEVER CHARACTERISTICS I THOUGHT WOULD BE **FUN.**
I WONDER WHY... I THOUGHT I WAS GOING TO DRAW A DEEP, PROFOUND DRAGON BASED ON MYTHS AND LEGENDS...
BUT THEN, THAT WOULD CHANGE THE ENTIRE GENRE OF THE STORY.
BUT ANYWAY...

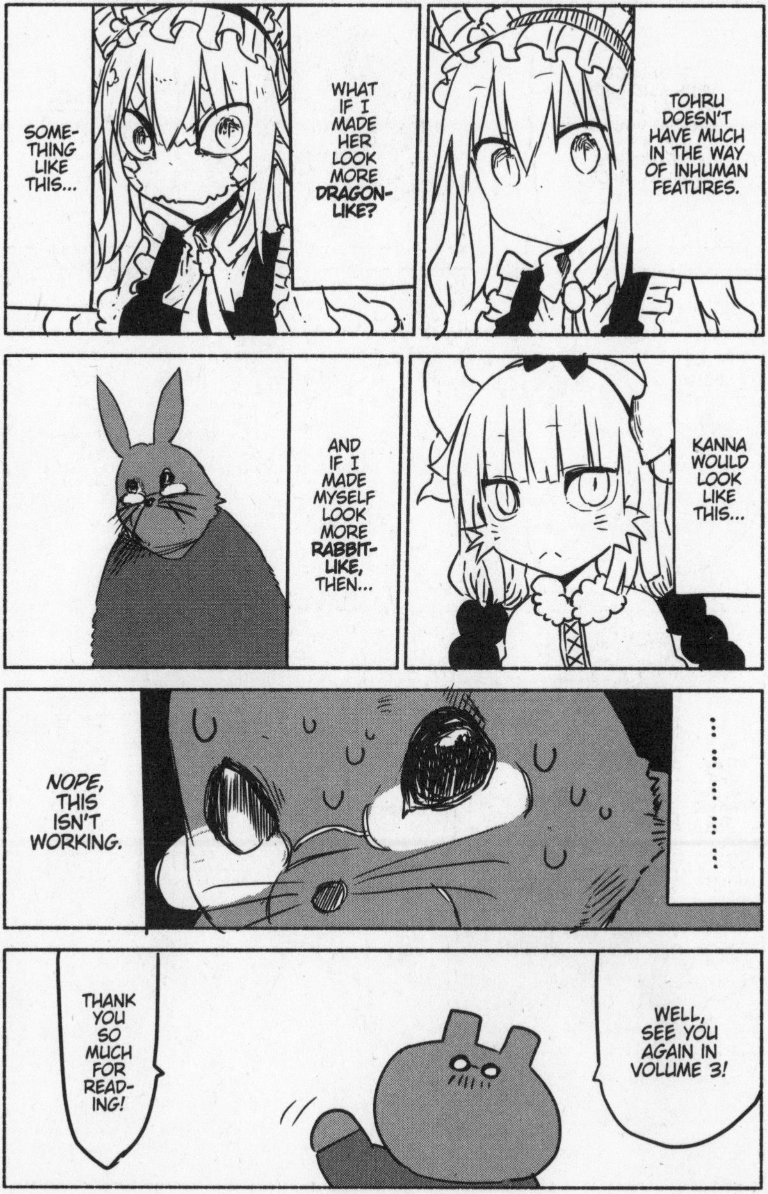
TOHRU DOESN'T HAVE MUCH IN THE WAY OF INHUMAN FEATURES.
WHAT IF I MADE HER LOOK MORE DRAGON-LIKE?
SOME-THING LIKE THIS...
KANNA WOULD LOOK LIKE THIS...
AND IF I MADE MYSELF LOOK MORE RABBIT-LIKE, THEN...
......
NOPE, THIS ISN'T WORKING.
WELL, SEE YOU AGAIN IN VOLUME 3!
THANK YOU SO MUCH FOR READ-ING!

Miss Kobayashi's
DRAGON MAID

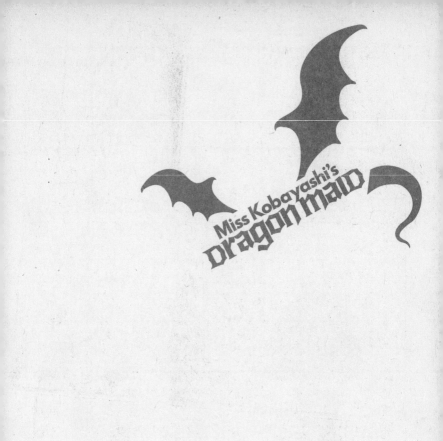

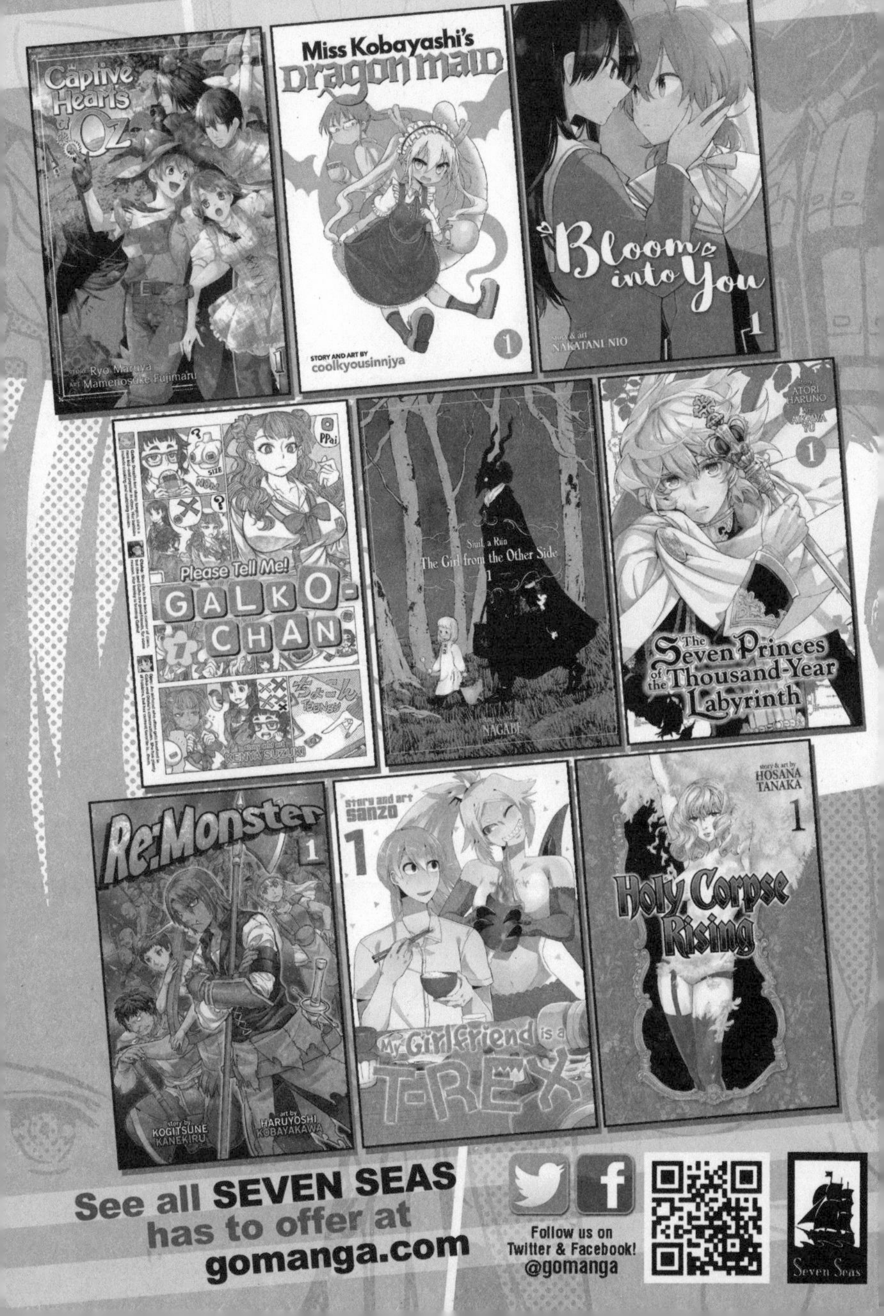

Captive Hearts of Oz
Story Ryo Maruya
Art Mamenosuke Fujimaru
1
Miss Kobayashi's Dragon Maid
STORY AND ART BY coolkyousinnjya
1
Bloom into You
Story & art NAKATANI NIO
1
Please Tell Me! GALKO-CHAN
story and art KENYA SUZUKI
Siúil, a Rún
The Girl from the Other Side
1
NAGABE
1
The Seven Princes of the Thousand-Year Labyrinth
Re:Monster
1
story by KOGITSUNE KANEKIRU
art by HARUYOSHI KOBAYAKAWA
Story and art sanzo
1
My Girlfriend is a T-REX
story & art by HOSANA TANAKA
1
Holy Corpse Rising

SEVEN SEAS ENTERTAINMENT PRESENTS

Miss Kobayashi's Dragon Maid VOL. 2

story and art by **coolkyousinnjya**

TRANSLATION
Jenny McKeon

ADAPTATION
Shanti Whitesides

LETTERING
Jennifer Skarupa

LOGO DESIGN
KC Fabellon

COVER DESIGN
Nicky Lim

PRODUCTION MANAGER
Lissa Pattillo

EDITOR-IN-CHIEF
Adam Arnold

PUBLISHER
Jason DeAngelis

MISS KOBAYASHI'S DRAGON MAID VOL. 2

First published in Japan in 2013 by Futabasha Publishers Ltd., Tokyo.
English version published by Seven Seas Entertainment, LLC.
Under license from Futabasha Publishers Ltd.

ISBN: 978-1-626924-31-4

Printed in Canada

First Printing: February 2017

10 9 8 7 6 5 4 3 2 1

FOLLOW US ONLINE: ***www.gomanga.com***

READING DIRECTIONS

This book reads from ***right to left***, Japanese style. If this is your first time reading manga, you start reading from the top right panel on each page and take it from there. If you get lost, just follow the numbered diagram here. It may seem backwards at first, but you'll get the hang of it! Have fun!!

1
2
3
4
5
6
7
8
9

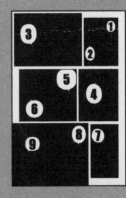